PENGUIN BOOKS
INDIA GROWS AT NIGHT

Gurcharan Das is a well-known author, commentator and public intellectual. His books include the much acclaimed *The Difficulty of Being Good* and the international bestseller *India Unbound*. He writes a regular column for a number of Indian newspapers and occasional guest columns for *Wall Street Journal*, *Foreign Affairs* and *Newsweek*. He graduated from Harvard University and was CEO of Procter & Gamble before taking early retirement to become a full-time writer. He lives in Delhi.

PRAISE FOR THE BOOK

'Why should it take us 15 years to get justice in the courts or 12 years to build a road?' argues Gurcharan Das . . . You need a strong state and a strong society, so the society can hold the state accountable. India will only get a strong state when the best of society join the government . . .— Tom Friedman, *New York Times*

'Das has written a timely book that deserves to be widely read. And it has its share of hard-headed proposals . . . Simply calling for less government is no answer, says Das. It needs also to be strong. Indian capitalism needs an honest referee . . . India has much to celebrate nowadays but also faces a cacophony of institutional challenges . . . Das's core argument is right and urgent'—Edward Luce, *Financial Times*

'An Indian political pamphlet of the 21st century . . . Das moves swiftly across centuries and continents, between anecdotal evidence and occasional factual detail, to outline his liberal case for a strong state. The essence of this argument is that while India has grown over the last two decades the state has not kept pace. And he does not see this as a recent phenomenon but a part of a longer term reality'—Narendar Pani, *The Hindu*

'It is hard to disagree with Das's bullish take on the future of the subcontinent. Indian middle classes are on the rise, and are increasingly becoming an interest group in their own right. As they grow in size, wealth and respectability, they will have a greater say in Indian politics and hopefully push for reforms improving government effectiveness and accountability'— Dalibor Rohac, *Mint / Wall Street Journal*

'The eclectic mixture of mythology, history, sociology and economics is overwhelming, but the reader can't disagree with Das's prescription of a strong liberal Indian state'—Dipankar Bhattacharyya, *Hindustan Times*

'Offers one significant new twist for the global discussions on markets and states . . . While the Western world wrings its hands about the loss of the moral on the way to the market, Das celebrates and promotes the discovery of a new version of an old moral compass, driven by and supportive of the market . . . If the state enables the market, the market will reshape society, and the weak state will become strong, in the sense of being compelled by public aspiration to push back on the illiberal aspects of the social order . . . In the end, this may be the underlying point of the book: the social system for shaping both markets and states toward development begins with the individual enterprise of introspection'—Jessica Seddon, *Caravan*

'Gurcharan Das's latest book captures the deep discord in today's India—a robust, aspiring society thriving in a flourishing economy held hostage by a flailing state and governance failures. Its focus on "what is to be done" to create a strong, liberal state in India makes it a brilliant read for all Indians hoping for a better India and keen to contribute to creating one'—N.R. Narayana Murthy

'Gurcharan Das has written a provocative book on the prospects of economic growth in India today. He writes in such a way that even those who disagree with him are forced to reconsider the grounds on which they base their views. This is a stimulating and challenging book'—André Béteille

'Excellent . . . gives a brief conspectus of the current working of our democracy . . . The moral component of the rule of law to justify it as dharma is perceptive'—J.S. Verma, Former Chief Justice of the Supreme Court

ALSO BY GURCHARAN DAS

NOVEL

A Fine Family (1990)

PLAYS

Larins Sahib: A Play in Three Acts (1970)

Mira: Rito de Krishna, tr. Enrique Hett (1971)

Three Plays (2001, 2011)

NON-FICTION

India Unbound: From Independence to the Global Information Age (2000)

The Elephant Paradigm: India Wrestles with Change (2002)

The Difficulty of Being Good: On the Subtle Art of Dharma (2009)

GENERAL EDITOR

THE STORY OF INDIAN BUSINESS

Tom Trautmann, *Arthashastra: The Science of Wealth*

Tirthankar Roy, *The East India Company: The World's Most Powerful Corporation*

Kanakalatha Mukund, *Merchants of Tamilakkam: Pioneers of International Trade*

Lakshmi Subramanian, *Three Merchants of Bombay: Doing Business in Times of Change*

GURCHARAN DAS

INDIA GROWS AT NIGHT

A LIBERAL CASE FOR A STRONG STATE

PENGUIN BOOKS

PENGUIN BOOKS

Published by the Penguin Group

Penguin Books India Pvt Ltd, 11 Community Centre, Panchsheel Park, New Delhi 110 017, India

Penguin Group (USA) Inc., 375 Hudson Street, New York, New York 10014, USA

Penguin Group (Canada), 90 Eglinton Avenue East, Suite 700, Toronto, Ontario, M4P 2Y3, Canada (a division of Pearson Penguin Canada Inc.)

Penguin Books Ltd, 80 Strand, London WC2R 0RL, England

Penguin Ireland, 25 St Stephen's Green, Dublin 2, Ireland (a division of Penguin Books Ltd)

Penguin Group (Australia), 707 Collins Street, Melbourne, Victoria 3008, Australia (a division of Pearson Australia Group Pty Ltd)

Penguin Group (NZ), 67 Apollo Drive, Rosedale, Auckland 0632, New Zealand (a division of Pearson New Zealand Ltd)

Penguin Books (South Africa) (Pty) Ltd, Block D, Rosebank Office Park, 181 Jan Smuts Avenue, Parktown North, Johannesburg 2193, South Africa

Penguin Books Ltd, Registered Offices: 80 Strand, London WC2R 0RL, England

First published in Allen Lane by Penguin Books India 2012
Published in Penguin Books 2013

ISBN 9780143421078

Typeset in Sabon Roman by SÜRYA, New Delhi
Printed at Thomson Press India Ltd, New Delhi

For

Maya Sukshma, Kabir, Nisha, Neha and Megha

If China must be regarded as nothing else but a State, Hindoo political existence presents us with a people but no state.

—G.W.F. Hegel

CONTENTS

INTRODUCTION

A Rising Economy, an Aspiring Society and a Declining State

The state exists for the sake of a good life,
not for the sake of life alone.

—Aristotle, *Politics*, 3.9

Indians wryly admit that 'India grows at night' when they sit down to sip chai and talk about their country's messy road into the future. But that is only half the saying. The complete sentence is: 'India grows at night while the government sleeps,' meaning that India may well be rising despite the state. Prosperity is, indeed, spreading across the country even as governance failure pervades public life. It is a tale of private success and public failure. The private home is neat, clean and energetic. The government office is slothful, suffocating with controls and filled with mind-bending red tape. If it were a home, dirty dishes would be flung about the bedroom, old shoes and newspapers would be piled high in the kitchen, and everyone would have chai all day long. The difference between the two is a sense of responsibility in the Indian home—if you don't work you don't eat. That accountability is missing in public life.

How can a nation become one of the world's emerging powers despite a weak, ineffective state? And should India not grow during the day as well? It is questions like these that led me to write this book. I grew up in the idealistic days after Independence when we passionately believed in Jawaharlal Nehru's dream of a modern and just India. We were all socialists then. As the years went by, I watched Nehru create a command economy which took us to a dead end. Instead of socialism we ended up with statism, and we sardonically called it the 'licence raj'. In my book *India Unbound*, I recounted the story of those four decades of missed opportunities and my own personal humiliation during the 'licence raj'. In 1991, India's economy was finally unshackled by liberal economic reforms, which lowered trade barriers and tax rates, broke state monopolies, unshackled industry and competition, and opened up to the rest of the world. Growth accelerated, prosperity began to spread and the world began to speak about 'the rise of India'.

No one in India quite understands how their noisy, chaotic democracy of a billion people has become one of the world's fastest growing economies. After all, sixty countries implemented the same reforms as India did. Clearly, suppressed energy burst out after 1991 but no one imagined that Indian entrepreneurs would respond so quickly to create innovative, red-blooded firms, who learned to compete brutally at home and have begun to stomp on to the global stage. India's is a 'bottom-up' story, unlike China's 'top-down' success that has been orchestrated by an authoritarian state.

After experiencing the pain of the 'licence raj', I became a libertarian, passionately committed to individual freedom and deeply suspicious of state power. The reforms were a defining moment in my narrative of national history in which India gained only its 'political' independence in 1947; it did not win 'economic' independence until 1991. India's rise has been enabled by two institutions of liberty— democracy and free markets. For our vibrant democracy, I give credit to Nehru, who laid its foundations. But India rose economically only after Nehru's over-regulating state stepped out of the way.

With my commitment to individual liberty, I began to believe that the state was 'a second-order phenomenon', at best a protector of what people choose to do in private life or in civil society and at worst capable of destroying those freedoms. I celebrated the heroic idea that India was rising despite the state. Two decades later, I have realized that I might have been wrong. I am now convinced that the state is of first-order importance. It can either allow human beings to flourish or it can become the biggest obstacle to their realizing their potential. To rise despite the state is courageous but it cannot be a long-term virtue. It only gets you so far. Prosperity does not magically appear 'when the government sleeps'. India's recent success has come about because the state has quietly provided through the shadows reasonable property rights, reasonable security and reasonable law and order. And now India has begun to experience the limits of 'growing without the state'. The growing-at-night strategy is no longer viable and the task is to reform the institutions of the state. The state must come out of the shadows and India should thrive during the day.

WHAT CONSTITUTES NATIONAL SUCCESS?

This raises a deeper question in my mind: what constitutes national success? A successful nation, it seems to me, has these attributes: politically, it is free, democratic and accountable, with a rule of law that is strictly enforced; economically, it is prosperous, dynamic and reasonably equitable; and socially, it is peaceful, cohesive and inclusive—striving to reduce hierarchy and increasing equality of opportunity. It is rare to find such a nation. Western democracies are free and prosperous but their societies appear to be disintegrating. The nations in the East are prosperous and socially cohesive but they are mostly un-free under authoritarian political regimes. Where does India stand?

For decades, India scored high as a political democracy, middling as a hierarchical society and poorly as an economy. But this changed after its economy was unfettered in 1991 and India went on to become the world's second fastest growing major economy in the first decade of the twenty-first century. Although prosperity has begun to spread and the middle class is growing rapidly, millions are still desperately poor and undernourished, with little access to clean water, good schools and functioning health services.

Socially, too, there have been considerable gains. Dalits and other backward castes have continued to rise through the ballot box and a surging economy. A middle class has begun to develop among the lower castes, and Mayawati, until recently the chief minister of India's largest state, Uttar Pradesh, is the proud symbol of their ascent. This virtuous circle has not yet touched the tribal areas where Maoist violence continues to rage. But the shadows of communal violence have receded, despite the events in Gujarat in 2002 and Delhi in 1984 and periodic provocations by extremists. The attraction of Hindutva as an electoral platform is also declining, especially among the young, and minorities in India feel more secure.

Politically, however, the Indian state has declined into a state of paralysis. Governance has become a serious problem and corruption is pervasive. Although elections have become fairer (thanks to the Election Commission) and local democracy continues its slow march down to the village (after the Seventy-third Amendment to the Constitution), the state's inability to deliver the most basic services provoked one observer to call India a 'flailing state', a theme that I elaborate in Chapter Four. While economic growth is a necessary condition for lifting the poor, it is not a sufficient condition. People also need honest policemen and diligent officials, functioning schools and primary health centres.

WHAT IS A LIBERAL, STRONG STATE?

A successful liberal democracy has three elements, according to Francis Fukuyama in a sparkling new book, *The Origins of Political Order*. It has a strong authority to allow quick and decisive action; a transparent rule of law to ensure the action is legitimate; and it is accountable to the people. This was the original conception of the state as imagined by the classical liberal thinkers, which inspired our founding fathers. Combining these three elements is never easy and only a few states get the balance right. In India, the rule of law has weakened partly as a result of democratic politics—corruption is a symptom of this weakness. At the same time, an aggressive civil society and media are enhancing accountability, for example, through the Right to Information Act. The state's ability to act has been undercut by enfeebled enforcement of the law; but also, ironically enough, by civil society's success in holding the state accountable. What was always a timid and soft state is now almost paralysed in its ability to make bold decisions. In an attempt to build enough checks and balances, India's founding fathers forgot that the government was created to act.

If John Stuart Mill, the celebrated nineteenth-century English thinker, were to appear suddenly in India today, the author of the famous essay 'On Liberty' would be delighted to see the amount of freedom that Indians enjoy. But as the author of 'Utilitarianism', who believed in the 'greatest good for the greatest number', he would get quickly depressed. The very same liberty results in taking eight years to build a road in India where it should take three; ten years to get justice instead of two. As a libertarian, he would applaud the protests and demonstrations of farmers over land rights or of Anna Hazare's over corruption. But as a sensible citizen, he would be dismayed by the paralysis in executive decision-making, by parliamentary gridlock and by the courts routinely dictating action to the executive.

It is a mistake to believe that the Indian state has weakened only in recent times because of coalition politics, weak leadership and economic liberalization. On the contrary, free markets depend on a strong rule of law with tough regulators and an impartial judiciary that enforces contracts quickly and fairly. The rule of law began to weaken in India in the 1970s as a result of Indira Gandhi's populist and patronage politics. Although it inherited at Independence the institutions of a strong state, India has historically had a weak state. But it has had a strong society, and the average Indian was defined by his place in that hierarchical society. It is quite unlike China which had a strong state and a weak society. India's history is one of political disunity with constant struggles between kingdoms, unlike China's history of strong empires. In Chapter Two, I develop this theme in a historical essay to try to come to grips with some of our contemporary dilemmas.

Given this past, it isn't surprising that after Independence India became a chaotic democracy in 1947, unlike the rule by autocrats in much of the third world. Gunnar Myrdal, the Swedish Nobel Prize winner, who studied India in the late 1950s and 1960s, called it a 'soft state'. In the twenty-first century, true to character, India is rising from below, quite unlike China whose success has been scripted from above by an amazing technocratic state that has built extraordinary infrastructure in such a short time.

Anna Hazare's movement in 2011 was the most recent example of a historically weak state colliding with a strong society. It reflected the continuing evolution of India from a traditional, hierarchical society to a modern civil society. Adam Smith had predicted in *The Wealth of Nations* that the growth of markets would lead to a division of labour and new social groups would emerge. The fluidity and open access of markets would undermine traditional social authorities and replace them with more flexible, voluntary forms of association. Two decades of high growth in India have been doing just that—and it is a positive thing. A modern democracy needs a vigorous civil society to keep it honest. But it is also dangerous when it fails to observe constitutional norms, and this is my principal anxiety over Anna Hazare's movement.

Generally, leftists desire a large state and rightists a small one, but what India needs is an effective state with a more robust rule of law and greater accountability. This book arises out of a quest for a strong, efficient and enabling state. Such a state is efficient in the sense that it enforces fairly and forcefully the rule of law, and contracts and rights guaranteed by the Constitution; it is strong because it has independent regulators who are tough on corruption and ensure that no one is above the law; it is enabling because it delivers services honestly to all citizens;

it is not intrusive as the 'licence raj' was, but is rules-based, with a light, invisible touch over citizens' lives. I could have used any of these adjectives in the subtitle of this book. In the end I settled for 'a liberal case for a strong state', hoping that readers would understand that I did not mean a benign dictatorship but a constitutional, accountable state that relentlessly and fairly enforces the rule of law.

I am at heart an old-fashioned liberal, the kind that mushroomed in the towns of India in the nineteenth century and whom Chris Bayly has described with gusto in his recent book, *Recovering Liberties: Indian Thought in the Age of Liberalism and Empire*. Like any liberal, I believe in liberty and equality. While I give priority to liberty over equality, I passionately believe in the 'equality of opportunity'. I am against attempts to achieve 'equality of result' because I do not think the human ego will shrink that far, and this is where I part company with my leftist friends. As I explain in Chapter Nine, my classical liberalism is different from what is called a 'left liberal'. My 'Indian liberalism' is also informed by a quiet toleration for all beliefs in our maddeningly diverse country where all paths seem to lead to the same divine unity and where among 330 million gods no god can afford to be jealous.

The big story of the twenty-first century's first decade is how China and India have embraced the market economy and have risen. The common mistake is to think that the race between China and India is about who will get rich first. The truth is that both countries will become prosperous and reach middle-income levels. The race is about who will fix its government first. India has law and China has order, but a successful nation needs both. If India fixes its governance before China fixes its politics, India will win the race, as Raghav Bahl says. If neither succeeds, then both may get stuck in the 'middle-income' trap. To avoid that fate India needs a stronger state and China needs a stronger society.

THE BOTTOM-UP STORY

India's 'bottom-up' success is not surprising given its historically weak state mechanism whose power was checked by a strong society. That society not only prevented state tyranny but never allowed state power to become too dominant, as in China and Russia, where despotic states were able to divest people of property and personal rights. Such repressive states have never existed in South Asia even during the periods of empire—the Mauryas, Guptas, Mughals and the British. China, on the other hand, has been held together by a strong state, and its history is that of strong empires but a weak society.

Two decades of high growth have brought dignity to the Indian middle class, and this means hope for the future. The Anna Hazare movement was a symbol of this dignity, and even if the movement fails, it has played its historic part. Dignity is a state of mind and for too long people in India have been denied dignity by public officials who ride around with lights flashing on their cars and make them wait in endless queues for the most basic services. Liberty without dignity is self-despising; dignity without liberty makes for status without hope; but liberty with dignity is hugely empowering. I shall elaborate on this theme in Chapter Six.

The success of democracy and free markets in India is consistent with its historical temper of pluralism and diversity. In their modern form, these two institutions came to India via the eighteenth-century European Enlightenment, carried on the utilitarian coat-tails of the British Raj. However, the roots of liberty are far older on the subcontinent, going back to the restraints placed on the ruler by raj dharma, 'dharma of the king', as I discuss in Chapter Three. Dharma can mean many things—duty, virtue, righteousness—but it is chiefly concerned with doing the right thing. Dharma also means law, and it preceded the state and placed limits on the king's power in pre-modern India. The king did not give the law as in China. Dharma was above the state, and the king was expected to uphold it for the benefit of the people. The king also did not interpret the law, unlike in China; it was the Brahmin who interpreted the law. Hence, a liberal division of powers was created early on, which contributed to a weak Indian state at birth. But it also prevented oppression by the state.

Myth-making is a part of the rhetoric of nation-building, and no one understood this better than Mohandas Gandhi. He adopted the universal aspect of dharma, called sadharana dharma, which consists of the duties expected of all human beings—duties such as ahimsa, 'not hurting others', satya, 'telling the truth', etc.—and thus he mobilized the masses in the cause of his liberal agenda to transform society. While India's society may be fragmented, he discovered that this dharma of conscience resonated with all Indians, including the minorities. In Chapter Three I ask if this universal dharma could be recovered as a 'modern myth' in the twenty-first century and help to translate the values of the Indian Constitution into meaningful language for the ordinary citizen and thereby instil the 'habits of the heart' required of a modern citizen. Sensible Indians understand that dharma is not a theocratic ideal but a secular, ethical idea, and the only reason I employ it here (rather than an anaemic English word such as 'moral') is to invoke the power of tradition on behalf of a liberal goal in the manner of Mahatma Gandhi.

Markets and merchants have been with us right through India's history—the Vaishya was a respected, 'twice-born' member of the varna-based society. At the heart of the market system is the idea of exchange—buying and selling—between free, self-interested human beings. I shall argue that people are able to trust each other and feel safe in transacting with strangers because of the shared restraints of that same sadharana dharma. In this context, dharma provides the underlying moral norms that promote trust and give people a sense of security when they cooperate in the marketplace. I explore this in Chapter Five. In contrast, the dirigiste socialist state or 'mai-baap sarkar' eroded this dharma capital. The idea of a 'limitless state' which occupied the 'commanding heights of the economy' for four decades in India was inconsistent with the country's historical temper and, not surprisingly, it failed.

IN TAHRIR SQUARE

This book was born on a visit to Egypt. On 8 April 2011, the day before Anna Hazare broke his fast, I was in Cairo to present the 'Indian model' for Egypt's future at a conference of liberals from their democracy movement. I had been reluctant to leave Delhi when history was in the making at home but I agreed in the end. It turned out that instead of teaching Egyptians something about democracy, I ended up learning something about India.

Cairo's Tahrir Square reminded me of Jantar Mantar in Delhi where I had seen the seventy-four-year-old Anna Hazare in a white villager's cap a few days earlier. Both were non-violent protests reminiscent of Mahatma Gandhi. Anna's hunger strike in particular was evocative of Gandhi's tactics. And like Gandhi, he had put a powerful government on the defensive. His fast was in support of a Lokpal, an anti-corruption agency to investigate complaints against politicians and officials. Clearly, Anna was no Gandhi—not even a pale copy—and while his movement had succeeded in creating awareness about corruption, I felt ambivalent because street revolutions are dangerous in a settled democracy.

A year earlier, however, no one in India could have imagined that Cabinet ministers, powerful politicians, senior officials and CEOs would be in jail awaiting trial for corruption. The credit for this belonged in no small part to Anna's movement, supported by determined justices of the Supreme Court, and a newly assertive Indian middle class. A series of scandals had enraged the middle class, the media and the opposition parties. These included graft-ridden purchases for the 2010 Commonwealth Games in Delhi, for which rolls of toilet paper worth Rs 40 had been purchased for Rs 400; mobile-phone spectrum had been 'given away' to favoured companies at prices so low that it had lost the government between Rs 40,000 crore and Rs 1,60,000 crore in licence fees; and pricey apartments in Mumbai had been 'grabbed' by politicians, officials and generals. These were some of the headline-grabbing examples of India's crisis of governance.

But the Egyptians did not want to hear about these things. They were too busy with their own problems and they asked me three difficult questions. First, how did India keep its generals out of politics? Second, how did it manage to create a sense of security for its minorities? (They explained that 11 per cent of Egypt was Coptic Christian while 13.5 per cent of India was Muslim; but why did Muslims in India feel secure while Christians in Egypt did not?) And third, what could Egypt learn from India's success in winning outsourcing business from the world's largest companies and become a rapidly growing economy? I did not have satisfactory answers to any of their questions, but they did force me to think about India in a fresh and new way.

When the conference got over in the evening, some of us wandered over to Tahrir Square nearby for a bit of sightseeing. We had heard that a massive demonstration had broken out that day against Hosni Mubarak, and we thought we might catch a moment in history. But through a twist of fate, I found myself on the podium, quite unexpectedly offering good wishes to 27,000 protesters from 'the people of Al Hind, the land of Mahatma Gandhi'. I was given three minutes to speak and in that brief time I spoke off the cuff about what I thought was the most important lesson from India's experience with democracy. I said to the crowd that democracy entails many things— elections, liberty, equality, accountability. But the hardest thing to achieve in practice is the 'rule of law' and the idea that no one is above it. To attain that, strong institutions of governance were needed.

'You would not be protesting today,' I added, 'if Egypt possessed the rule of law and if Hosni Mubarak did not think he was above it.' Then I told the Egyptians that while India was a proud democracy, its governance institutions had weakened, corruption had grown and indeed we had our own Tahrir Square movement.

I woke up that night at three to the sound of gunfire. At first I thought they were bursting crackers in the square. Soon there was a knock on the door. It was my host, who whispered that the army had moved into Tahrir Square and I should be prepared to flee as my 'three minutes of fame' had been posted on YouTube. Filled with fear, I changed quickly, picked up my laptop and passport, and sat and waited. I must have fallen asleep because the next thing I remember is that it was seven o'clock. I was still alive. I saw a cloud of smoke above Tahrir Square; I switched on the television to learn that the army had indeed come, but it had left as quickly, leaving two persons dead. It had been searching for soldier-protesters.

I returned home the following day, much relieved. I

picked up the morning newspapers in Delhi to find a number of editorials and op-eds comparing, somewhat simplistically, Jantar Mantar to Tahrir Square. They were wrong to do so. The defiant faces in Tahrir Square returned to me hauntingly: in their eyes was rebellion but there was also fear. They had been right to be afraid as it turned out. I had never had to fear the army in India, nor had to think about the first question of the Egyptians. India was not that kind of a state. What those eyes in Tahrir Square did not comprehend was that self-government is a slow, painful and demanding process, and ultimately depends on certain 'habits of the heart'. Indians still needed to learn those habits. But the Egyptians did provide me a new perspective on India, which I explain at the end of Chapter One.

What Anna Hazare's campaign against corruption had in common with the Arab Spring was an awakening in both countries of the new middle classes, especially the young, who had begun to believe that they mattered politically and were now demanding accountability from the state. Anna had also seeded the idea that accountability could only begin when each watchful citizen became aware of his personal dharma. 'I Am Anna', written on the Gandhi caps worn by the members of the Anna movement, symbolized this moral revolution. Those who vilified his campaign for attempting to usurp the Parliament's authority forgot in their arrogance that in the eyes of the ordinary citizen he was a reflection of public dharma—the same one whose symbol was placed in the middle of the Indian flag in the form of the Ashok Chakra. This dharma had been wounded by corruption.

AN OLD-FASHIONED PAMPHLETEER

This is not a 'how to' book with five quick answers to what India should do in the next five years. It is a moral essay which belongs to the tradition of the eighteenth-century English pamphleteers about whom George Orwell wrote so eloquently. Although it seeks mainly to understand the travails of Indian democracy, it is not shy on advocacy, with specific suggestions for good governance and prosperity. I have summarized the most important ones in Chapter Nine, 'What Is to Be Done', a title inspired by Lenin's bias for action. My ambition as a writer of non-fiction is to try to combine narrative writing of day-to-day events with economic, social and political thought. Finding a balance is a continuous struggle; each needs the other to be satisfying and my writing is poorer without it. I acquired a liberal perspective on life at the university from reading Rousseau, Kant and Locke. From their ideas I also gained an optimistic view of history, believing that the growth of liberty, prosperity and democracy was inevitable. What I did not realize is that progress in that direction might also lead to detours along the way—for example, to Chinese authoritarianism, Russian corruption, the Indian 'licence raj' and Nigerian perfidy.

As someone who writes columns regularly in newspapers, I have to be careful about my perspective. The 800-word rectangles are ephemeral by nature but a book of non-fiction endures (hopefully). With a beginning, middle and an end, it has to capture the big picture within the framework of an overarching thesis. The reader expects a continuity of ideas, and needs a single argument to run through the whole, unfolding chapter by chapter. Only then is it wholesome and satisfying. In the obsession with day-to-day events, it is easy to lose sight of this big picture. A Londoner in the 1820s, for example, would not have seen one of the greatest events unfolding in world history: the industrial revolution. If you were at the docks, you might have noticed rising textile exports; MPs from the North would have told you that the mills in Lancashire were expanding; you might have heard at the India Office about the plight of Indian weavers. But no one could see the big picture. So it is with contemporary India; it is difficult to see the silent but grand transformation that is under way.

There is also the problem of balance between idealism and realism for a writer. I am sometimes accused of being optimistic. Yes, I do have a positive view of the universe and of human beings; my goal in life is to further human freedom and well-being. But I am also aware of the unintended consequences of good intentions. The problem is that one never really knows enough about something, especially when it is near in time and place. Since my subject is India, there are good reasons to be optimistic. Warts and all, India is not only reasonably stable and united, but it is quite miraculously a secular democracy that in the past two decades has become a successful economy. Its citizens live together in greater hope than those of almost any other developing nation.

All writing is subjective and inevitably distorts the world, and this is also a balance that a writer has to worry about. V.S. Naipaul wrote two scathing, venomous, almost hysterical descriptions of India, and then went on to express a curious optimism about the same subject in his third book, *India: A Million Mutinies Now*. Had Naipaul changed or had India changed? In the first two books he described a 'half-made' postcolonial society stripped of history by the colonial encounter, insecure of its identity, situated at a distant periphery of the developed world. In his third book, he saw a different nation. That insecure, 'half-made society' was now threatened by 'a million mutinies'—the strident assertions of caste, class and religion—which to the Naipaul of the two earlier books might have suggested social and political anarchy. But to the later Naipaul these acts of rebellion were signs of a new self-confidence. They were signals of renewal and of India's rediscovery of itself. He now displayed an uncharacteristic sympathy for the actors in this regenerated India.

One may not agree with Naipaul's crude political judgements; one may be angry with his politics; but I find something to admire in his courageous, subjective approach to the world. Both India and Naipaul had, in fact, changed. The point is not to hastily condemn a work because it is excessively subjective. The writer of non-fiction must, of course, strive for as much 'objectivity' as possible. But in the end, the unforgiving truth is that all writing—both fiction and non-fiction—is an autobiographical project of self-fashioning.

I

THE INDIA MODEL

Good laws, if they are not obeyed,
do not constitute good government.

—Aristotle, *Politics*, 4.8

A BAFFLING STORY

Kushal Pal Singh, 'KP' to his friends, is a hugely successful builder who is fond of narrating the tale of two adjoining towns on the outskirts of Delhi—Faridabad and Gurgaon. In 1979, Faridabad had an active municipal government, fertile agriculture and a direct railway line to the national capital. It also had a host of industries—including one owned by KP—and a state government that was determined to make it a showcase for the future. Gurgaon, on the other hand, was a sleepy village with rocky soil and pitiable agriculture. It had no local government, no railway link, no industries, and its farmers were impoverished. Compared to pampered Faridabad, it was wilderness.

In 1979, the state of Haryana divided the old political district adjoining Delhi. It gave the better half to Faridabad; the worse half became Gurgaon. When an official of the Haryana government in the early 1980s made a presentation to investors about making Gurgaon a city of the future, he was laughed out of the room. Anyone in Delhi, including my brother, who wanted to invest in industry or in real estate, was advised by their friends to go to Faridabad.

Thirty years later, Gurgaon has become the symbol of a rising India. Called 'Millennium City', it has dozens of shiny skyscrapers, twenty-six shopping malls, seven golf courses, countless luxury shops belonging to Chanel, Louis Vuitton and others, and automobile showrooms of Mercedes-Benz, BMW and Audi. It has 30 million square feet of commercial space and is home to the world's largest corporations—Coca-Cola, PepsiCo, GE, Motorola, Ericsson and Nestlé among them. Its racing economy is reflected in its fabled apartment complexes with swimming pools, spas and saunas, which vie with the best gated communities anywhere.

Faridabad remains a sad, scraggly, would-be town, groaning under a corrupt, self-important municipality; it is still struggling to catch up with India's first wave of modernization after 1991. Gurgaon's disadvantage has turned into an advantage. It had no local government, nor planning authority. It was more or less ignored by the state government until it became successful and then only as a source of graft. This meant less red tape and fewer bureaucrats who could block development in Gurgaon.

But Gurgaon had destiny. Meaning 'village of the guru', it belonged according to legend to Guru Dronacharya, the martial arts guru in the *Mahabharata*. In the epic, the kingdom of the Bharatas is also divided: the better half goes to the Kauravas and the worse half to their cousins, the Pandavas. But the Pandavas are diligent, hard-working and determined; they clear the land, make shrewd alliances, and build a magical city, Indraprastha. Archaeologists believe this city may be buried under South Delhi or close to it. Could Gurgaon be the twenty-first-century equivalent of the magical Indraprastha?

Gurgaon has risen with little help from the state. It only got its municipal corporation in 2008. Its ineffectual but arrogant planning authority, Haryana Urban Development Authority (HUDA), was continuously overshadowed by the speed and energy of private developers like K.P. Singh, whose company Delhi Land and Finance Ltd (DLF) is one of the secrets behind the miracle. Instead of planning for the future, HUDA was always planning for the past; it had collected more than Rs 10,000 crore in infrastructure fees—an impressive sum—but few could say that the money had benefited the city or its residents.

The downside of rising without the state is that Gurgaon does not have a functioning sewage or drainage system; no reliable electricity or water supply; no public sidewalks; no decent roads; and no organized public transport. Garbage is regularly thrown into empty plots of land or by the side of the road. So, here is the puzzle: how did spanking new Gurgaon become an international engine of economic growth with minimal public services?

Gurgaon manages to flourish without public infrastructure because of its self-reliant, resilient citizens. They don't sit around and wait. They dig bore wells to get water when government pipes run dry. They put in diesel generators when power from the state electricity board fails. They use cell phones from private providers rather than landlines of the state company, Bharat Sanchar Nigam Ltd (BSNL). They use couriers rather than the post office. Many companies have even installed their own sewage treatment plants. Apartment complexes and companies employ tens of thousands of security guards rather than depend on the police. When teachers and doctors do not show up at government primary schools and health centres, people open up cheap private schools and clinics, even in the slums. Private schools of all kinds are flourishing on every street—even the poor can find one to fit their pocket, where fees are as low as Rs 150 per month.

To rise without the state, as Gurgaon has done, is a brave thing, but it is not sustainable. Gurgaon would be better off with a functioning drainage system, reliable water and electricity supplies, public sidewalks and parks and a decent public transport system. Indeed, it should also 'grow during the day'. Moreover, the truth is that the state has not been entirely absent in Gurgaon. It has just not been effective. It has managed to provide a degree of security, law and order, property rights, town planning and even some infrastructure. Gurgaon would be a happier place if the state were to begin functioning effectively and honestly, and helped to improve infrastructure.

Modern India is in some ways Gurgaon writ large. The nation's ascent also baffles Indians, and it was reflected in my inadequate, hesitating responses to the Egyptians. Middle-class Indians, who now constitute almost a third of the country, believe that their nation is doing well because the pre-1991 over-regulating state has gradually liberalized. They point to the information technology (IT) industry as the quintessential example of India's rise after 1991 without interference from the state. To them, the entrepreneur is at the centre of this success story as India now has dozens of highly competitive private companies that have become globally competitive. Meanwhile, the state has not kept pace. It has not provided enough electric power, roads, ports, water, schools and hospitals—the entire infrastructure needed for a rising nation. Nor has it allowed the private sector to build it in adequate quantity. The middle class envies China's extraordinary infrastructure, which has enabled it to rise.

THE MODEL IS UNIQUE

There are many paths to modernity. East Asia adopted a state-directed model of development. China's is a path of authoritarian capitalism. The West's rise was slower, over several hundred years, and combined market capitalism and a centralized bureaucratic state that gradually evolved into a liberal democracy. The capitalist division of labour led to an industrial revolution, the rise of a middle class and mobility, which in turn transformed rural kinship relations to impersonal connections of the city and produced an ethos of individualism.

India offers a new model. First, it got democracy before capitalism; the rest of the world did it the other way around. Second, its economic rise has been driven from 'below' through its people, rather than forced from 'above' by the state. Third, its economy has been impelled by domestic demand rather than exports, by services rather than manufacturing, and by consumption more than by investment. Although historically a weak state, India possessed at Independence sturdy institutions of a centralized bureaucratic government which had evolved during the years of colonial rule. These institutions helped the new nation to establish a successful democracy after 1950—even before it had the economic base or administrative capacity to support such a system with universal franchise. In most countries, except perhaps the United States, capitalism had preceded democracy. After 1950, India tried to industrialize through the agency of the state by placing the public sector at the 'commanding heights' while controlling private enterprise tightly. But it did not have the capacity or the disposition to manage a command economy. Moreover, its centralized bureaucratic state was not in keeping with the country's historical, decentralized temper.

Because democracy came before capitalism in India, the constitutional restraints and fiscal discipline of a modern state were quickly challenged by the rough and tumble of competitive politics. Politicians were happy to create the illusion of a limitless state with populist giveaways at the ballot box. Nehru's choice of a socialist economy reinforced this illusion. Thus, a large government came into being with far too many opportunities for bureaucrats and politicians to be corrupt. After forty years, this state became bankrupt and was forced to make a U-turn. Beginning in 1991, through a series of reforms, it dismantled socialist institutions and replaced them with market-oriented ones. These gained legitimacy quickly because the economy responded and other command economies also collapsed around the world at the same time. Twenty years of capitalist growth has stimulated a broad transformation of society in India, resulting in the rapid rise of the middle class. Mobility and urbanization are contributing to the weakening of old kinship bonds of the village; India's traditional society is gradually changing into a more vocal civil society. Supported by a strapping and independent media, it has begun to hold the state more accountable.

Meanwhile, the robust institutions of the state, inherited from the British, have gone into steady decline. The rule of law has eroded, and governance and corruption have become a serious problem. Too many interactions with the government are morally ambiguous. In some regions, a citizen cannot obtain a birth certificate without paying a bribe; a rickshaw driver pays the police a sixth of his daily earnings; a farmer cannot get a clear title to his land without having to bribe a revenue official; a parent finds that the teacher is absent in a government primary school; a sick person has to cope with an absent doctor at the state primary health centre. These are some of the areas where the state touches citizens' lives, leaving them mostly disappointed. The local institutions of accountability are too weak and in the eyes of the helpless citizen, there is a pervasive feeling of the failure of the general restraint of 'public dharma'.

According to a study by Harvard University's Michael Kremer, one out of four teachers in India's government elementary schools is absent, and one out of two present is not teaching. Even as the famed Indian Institutes of Technology (IITs) have acquired a global reputation, less than half the children in the fifth grade in India can do second grade reading and maths, according to the Annual Status of Education Report (ASER). Hence, even the poor are exiting state schools and moving to budget private schools which charge Rs 100 to 400 a month in fees. Around 35 per cent of Indian children are now in private primary schools—almost 50 per cent in urban India. The same failure of delivery is reflected in the most tragic of all statistics—half the children in India do not get enough or the right food or adequate care. One-third of the babies in India are born with low birthweight. This is heartbreaking given that India has 'sustained the greatest effort in history to improve nutritional standards' according to UNICEF, through its Integrated Child Development Services programme.

India's economic success has not been equally shared. Cities have done better than villages; some states have done better than others; the economy has not created jobs commensurate with its rate of growth; only a small fraction of Indians are employed in the modern, unionized sector. People are willing to accept this inequality because a vast number have indeed seen their lot improve and there is hope for an even better future for their children. But a weak and corrupt state adds salt to the wounds of those who feel left out. Social scientists think of failures of the state as a problem of institutions, and the solution, they rightly say, lies in changing the incentive structure. But these failings also have a moral dimension. 'Dharma has been wounded' has been a common refrain right through the Anna Hazare movement against corruption.

Millions of Indians are stuck between the factory and the farm but they do not sit around and complain. Each morning they pull themselves up and go out and create a livelihood in the informal sector. This too is part of the Indian model. Regulations do not make it easy. Eighteen years of slow, incremental economic reforms have fashioned a certain kind of nation which was captured in the film *Slumdog Millionaire*. If the movie caught the character of the nation's entrepreneurial poor, the Indian Premier League (IPL) of cricket mirrors the entrepreneurial energy of the middle class. The character quite simply is of a vibrant and energetic people who are hemmed in by an arid ecosystem of weak governance. In the World Bank's new study, *Moving Out of Poverty*, most Indians claimed to have moved out of poverty through their own initiative. The poor prefer an enabling environment that lets them work with dignity rather than depend on handouts of the government.

REFORMS LEAD TO A MIRACLE ECONOMY

India's economy has been growing rapidly for a quarter of a century. After three post-Independence decades of meagre progress, the country's economy responded in the 1980s to Rajiv Gandhi's modest reforms, and annual growth picked up to 5.5 per cent; it rose to 6.2 per cent in the 1990s and to 8.5 per cent from 2003 to 2010, when India became the second fastest growing economy in the world. However, it hit a wall as growth plunged to 6.4 per cent in 2011–12.

In the quarter century of high growth, the middle class in India quadrupled to almost 300 million people. By 2022, half of India's 1.3 billion people will be middle class based on these trends. It will not be a western-style car-owning middle class but its values will be the same. Meanwhile, 1 per cent of the country's poor have been climbing out of poverty each year since the mid-1980s, according to the late economist Suresh Tendulkar, and this too has added up to 220 million people to the middle class. Population growth had also slowed from its historic rate of 2.2 per cent to 1.4 per cent by 2010. This means that per capita income has almost quadrupled since 1985, and India has gone from being the world's fourteenth largest economy in 2000 to the ninth in 2010, and if high growth continues, it will be fifth in 2020 and third in 2030.

It is true that the reforms have been behind India's economic rise. While the pace of reform has been frustratingly slow, every succeeding government from 1991 to 2004 persisted in reforming. And even slow reforms added up to make India the world's second fastest growing economy. An intriguing question is: dozens of countries (beyond East and Southeast Asia) adopted the same reforms, but why did India become more successful? No one seems to have an answer. My untested hypothesis is that if you reform in a society where there are people who know how to conserve and accumulate capital, then those reforms will have a bigger impact. India is fortunate to have abundant Vaishya or Bania communities of the merchant caste—Marwaris, Chettiars, Khojas, Jains, Agarwals, Guptas and more. The much-maligned caste system may thus have turned into a competitive advantage. This is also why, perhaps, more than 50 per cent of the Indian names in the Forbes 2012 billionaires list had Vaishya surnames.

As I mentioned, India's economic path is unique. Rather than adopting the classic Asian strategy—exporting labour-intensive, low-priced manufactured goods to the West—India has relied on its domestic market more than exports, on consumption more than investment, on services more than industry and on high-tech more than low-skilled manufacturing. The consumption-driven model has meant that the Indian economy has been more insulated from global downturns. Moreover, 30 to 40 per cent of GDP growth has been due to rising productivity—a true sign of an economy's health and progress—rather than to increases in the amount of capital or labour.

For half a century before Independence, the Indian economy had been stagnant. Between 1900 and 1950, economic growth averaged 0.8 per cent a year—exactly the same rate as the population growth, resulting in no increase in per capita income. In the first decades after Independence, economic growth picked up, averaging 3.5 per cent from 1950 to 1980, but population growth accelerated as well. The net effect on per capita income was an average annual increase of just 1.3 per cent. Indians mournfully called this 'the Hindu rate of growth'. Of course, it had nothing to do with being Hindu; it had everything to do with the Fabian socialist policies of Nehru.

After Nehru, those socialist policies became more rigid during the rule of his imperious daughter, Indira Gandhi, when India experienced its darkest economic decades. Nationalization of the wholesale trade in grain in 1973 was the high-water mark of the command economy. Its consequences were so horrendous that it was repealed within six months. Per capita income growth plunged and was half of the rest of the developing world's from 1965 to 1980. Father and daughter had shackled the energies of the Indian people under a 'mixed' economy that combined the worst features of capitalism and socialism. Their model was inward-looking and import-substituting rather than outward-looking and export-promoting, denying India a share in the prosperity generated by a massive expansion in global trade after the Second World War. They set up an inefficient and monopolistic public sector, over-regulated private enterprise with the most stringent price and production controls in the world, and discouraged foreign investment—thereby causing India to lose out on the benefits of both foreign technology and foreign competition. Their approach pampered organized labour to the point of significantly lowering productivity and they ignored the education of India's children.

But even this system could have delivered more had it been better implemented. It did not have to degenerate into a 'licence-permit-quota raj', as C. Rajagopalachari, the last governor general of India and later chief minister of Madras, put it in the late 1950s. The demands of a dirigiste policy stretched the competence of the state to its limits, and institutions began to decline. It is hard to blame Nehru because socialism was the received wisdom of his day, but by Indira Gandhi's time the wisdom had changed. She is rightly condemned for decreeing a state of political emergency, from 1975 to 1977, which curtailed human rights, but she deserves equal censure for the lost decades of India's economy.

In the mid-1980s, the government's attitude towards the private sector began to change, thanks to the underappreciated efforts of Prime Minister Rajiv Gandhi. Modest liberal reforms—lowering marginal tax rates and tariffs and giving some leeway to manufacturers—spurred growth. But the policies of the 1980s were profligate and brought India a fiscal crisis by the start of the 1990s. That crisis triggered the reforms of 1991, which finally allowed India's integration into the global economy—and laid the groundwork for the high growth of today. Those reforms signalled a decisive break with four decades of dirigisme. The economy quickly returned the favour: growth jumped, inflation plummeted and exports and currency reserves shot up.

At the end of the first decade of the twenty-first century, growth had slowed down and the nation plunged into a crisis of confidence. Unprecedented corruption was matched by an economic crisis that brought the nation to its knees. Inflation was unacceptably high, the rupee had weakened more than any currency in Asia, and both the fiscal and current account deficits were in a dangerous zone. Investment by private business declined significantly. Some feared that India may be at a tipping point similar to the one in 1991. The government blamed the debt crisis in the eurozone, but insiders knew that the culprit was the lack of reforms in the past five years and a paralysis in decision-making and red tape—especially the lack of approvals for land acquisition in the steel and power sectors—combined with unsustainable subsidies that were crowding out private investment. Whether India could return to a path of high growth depended on its ability to implement economic reforms and initiate the more difficult reforms of governance.

CAN INDIA SKIP THE INDUSTRIAL REVOLUTION?

India's competitiveness improved dramatically after 1991 despite poor infrastructure, high fiscal deficits and appalling governance. Growth was driven by services and domestic consumption. India had one of the world's highest consumption rates, accounting for 64 per cent of India's GDP, compared to 58 per cent for Europe and 38 per cent for China. That consumption might be a virtue embarrassed those Indians with an ascetic streak, but as the economist

Stephen Roach of Morgan Stanley put it, 'India's consumption-led approach to growth may be better balanced than the resource-mobilization model of China.' The contrast between India's entrepreneur-driven growth and China's state-centred model was stark. China's success was largely based on exports by state enterprises or foreign companies. Beijing remained highly suspicious of entrepreneurs. Only 10 per cent of credit went to the private sector in China, even though the private sector employed 40 per cent of the Chinese workforce. In India, entrepreneurs got more than 80 per cent of all loans.

What is peculiar about India's model is that high growth has not been accompanied by a labour-intensive industrial revolution that could transform the lives of the tens of millions of Indians still trapped in rural poverty. Many Indians watched mesmerized as China created an endless flow of low-end manufacturing jobs by exporting goods such as electronic gadgets, toys and clothes, whereas their own better-educated compatriots exported knowledge services to the rest of the world. They wondered fearfully if India might skip an industrial revolution altogether, jumping straight from an agricultural economy to a service economy. The rest of the world had evolved from agriculture to industry to services. India appeared to have a weak middle step. Services already accounted for 58 per cent of India's GDP in 2010, whereas agriculture and manufacturing were each less than 20 per cent.

The failure to create an 'industrial revolution' stemmed in part from bad policies. The most egregious one was made in the name of Mahatma Gandhi in 1970 when around 800 industries were reserved for the small-scale sector. In these 800 industries only tiny companies were allowed to compete. But of course they could not do so against the large firms of competitor nations. Large firms were barred from making products of daily use such as pencils, boot polish, candles, shoes, garments and toys— all the products that had helped East Asia and China create millions of jobs. Even after 1991, Indian governments were afraid to touch this holy cow. In the end, the fear turned out to be false—little more than bureaucrats scaring politicians by warning of a backlash. It took fifteen years to get rid of this suicidal law.

Another obstacle is the rigid labour laws that make it almost impossible to lay off a worker. The infamous case of Uttam Nakate illustrates this well. In early 1984, Nakate was found at 11.40 a.m. sleeping soundly on the floor of a factory in Pune while on duty. His employer, Bharat Forge, let him off with a warning. But he was caught napping again, and then again. On the fourth occasion, the factory began disciplinary proceedings, and after five months of hearings, he was found guilty and sacked. But Nakate went to a labour court, which forced the factory to take him back and pay him 50 per cent of his lost wages. Seventeen years later, after appeals to the Bombay High Court and the Supreme Court, the factory finally won the right to fire an employee who had repeatedly been caught sleeping on the job.

Aside from highlighting a lethargic legal system, Nakate's case dramatizes how the country's labour laws actually reduce employment, by making employers afraid to hire workers in the first place. The rules protect existing unionized workers—sometimes referred to as 'organized labour'—at the expense of everyone else. This is why organized labour comprises less than 10 per cent of India's workforce.

In the short term, the best way for India to improve the lot of the rural poor might be to promote a second green revolution. Unlike in manufacturing, India has a competitive advantage in agriculture, with plenty of arable land, sunshine and water. To achieve such a change, however, India would need to shift its focus from peasant farming to agribusiness, and encourage private capital to lease land from farmers and to bring in the latest technology. It would need to lift onerous distribution controls, allow large retailers to buy crops directly from farmers, and invest in a cold chain so that a quarter of India's crop could be saved from going rotten in the field.

Indian entrepreneurs still face plenty of other obstacles. Electric power is less than reliable and more expensive in India than in competitor nations. Checkpoints ('octroi nakas') keep trucks waiting for hours. Taxes and import duties may have come down, but the cascading effect of indirect taxes continues to burden Indian manufacturers. This is why a pending goods and services tax legislation will make such a difference. Stringent labour laws continue to deter entrepreneurs from hiring workers. The biggest deterrent is still government officials. The 'licence raj' may be gone, but an 'inspector raj' is alive and well in many states; the 'midnight knock' from an excise, customs, labour or factory inspector still haunts the small entrepreneur. Industry studies show that bribes constitute a significant cost of doing business; more than the money, it is the fear of harassment and humiliation by officials that deters a young person from becoming a manufacturing entrepreneur.

The troubling question remains: can India skip a labour-intensive manufacturing and industrial revolution? If so, how would it take its army of peasants from the villages to the cities?

THE NEED FOR A STRONG, EFFECTIVE STATE

It is an amazing spectacle to see the country turning middle class alongside the most appalling governance. In the midst of a booming private economy, Indians despair over the delivery of the simplest public goods. It used to be the other way around: during the 1950s and 1960s, Indians worried about economic growth but were rather proud of their judiciary, bureaucracy and police. Now, the old centralized bureaucratic Indian state is in steady decline. Institutions have frayed. Where the state is desperately needed—in providing basic education, health care and drinking water—it has performed dismally. Where it is not needed, it is still hyperactive in stifling small private enterprise through red tape and the 'inspector raj'.

The modern Indian state was formed in the early 1860s, soon after the British Crown took over the rule of India from the East India Company and set up a rule of law with clear, written-down rules in a set of elaborate codes. It was well administered but it was not accountable to the citizens. In 1947, this state became answerable to the people. Independent India inherited robust institutions of governance, which were considered by many to be among the best in the world. Partly enabled by these institutions, India went on to become a dynamic democracy with a vibrant civil society, and after 1991 it became a rapidly growing economy. However, those inherited institutions have not been renewed, reformed or modernized, despite the repeated recommendations of expert committees. This is the crux of the problem.

The puzzle is this: how can a vibrant democracy with a rising economy and an energetic civil society have allowed the state and governance to decay in this way? India has discovered that democracy does not necessarily lead to economic development without the right policies—it had to take a U-turn in 1991, adopt market-oriented policies, and only then did prosperity begin to spread. Now it is learning that high growth and prosperity do not ensure good governance. It has also begun to realize that it cannot take growth for granted. Optimists think that it is the country's destiny to reach the high income levels of the West and Japan. This will not happen unless the country fixes its institutions of governance. If it doesn't, it will more than likely be caught in a 'middle-income trap' like some Latin American countries which lost decades mostly for the same reason.

Another lesson from this overview of India's unique model of modernization is that a nation cannot rise forever at night. It needs a solid, effective state to provide a rule of law to support a rapidly growing economy and a rising society. The 1991 reforms did not happen spontaneously. They were in the end initiated by the state—even though it took a crisis, and the government was kicked and dragged into doing them. Moreover, markets have not entirely worked in a vacuum after 1991. Although institutions have deteriorated, a reasonable degree of property rights, security, and law and order have been undoubtedly important to India's rise.

Markets need a network of regulations and institutions and umpires to settle disputes. In the past two decades some good regulators have emerged. In the capital markets, the Securities and Exchange Board of India (SEBI) has matured and brought transparency; the Reserve Bank of India (RBI) has become less arbitrary in its oversight of banking; the telecom revolution, ushered in by the revenue sharing model of the Vajpayee government, was ably supported by the Telecom Regulatory Authority of India (TRAI) which withstood pressures from the telecom department to weaken the private sector. Similarly, insurance and pension regulators have also struck the right note; the new National Stock Exchange (NSE) forced reform on all the other stock exchanges. On the other hand, reforms of electric power failed because of weak and spineless regulators, and the later troubles in telecom relating to the radio spectrum were exacerbated by poor regulators.

Despite some real achievements, such as the setting up of some world-class institutions of higher learning during Nehru's time, the truth is that the Indian state is in serious trouble. After 2010, India began to experience the limits of 'growing without the state'. Investment slowed down because investors lost trust in the ability of the state to provide a reliable and predictable environment. Red tape reared its ugly head as the government became paralysed. Crony capitalism also became a real worry in the unreformed sectors of the economy. With high growth, tax revenues had risen for two decades, but they were not used to improve the capacity of the state or modernize governance. Infrastructure spending did rise but far too much still went into subsidies and 'premature welfarism'. The state did not hire more judges or police officials, or significantly upgrade technology or change obsolete systems in the bureaucracy and other functions that could have improved governance.

BACK TO THE EGYPTIAN QUESTIONS

My visit to Egypt brought about a change in my perspective. I had been too close to India and too impatient with its deficiencies. But after seeing the yearning for democracy in Tahrir Square, I felt that the persistence of democracy in India was an extraordinary achievement. India had held free and fair elections without interruption for sixty-five years. Of its 3.5 million village legislators, 1.2 million were women, who ruled over the world's most diverse country peacefully. This is a proud achievement for an often bungling state. The three questions of the Egyptians also helped me to understand the Indian model better.

No one in India ever asks the first question of the

Egyptians: 'How did you keep the generals out of politics?' The idea is inconceivable after sixty-five years of robust civilian Indian rule in which there have been periodic and peaceful changes of government. One answer might be plain 'luck'. Another speaks to the restrained behaviour of India's first generation of rulers, especially the charismatic Jawaharlal Nehru, who invited profound respect from the armed forces. Having fought for India's freedom, this generation went on to nurture the institutions of democracy, and this brought legitimacy to civilian rule.

The pattern of civilian control was set early. When power was being transferred from Britain to independent India, the British military commander wanted the public to be kept away from the ceremony for security reasons. Nehru politely informed him that India was now ruled by the people and he cancelled the general's order. Soon after, Sardar Vallabhbhai Patel, the home minister, was less polite in turning down the advice of the commanding general, who opposed military action in Hyderabad:

> As the decision was being deliberated in the cabinet, General Bucher stood up and said, 'Gentlemen, you have taken a decision in a difficult matter. I must give you my warning. We are also committed in Kashmir. We cannot say how long it will take so we will end up having two operations on our hands. This is not advisable, so as your C-in-C I ask you not to start the operations.' He offered his resignation if his advice was not heeded.

In the silence that ensued, Nehru looked distressed and helpless. Patel quietly told the general that he could resign but the police action would start the next day. The historian Ramachandra Guha cites another example to illustrate the culture of the armed forces. Referring to General J.S. Aurora, a war hero after the liberation of Bangladesh, he wrote: 'The striking fact is that no army commander has ever fought an election . . . [or] convert[ed] glory won on the battlefield into political advantage.'

By contrast, Pakistan, next door, experienced ten self-seeking, corrupt civilian governments in the first decade after Independence, and this made people lose respect for democracy. The army that seized power in 1958 in Pakistan had been part of the same proud, professional organization that India had inherited from the departing Britain at Partition in 1947; today that army is self-serving and corrupt and the main obstacle to peace.

Thanks to our vigorous democracy I do not fear the army in India. But I do fear a limp state which cannot implement its own laws or control its functionaries. The real danger to India, as I have noted, are decaying institutions of the state which are responsible for rampant corruption. Unless they are reformed, people might become impatient, and might be tempted to support a military adventurer. This is the true lesson from Pakistan's experience. The challenge is this: how to achieve disciplined governance without turning to authoritarian coercion?

The second question of the Egyptians also took me by surprise. India is indeed a *secular* democracy. The killing of around 3000 Sikhs provoked by Indira Gandhi's murder by two Sikhs in 1984 and the death of around 2000 Muslims after the burning of Hindu pilgrims in a train in Godhra in Gujarat in 2002 were horrendous events, but they were aberrations in six and a half decades of independent India. The relative success of secularism may have more to do with the nation's past traditions of tolerance. But democracy too, like a safety valve, has contributed to maintaining India's secularism.

Although more than 80 per cent Hindu, India is not a 'Hindu Pakistan' as Nehru put it. Despite periodic riots in the past sixty-five years, Indian Muslims have not turned fundamentalist, and overwhelmingly they approve of India's secular democracy. And as Guha says, 'as long as Pakistan exists there will be Hindu fundamentalists in India'. He adds that the Bharatiya Janata Party (BJP), the Hindu nationalist party, is not a 'fascist party' as some think. In 2004, the BJP alliance lost power in a general election and left office with dignity; fascists do not behave in that way. In fact, the riots in Gujarat in 2002 might have been the 'death rattle' of Hindu nationalism in its virulent form. The risk in India is not of a theocratic party seizing power but of politicians being tempted to play the identity card and making people feel insecure about their differences.

Liberals in Egypt and elsewhere in the Middle East have good reasons to fear the capture of the Arab Spring by political Islam. Egypt is profoundly Arab, and Arab societies are among the most tribal in the world. A state built on tribal foundations is inherently unstable because kinship ties reassert themselves. Egypt, however, is one of the few that did manage to create a modern state. The Mamluk Sultanate from 1517 to 1805 created a miraculously effective state which broke the tribal 'tyranny of cousins' via a unique institution of military slavery. Originally slaves, the Mamluks were expected to protect the state from Arab tribalism, but in the end they also fell victim to partiality and kinship and eventually took over the state. In the same way, the army took over the Egyptian state in the twentieth century.

The third question of the Egyptians goes to the heart of the India model: how to get the economy moving by becoming the world's back office. India became a high-growth economy partly as a result of the economic reforms. Egypt too will have to free its private sector from the tentacles of the state. Although India's success in software and business process outsourcing was enabled by removing some red tape in the telecom sector, the knowledge economy became a driver of India's growth because of benign neglect by the state. Bureaucrats did not know how to regulate it and could not choke it with red tape, in the way they stifled India's industrial revolution through licences, permits and inspectors. Customs inspectors could not stop the export of software through telephone lines; labour inspectors could not stop software engineers from talking to customers in America at night; excise inspectors could not harass the IT firms because the government did not levy tax on services. Much like Gurgaon, India's knowledge economy literally grew at night when the government slept.

A less appreciated reason for India's economic success

has been a mental change among the young. In *India Unbound*, I recounted the story of a fourteen-year-old low-caste boy named Raju, who was taking computer lessons in a Tamil village and wanted to grow up to be 'Bilgay, the richest man in the world'. Raju claimed to have found the secret of success: 'First, you must learn Windows; and next, you must learn four hundred words of English.'

'Why four hundred words?' I asked.

'To pass TOEFL!'

I should have known. Raju is the symbol of a mental revolution that swept India in the 1990s. Raju's generation had lost my generation's hypocrisy over money; in his priorities, Windows precedes English, which is only a skill and 400 words are enough. When I was growing up, the English language paralysed us. Raju's mind was liberated and decolonized—as emancipating as the rise of Hinglish.

One evening I heard the newscaster on the 9 o'clock Zee News announce: '*Aaj* Middle East *mein* peace *ho gayi*'— three words of English and four of Hindi, spoken as though it was the only way. That too is freedom. For generations, Indians have mixed their mother tongue with English, but earlier it was an expression of upward mobility. Now Hinglish has become the fashionable language of South Bombay and South Delhi, of Bollywood, FM radio and advertising. Who knows, perhaps one day Hinglish will produce its Shakespeare, and go on to become the proud language of India. David Crystal, a world authority on English and editor of the *Cambridge Encyclopedia of the English Language*, predicts that India will soon have the world's largest number of English speakers, and he claims that when tens of millions of middle-class Indians speak English in a certain way, it will be the way that global advertisers will have to speak it. This too is a part of the India model, and it is the result of the free debate of democracy that John Stuart Mill predicted would lead to the 'self-development of individuals as reasonable persons'.

BETTER THAN 'PHIPTY PHIPTY'

My Egyptian adventure left me feeling that warts and all, India had done reasonably well on balance—a thought that did not sit easily when I was up close to India's corruption and red tape. Although both India and Egypt were powerful societies with fragile states, their histories and backgrounds were unique. But both needed to strengthen the rule of law. Egypt had a highly efficient internal security apparatus but could not execute simple tasks like processing visa applications or licensing small businesses efficiently. What was in common between Tahrir Square and Ramlila Maidan was that both represented a middle-class awakening—a symbol of hope for both India and Egypt. As for India, Anna Hazare might fade away but the new-found voice and power of the middle class would not, and it might well script the political future of India as it had its economic rise.

Because India has historically had a frail state, strengthening state institutions will not be easy. Twenty million state employees constitute a formidable vested interest. A fractured Parliament cannot be depended on when 150 out of 542 seats were occupied by members with criminal records after the 2009 general election. Yes, the higher judiciary can be relied on to give reasonably fair justice, but it takes forever. Clearly, the 'flailing state' would have to be kicked and dragged to initiate governance reforms. The ray of hope lies in the newly awakened, rapidly growing middle class. Backed by an aggressive media, it constitutes a powerful countervailing force. When the middle class becomes 50 per cent of the Indian population, as it will in the early 2020s, the politics of India will also have to change.

On balance, India has managed to achieve a degree of success by the standards I have suggested in the Introduction. Paraphrasing Johnny Walker, the famous comedian of Hindi cinema, Ramachandra Guha concluded in *India after Gandhi* that India is a 'phipty-phipty democracy'. I believe India has done better than that. It has allowed most of its citizens to live together with a large measure of liberty—more freedom, certainly, than that available in most new nation states. It has had regular, peaceful transfers of power via the ballot box. Its economy has risen rapidly in the past twenty-five years. Although prosperity has not been evenly shared and there are still too many poor, there is now hope for the conquest of poverty. Socially, hierarchy has continued to weaken; caste matters less in the modern, urban economy, although it remains a vigorous marker of political identity. There would have been greater equality of opportunity had the state paid the same attention to the quality of education as it did to its quantity; prosperity then would also have been more equally shared. What mars this story of relative achievement has been the decline in governance and a weakening rule of law. Until it is fixed, India will remain a story of private success and public failure; it will not be able to call itself a truly successful nation, let alone a great power.

2

A PEOPLE BUT NO STATE

*When there was neither kingdom, nor king; there was
neither governance, nor governor, the people protected
themselves by dharma.*

—*Mahabharata*, XII.59.14

A few months after his first fast at Jantar Mantar in
April 2011, Anna Hazare staged a second one, this
time at the larger and more popular Ramlila Maidan. The
government caved in a second time and went back
humiliated to the drawing board to draft legislation for a
stronger Lokpal. It was hard to believe that a frail, seventy-
four-year-old villager in a Gandhi cap could hold the
sovereign government of a rising power to ransom.

As I was returning home from Ramlila Maidan, I decided
on an impulse to drop in on an old friend, a grandee of the

Congress party, who lived in a sprawling bungalow in Lutyens' Delhi. I wanted his reaction to Anna Hazare. Just as I turned into his gate, I saw on the opposite side of the street two young men, who were also returning home from the same spectacle. They were obviously in good spirits and were singing away in full-throated glory the line emblazoned on their caps: 'I Am Anna'. It had been inspired most likely by a slogan from the Egyptian uprising, 'We are all Khaled Said'. My friend, meanwhile, had just arrived from campaigning in a private jet and was emerging out of his black SUV, surrounded by half a dozen cars of his security detail with flashing blue lights. The overall effect was of intimidating power. I wondered if he had heard the boisterous crooning on the other side of the street.

I felt extremely ambivalent about Anna Hazare and his methods. I was not sure whether his supporters wanted to strengthen the state or to abolish it. But I was not prepared for a relentless onslaught against his anti-corruption movement. Over the next ten minutes I was subjected to an insistent monologue, punctuated by succulent swear words and occasional reminders of his own self-importance. He tried to smear Ralegon Siddhi, Hazare's village, calling it a 'mini state' with Anna Hazare as its quasi-dictatorial leader. I thought his attack pathetic, even more than his exhausted government's abject surrender to Anna Hazare's demands.

'Why blame him?' I said. 'Your government is corrupt—that's what is behind it.'

'Don't be naive, the entire political class is corrupt!' he said with irritation.

There was a long pause, which was followed by a brief moment of candour when the éminence grise let his guard down. 'Our government is not any more corrupt than the others, it is just weaker.'

I wanted to tell him that only feeble governments were corrupt; sturdy governments do not allow people to steal from them. Instead, I asked him about a story in that morning's *Times of India* about 'policy paralysis' in his government. The story had catalogued twenty-eight major projects of the government in key areas of infrastructure that had been stuck *after* permission had been granted by the government. One of these was a 12 million ton steel plant by the Korean company POSCO, which was the largest foreign investment in India and a 'showcase'—and had been caught in red tape for five years. In addition there were 168 projects of Coal India, a government-owned company, which were awaiting clearance of the environment ministry, according to its chairman, N.C. Jha. The approval was supposed to come in 300 days but was, in fact, taking as long as six years. As a result there were power shortages, blackouts in many parts of the country. Despite vast coal reserves, India had now become an importer of coal. Some of the responsibility lay with green activists, but the major problem, according to those in the know, was red tape and inter-ministerial wrangling.

'Is it as bad as that?' he asked. After a pause, he said, 'The problem is a weak coalition government and a feeble prime minister.'

As I sat listening to my friend, I realized that he was making the common mistake in thinking that the Indian state had weakened only in recent times because of coalitions and weak leaders. He was unaware of its inherently feeble nature. The Anna Hazare movement against corruption was only the most recent example of a historically frail state bumping up against a traditionally stout Indian society. If India had always had an anaemic state, it had always had a strong society, which was now morphing rapidly from a traditional to a modern civil society.

A WEAK STATE, A STRONG SOCIETY

The king in Indian history was a distant figure and did not touch the life of the ordinary person, who was defined by the village, the caste and the joint family. This realization came to me while I was editing an economic and business history of India in fifteen slim volumes. The type of despotic and intrusive governments that emerged in China, which divested people of their property and their rights, hardly existed in India. India's past was a history of competing kingdoms and of political disunity in contrast to China's history of muscular empires. The German philosopher G.W.F. Hegel made the same observation in his typically extravagant way: 'If China must be regarded as nothing else but a State, Hindoo political existence presents us with a people but no state.'

Of course, such a generalization is by definition simplistic. Some Indian kingdoms, especially in the south, were extremely strong, but the vast majority were comparatively weak. Others did the sensible thing and decentralized decision-making and they ended up with strong governments at the local level. Overall, however, there is a germ of truth in Hegel's statement. India had few empires and even these were weaker than the state in China, which had cultivated a highly trained central bureaucracy for thousands of years.

To come to grips with the Indian conception of the state, the political scientists Lloyd and Susanne Rudolph contrasted it with the European ideal in a recent volume, *The Realm of Institutions: State Formation and Institutional Change*, which summarized fifty years of their ruminations about the Indian state. In Europe, the modern state was based on three ideals: the Greek idea of common citizenship, the Christian ideal of a moral community and the seventeenth-century concept of a civil society. In contrast, the classical Indian conception was of limited state power, whose main purpose was to protect the 'ordered heterogeneity' of Indian society. India's society consisted of diverse cultural communities that shared a sense of brotherhood within themselves but existed distinctly apart in their relationship to each other. Yet they lived harmoniously in what André Béteille has called 'non-antagonistic strata'. The state was meant to uphold this peaceful order. Unlike Europe, the diverse social groups in India did not participate in a single civil society. Instead, India's diverse social groups had their own laws and customs which existed prior to the state. The duty of the ruler was to protect the respective customs and laws of this self-regulating social order.

Because India generally had a frail state, it is not

surprising that it went on to become a chaotic democracy after Independence in 1947. Although it had the appearance of a centralized modern nation state, it was, in fact, loosely structured, segmentary, with considerable sharing of powers with the regional states. It was characteristic of Indian state formation. In the 1960s, Gunnar Myrdal, the Swedish economist, in frustration at the Indian state's inability to get things done, dubbed it a 'soft state' in his monumental three-volume *Asian Drama*. And it is not surprising that in the twenty-first century India appears to be rising from below, quite unlike China, whose success has been scripted by a technocratic state.

Myrdal had come to Delhi at the height of India's experiment with a dirigiste socialist state and felt irritated by the 'soft' Indian state, which lacked the determination and ability to change institutions that stood in the way of development. He felt that it could not eradicate corruption, enact land reform and get people to pay taxes. He found a great gap between ideals and reality, between legislating laws and implementing them. He rightly predicted that the gap would make Indians contemptuous of state power, and this would make reforms more difficult in the future. The most scornful turned out to be the Naxalites or Maoists, whose activities had spread over the previous decade to 150 districts, covering nearly 40 per cent of India's geographical area and 35 per cent of its population.

A 'soft' state, Myrdal wrote, is unwilling to 'impose obligations on the governed' and there is correspondingly 'unwillingness on the part of the governed to obey rules'. Carrots are preferred to the stick, despite the exhortation on behalf of danda-niti, 'punishment', in the classical texts. As a result, there is low social discipline. Western nations, he felt, had much higher discipline at a similar stage in their industrialization. This was an unfashionable message to give to Indians who had recently become free of colonial rule.

Although the author went on to win a Nobel Prize, his book was not received well in India's intellectual circles. Its insights and suggestions remained forgotten for four decades, especially with regard to what Myrdal called the 'folklore of corruption'. Since corruption was ubiquitous in people's day-to-day conversation and gossip, he claimed that Indians had got so used to it that they had become prey to petty corruption at the slightest temptation, and breaking rules and flouting laws had become a cultural norm. During the freedom struggle, flouting of laws had been a heroic act of resistance to colonial authority but it had become a debilitating habit.

While the state has always been feeble, India has been held together by a sturdy society. Jawaharlal Nehru, in his book *The Discovery of India*, defined this society in three words: village, caste and family. India's society consisted of over half a million more or less autonomous villages that were once reasonably self-sufficient; more than two thousand jatis, or endogamous, occupational castes; and the joint family. India's atomistic society is thus more like a biryani or a salad bowl compared to China's melting pot. Both India and China were created by the historic wanderings of peoples and tribes from across Asia over thousands of years. India tended to 'accumulate' its diverse groups who retained their distinctiveness while identifying themselves as Indian. China tended to 'assimilate' its people into a common, homogeneous Han identity. True, people on the periphery resisted Han assimilation; its spoken language was, until recently, highly diverse (although the written language was universal).

Nevertheless, China is more of a melting pot in which differences disappear while India is like a salad bowl in which constituents retain their identity. India accommodated its migrant minorities by allowing them to become a separate jati or caste—the Jats, the Rajputs and so on—and this made it possible for a vast variety of people to live together. India is a plural society, which means that loyalty is fragmented in favour of the joint family, the caste, the religion and the linguistic state. There is less loyalty to the whole which manifests itself in a temptation for a special type of corruption called nepotism.

Nehru did not emphasize the particularistic loyalties of Indian society, nor its hierarchical nature, but focused instead on its communitarian character—the idea that the group is more important than the individual. This is why B.R. Ambedkar, one of the creators of the Indian Constitution, insisted that the individual rather than the village should be the moral unit of the Constitution. His famous remark in the constituent assembly is widely quoted today: 'What is the village but a sink of localism, a den of ignorance, narrow-mindedness and communalism? I am glad that the Draft Constitution has discarded the village and adopted the individual as its unit.'

Ambedkar helped me understand why an individual's autonomy in India has been traditionally limited not by the state but by kinship ties, caste rules and religious obligations. These institutions of society also limited the control of the state on the individual. Caste, in particular, was antithetical to the development of a strong nation state, according to Hegel. The task of modern citizenship was to convert the partial loyalties of society to a loyalty to the modern, impartial state.

While a solid society helped to check state power, a feeble state did not return the favour. Obligations of caste, rules of religion and duties of kinship limited the ordinary person's freedom. The social anthropologist Ernest Gellner labelled this 'tyranny of the cousins' in which one's social world was narrow and limited to a circle of relatives, caste brethren and the priest, and they determined who one married, how one worshipped and just about anything that really mattered. A weak state was unable to provide a balance and protect the individual from social oppression. In China, on the other hand, social actors were much weaker than in India and were not able to resist a state that was very powerful and often oppressive. The contrast is as true today as it was in the third century BCE, when Qin Shih Huangdi and Ashoka were building empires. Protests against injustice in India were generally not aimed at the state as they were in China. They were aimed normally at the social order, dominated by Brahmins.

India's answer to oppression from Brahmins was the guru, a spiritual entrepreneur, who created a dissident religious movement. Buddha was the most famous, but gurus are ubiquitous even today—you can encounter one every fifty kilometres. India in the sixth century BCE experienced a flowering of spiritual entrepreneurs. Aside from the Buddha, there was Mahavira of Jainism, which is still a remarkably popular religion in Gujarat and Rajasthan. Other yoga sects also emerged within Hinduism. Over time the most important of these were the egalitarian bhakti sects, which enjoyed an important revival in medieval and colonial times, and are still popular today. My father belonged to one such sect, Radha Soami, whose ashram is situated on the banks of the Beas in Punjab.

As India modernizes, its traditional society is changing. It is evolving into an urban civil society and challenging the state. The latest example of this is Anna Hazare's movement against corruption, which is following in Jayaprakash Narayan's footsteps in the 1970s and of course Mahatma Gandhi's in pre-Independence India. (Ambedkar did not approve of Gandhi's 'chanting crowds' and would have condemned Hazare as being anarchical and subversive of the Constitution.) The traditional self-sufficient village is now producing for a national market. The customary governance institution of the village is giving way to a democratically elected panchayat. Ritual segregation between castes has weakened, helped by legislation against untouchability. Caste hierarchy is waning as the demand for talent in the modern economy undermines traditional claims for status. While atrocities against Dalits persist in villages, their status has risen through the ballot box and a Dalit middle class has come up through affirmative action. The joint family is also fading with urbanization and mobility, but ties of kinship still assert themselves when it comes to a marriage partner.

THE PARTING OF POWER AND STATUS

The idea that human beings once existed in isolation in a state of nature is an early modern western myth. There never was a paradise of free-spirited individuals roaming contentedly through the primordial forests, as Rousseau claimed. In India too, despite our perennial fascination with the sanyasi, the 'renouncer' who is a 'theatrical figure in ochre robes', human beings have always lived in kin-based social groups much as in the rest of the world. Living thus for thousands of years taught people to cooperate socially. The rules of social cooperation are the rules of dharma.

The Indian state, like most states in the world, evolved from a tribal society. Historians differ in dating this transition but it probably occurred on the Indo-Gangetic plain early in the first millennium BCE. During the early Vedic period India consisted of tribes and clans, organized as *gana-sangha*, ruled by a raja or a tribal chief, who was more often 'first among equals' and his authority was limited by sabhas or samitis of his kinsmen. The land did not belong to the king but to clan families, such as the Kurus and Panchalas whom we remember from the *Mahabharata*. The raja did not own the land, nor had taxing authority in the modern sense; ownership was vested in the clan.

With the coming of cities and merchants the mahajanapada, 'the state', emerged in the sixth century BCE. Kashi and Kosala were the first to come up but Magadha in south Bihar went on to become the strongest and most famous. The raja of the tribal clan now became a more powerful king, but even now his power was limited by dharma, 'the law', and by the priest, who interpreted the law. The law was above the monarch. The raja was expected to uphold or protect dharma, as the Dharmashastras, 'dharma texts', make amply clear. When the king violates dharma in the *Mahabharata*, he is called a 'mad dog', and the epic encourages people to revolt against him.

Dharma was rooted in culture and religion rather than in politics. The word derives from the Sanskrit root *dhr̥*, meaning to 'sustain' and 'hold up' like a foundation. It is the moral law that sustains an individual, society and the cosmos. The earliest law books, the Dharmashastras, were not edicts of emperors as in China, but documents written by religious authorities. Subsequently, the law evolved in India somewhat like British Common Law, based not only on the dharma texts but on case law linked to precedents generated by pandits and other religious authorities. Thus, dharma developed in an unplanned, evolutionary manner independently of anyone's will. A major discontinuity came with Britain's colonial rule when India transitioned from a particularistic dharma of myriad customary rules in the different regions to a single Common Law.

The early social division of society into four varnas, 'social classes', also limited the power of the state by separating secular and religious authority. While Kshatriyas, 'warriors and landholders', ruled, the Brahmin had a higher status and the power to interpret dharma. Brahmins in India were not organized hierarchically, as in the Roman Catholic Church, but they were aware of their moral authority as guardians of the sacred law. Unlike China and other societies, the religious elite in India were able to challenge the political and economic elite. Thus, power and status were separate, as Louis Dumont has so eloquently described, and this led to a liberal division of powers early in India's history and served the purpose of checking the tyranny of the state.

ORDERED HETEROGENEITY

The most important empires on the Indian subcontinent—Maurya, Gupta or Mughal—were far weaker, as I have mentioned, than the Chinese. None was able to do what the Qin dynasty could, which was to build one of many fortifications that subsequently became the Great Wall of China to keep invaders out. The wall forced the nomadic Xiongnu back into Central Asia, where they displaced a series of other tribes. In a knock-on effect, this led the Scythians, or Sakas, to invade northern India, to be followed by the Yuezhi, who established the Kushan dynasty. The Guptas could not prevent India from being invaded by another group of tribal nomads from Central Asia, the Huns. Foreign invaders were able to conquer

India partly because of political disunity, but also because no ruler had been able to penetrate Indian society and had left the internal social order untouched. Just as the Aryas of the Rig Veda could not erase the traditions of the indigenous Dasas, so too were the later invaders, including the Muslims and the British, unable to effect social change.

The strong Indian society assimilated the subsequent waves of conquests and migrations—Greeks, Sakas, Kushans, Huns—in the manner prescribed by the dharma texts. It compartmentalized them rather than homogenizing them. Since the laws and customs of the new social groups existed prior to the state, kings were enjoined to uphold the diverse customs of the new social groups. Militant Islamic conquerors also succumbed to the principle of 'ordered heterogeneity'. The early Turkic invaders in the twelfth century, who were required to convert wholesale the conquered peoples by the sword, found the Indian society too stubborn. Thus, the subcontinent did not become a homogenized Islamic country. Instead, Indian society compartmentalized the new migrants. Badaoni, writing in the sixteenth century during Akbar's rule, says, 'As a result of all the influences which were brought to bear on his Majesty, there grew—gradually as the outline on a stone, the conviction in his heart that there were sensible men in all religions.' Later, Aurangzeb tried to deviate from the principle of 'ordered heterogeneity' and endangered the foundations of the Mughal Empire. The British, too, after some trial and error, yielded to the accepted practice of the subcontinent and protected the personal laws and customs of the different communities.

The ideal of a subcontinental empire, however, continued to exist throughout history even though it was indifferently realized. It went back to the Mauryan Empire in fourth century BCE. Mauryan rulers identified themselves as chakravartin, 'universal emperor', symbolically depicted as the centre of the great wheel that represented the political universe. Ashoka Maurya, a devoted convert to Buddhism, ruled two-thirds of the subcontinent with the aid of an elaborate official hierarchy, an intelligence service and a paid army. The imperial idea reappeared in the Gupta dynasty (320–535 CE) and was powerfully restored by the Mughals (1556–1707/1857), whose Mongol Turkic origins and Persian borrowings brought external ideas, men and practices to the process of state formation on the subcontinent.

After the Gupta Empire, regional kingdoms and segmented local authorities ruled India for six centuries. From the thirteenth to the sixteenth centuries, the Muslim Sultanate attempted to displace them by independent nobility and a sophisticated revenue apparatus influenced by Abbasid and Saffavid models. The Mughals added a more rationalized imperial service (the mansabdari system) to this under the direct control of the emperor. The Mughal state combined a mixture of direct and indirect rule—for example, direct in Gujarat and Awadh, and indirect in Rajputana, where Rajput rulers had extensive autonomy. British rule, after that, blended the ideas and institutions of the European nation state with Indian reality. It adapted Mughal ceremony with modern administrative arrangements and liberal, utilitarian ideas to create a centralized, imperial state. But it too did not directly rule many princely states, over which it exercised an indirect paramountcy.

Thus, when the subcontinental empire existed in India, it invariably did so by preserving aspects of the regional kingdom as part of the system of 'ordered heterogeneity' which has dominated India's history. Unlike the Chinese empire or the European sovereign state which obliterated lower authority, the Indian state preserved secondary jurisdictions. It remained a layered and segmented authority. Both the Mughal and the British states formed alliances with kingdoms, such as the Rajputs, who helped them to rule their empire. The failure of Mughal officials to incorporate the rulers of the south is partly responsible for the collapse of Mughal rule. Today's Indian state has endured because its founding fathers recognized early the principle of 'ordered heterogeneity'. In the 1950s, they accepted linguistic states as contemporary expression of the regional kingdom.

Why India ended with a robust society is not easy to explain. Society emerged on the subcontinent, as it did everywhere, as a 'spontaneous order' without conscious design (to use the language of the Nobel Prize winner Friedrich Hayek). Language, the market and moral rules have also evolved in this spontaneous manner. Indeed, life's evolution on earth is another dramatic example. The latest illustration of 'spontaneous order' is the Internet. Even so, the ability of India's society for self-organization has been exceptional. Highly elaborate ritual practices—a 'performative society'—may also have contributed to the stability and continuity of India's society.

Why a strong state did not develop in India may have something to do with the relative absence of violence in India. To quote Charles Tilly's pithy formulation: the state made war and war made the state. A strong state emerged early in China because of the desperate conditions created by continuous warfare among feuding warlords. A powerful state under a tough king or emperor was needed to keep the warlords in check. In Europe, the modern state—which governed a large territory with a centralized bureaucracy, deployed large armies and taxed its people uniformly—emerged much later than in China, around the sixteenth century.

The conditions on the Indian subcontinent were more peaceful. Although the Vedas describe skirmishes between the Aryas and Dasas, India never experienced the 'centuries-long periods of continuous violence comparable to China's Spring and Autumn and Warring States periods . . . or a five-hundred-year period of continuous warfare . . . during the Western Zhou Dynasty', according to Fukuyama. India's relative peace may have been due possibly to the lower density of population in the Indus and Ganges river valleys. If people were unhappy or felt coerced by a ruler, they simply packed up and moved on. They migrated to a new place rather than submit to the whims of a tyrannical king.

More recently, people did experience considerable hostilities—for example, in the sixteenth to the eighteenth centuries—but the subcontinent has been remarkably free of violence since 1857. It managed to escape both the world wars in the twentieth century. Its struggle for freedom from colonial rule was also non-violent, thanks to Mahatma Gandhi. Yes, there was a horrific bout of bloodshed at Partition but it was not state sponsored. India also escaped the horrendous carnage of Mao's China or Stalin's Russia, and for this some credit should go to the extraordinary vision of the first generation of leaders of free India. But the question is: has this remarkable record of peace contributed to a weak state? If it has, does it present a major obstacle to strengthening the Indian state in circumstances of peace?

Clearly, Indians have had an ambivalent relationship to power. They would never have allowed an amoral doctrine such as Chinese Legalism, which regards the only goal of politics to be the naked accumulation of power, to flourish. The exact opposite ideas, such as ahimsa, 'non-violence', emerged early on the Indian subcontinent during the time when the Vedic texts were written. They were developed in the Upanishads and flowered with the Buddha. The constant refrain has been that killing living beings has bad consequences for one's karma. Although there is no lack of pragmatic advice to the king, exhorting him to practise realpolitik in texts such as the *Arthashastra*, it was always trumped by constant reminders that the dharma of the king is to protect his people against external aggression. Thus, Bhishma tells King Yudhishthira, who is inclined to 'non-violence' after the terrible war in the *Mahabharata*, not to ignore danda, the 'rod of power', in order to protect his people—sensible advice.

VIBRANT BAZAARS, DECADENT RULERS

When European travellers came to India they were struck by the weakness of political authority. They noted the contrast between the energy, colour and sophistication of the Indian bazaar and the decadence of the rulers. When the Mughal Empire collapsed in the eighteenth century, India reverted to its usual norm—a dynamic, decentralized society with a weak state. The historian Chris Bayly offers a rich picture of day-to-day life during this period of so-called anarchy. He shows in his book *Rulers, Townsmen and Bazaars* that life continued to thrive in north India's bazaars as merchant communities quickly adjusted to new circumstances and new opportunities, and he rectifies the old Victorian stereotype of a 'static native society as a backdrop to British exploits'. Colonial historians called the eighteenth century India's 'black century', in which anarchy had followed the collapse of Mughal authority. This in turn had given impetus to European expansion, leading eventually to the 'British Peace' after 1857. Rather than chaos, Bayly calls this time of trouble a period when society was resurgent, as power became decentralized and commercial. Regional kingdoms emerged after the Mughal Empire—in particular, peasant kingdoms of the Jats, Marathas and Sikhs were based on a creative interaction between the state and an agrarian society, as new political entrepreneurs found financial support from merchants and other intermediaries in the bazaar.

The limited nature of the Indian state explains why the Portuguese were able to move into the west coast of India fairly easily in the fifteenth and sixteenth centuries. The kings ignored the Portuguese traders until it was too late. The Mughals did not regard the Europeans as a threat but as 'pimples on the outer skin of the Empire'. They did not feel threatened because maritime trade was not worth bothering about. In China, by contrast, the empire controlled the ports strictly and the Europeans were forced to launch an attack on the Chinese state in order to prise out commercial privileges. In India, the relationship between the king and the merchant was more ambiguous, and Europeans exploited this fuzziness to make inroads. When the king was short of cash, he would even 'outsource' or 'farm' his right to tax to a merchant or a landowner without losing his status as king. Since trade requires protection, if the king is too weak to give security, merchants will create a security force, and this force can sometimes become an army. Before the king realizes it the trader becomes a rival, and this is not an implausible script for the rise of the British Empire in India.

Bayly reminds us that India's political culture depended on legitimacy. If a ruler insisted on a higher share of revenue from the community, he had to deliver better services and infrastructure. Ordinary people regarded the state as beneficent when it built roads and canals. People praised the ruler, whether Muslim or Hindu, when he performed. The British Raj won the grudging respect of Indians for this reason—it did what the Maurya, Gupta and Mughal empires had done only in a limited way. The British enacted the Police Act of 1861, which resulted in posting a policeman with a common code of conduct in every village. In this way they managed to penetrate the village. In his book *Strong Societies and Weak States*, the political scientist Joel Migdal cites other examples, such as the building of the railway in the nineteenth century which gave legitimacy to the idea of a strapping, centralized state. But the British were careful when it came to social norms and beliefs. When they attempted social reform, such as the change in the age of consent for marriage, it backfired and strengthened anti-colonial sentiment. Thus, they were reluctant to touch the old system of obligations based on relationships between joint families and castes, and shift to one based on individualism—from what sociologists call 'status' to 'contract', as had occurred during the eighteenth and nineteenth centuries in the West.

A STATE CREATED BY SAINTS

After Independence, India adopted a modern, liberal Constitution based on the rule of law, enforced by a well-built centralized state. Its liberal ideas were founded on concepts that had come via the British Raj but had been internalized by a small middle class over a hundred years and especially during the freedom struggle. Indians embraced their Constitution enthusiastically. It was truly a 'bridgehead of effervescent liberty on the Asian continent' in the words of the political thinker Sunil Khilnani, but that liberty did not begin to fully flower until Indians gained economic freedom from a quasi-socialist state with the economic reforms in 1991.

In the excitement after Independence there was a shared

sense of a moral, unifying India. After all, 'India had been created by saints in the shadows of Hitler, Stalin and Mao', as Andre Malraux put it. Thanks to the freedom movement, a sense of unity had emerged both in the elite and the popular consciousness. This sense of commonality gave a new meaning to the separate communities and identities of the subcontinent, which had been energized by Gandhi's strategy of nurturing national unity through the medium of regional languages and symbols. But this sense of unity has since become more complex in two distinct ways. One, at the intellectual level, many have been persuaded by a new generation of historians to acknowledge the 'little traditions' of the local regions and lower-caste identities in contrast to a unifying pan-Indian, Sanskritic 'great tradition'. Two, the pressure of electoral politics has brought into being linguistic states, which have gradually become strong and have accelerated the shift in power from the Centre to the states. This may have contributed to weakening the central authority but it has strengthened India's democracy.

Soon after Independence, a relatively strong state posed the greatest challenge to the traditional hierarchical society. It abolished untouchability and enacted affirmative action on behalf of Dalits through reservations in public sector jobs and educational institutions. It passed the far-reaching Hindu Code Bill, which brought about, among others, far greater equity in the inheritance of a son and daughter. With democratic and populist pressures, the state also tried to emulate what became features of a western welfare state after the Second World War. This included sensible policies on education, public health and social welfare. The powerful influence of the thinking of Fabian socialists and the economist John Maynard Keynes played an important role. But the problem was that the Indian state was revenue poor and did not have the financial base for supporting such ambitions. Nor did it expand its administrative capacity.

A missed opportunity at the early stage of the republic was not to have embedded vigorous local democracy. Only in 1992 was Panchayati Raj legislated after several amendments to the Constitution, and then implemented only reluctantly. Self-government is a slow and demanding process, and participation at the local level is a 'school of democracy' in which people learn civic habits, duties and attitudes. These civic virtues help build the self-restraint that eventually strengthens the rule of law. Thus, there remains a gap between the ideals of the western liberal Constitution and the existing prejudices of the people. The politicians after Independence did not do a good job in bridging this gap. Nor was there, alas, a Mohandas Gandhi in independent India—a person with real moral authority who would have the genius to translate the constitutional ideals in a meaningful way into the world view of the people, so that they could call the Constitution their own rather than something imposed from above.

What emerges from this brief historical overview is a picture of a weak state and a strong society. This account was never meant to be comprehensive; otherwise it would have dwelt on the Mughals and the other large and long-enduring kingdoms—the Cholas, the Eastern Chalukyas, the Palas, etc. My purpose has been to tease out of the evanescent Indian past a shy, hesitant attitude to centralized authority on the subcontinent. This historical temper will explain among other things why a federal system has evolved in contemporary times in which chief ministers of states are often more powerful than the prime minister in Delhi. This disposition is also consistent with a plural, syncretic and resilient culture with a continuous and uninterrupted history of thousands of years. The secret of its unique persistence may lie in its ability to borrow and accommodate variety. Barely a century after the rule by Muslims got going, for example, India produced the extraordinary Amir Khusro who reflected the fusion of Hindu and Islamic traditions. The Indian mind instinctively recoils from centralized and rigid approaches to life. Hinduism has never defined itself by inflexible dogma. Despite the lack of political unity, people have felt bound by a common culture since ancient times. A sense of a 'sacred landscape' and widespread pilgrimage networks may have something to do with this, as Diana Eck suggests in her recent book, *India: A Sacred Geography*.

A STRONG STATE, A STRONG SOCIETY

It was after a gap of almost five months that I once again ran into the grey eminence of the Congress party, this time at a book launch at the India Habitat Centre in Delhi. Both of us were glad for the chance of a chat over chai after all the speeches. He confessed that he had been impatient and irritated the last time we had met. But now that Anna Hazare had receded from the front pages, he seemed more relaxed. With a smile he told me that he had dutifully gone to Bahri in Khan Market and bought the books I had recommended.

'So, do you agree that a successful nation needs both a strong state and a strong society?'

We quibbled over the word 'strong', but soon concurred that a 'strong state', at least in the sense that the classical liberal thinkers had thought of it, did not have to be oppressive. Moreover, our historical temper would never allow a state to become oppressive in that sense. It was an effective and competent state which enforced its laws strictly and fairly, and was relentless in upholding the rule of law. While observing due process, it would be efficient in delivering timely outcomes, especially as they related to justice and the courts. It was a constitutional state above all, not a populist one, that competitive politics had created.

'A strong state cannot be a limitless state if it wants to perform its core governance functions with excellence,' I added. The sight of the finance minister getting up to announce two dozen welfare schemes each March in the Budget was every bureaucrat's nightmare. We needed to be humbler in our ambition and our ability to re-engineer society. Economic growth was creating opportunities and if the state could only enable access to good schools and health care, equity would follow. One of the great scandals of our age was the appalling quality of the average government school and primary health centre. He did not agree with a 'limited state' but both of us felt that a limp state like India's with a feeble rule of law created uncertainty in people's minds. A weak rule of law allowed policemen, ministers and judges to be bought. When people see the powerful and rich get away, they lose respect for the state and turn back to their parochial interests.

'This is why we needed Anna Hazare to come and remind us of this truth,' I said.

He did not flare up at the mention of Anna Hazare's name, and so I continued. I explained that a successful society needed both a strong state and a strong society. Anna's movement may not endure but its legacy would. One may not approve of his non-constitutional tactics, but he had awakened the new Indian middle class in order to help clean up public life. The cleansing had to come from within, with each citizen becoming aware of his dharma. Anna's cap, like the Gandhi topi, was symbolic of this moral revolution. He had bequeathed to the young the idea that they mattered politically. But he had also demonstrated that India's old hierarchical society was changing, and one of its consequences was an assertive civil society. The old order had been unequal but stable and people knew what was expected of them at different stages of life. All this was in flux. In the midst of a million mutinies, people were revolting against inequality and hierarchy, but they did not yet have a new set of working rules to reduce the confusion and the pain. There was no new widely accepted idea of public dharma to replace the old one. Hence, the flagrant lack of respect for the rule of law and rampant corruption.

3

A CRISIS IN THE RULE
OF LAW

*Although the king is invested with
authority and power, true sovereignty
belongs to dharma, not the king.*

—*Mahabharata*, XII.71.26

NO ONE IS ABOVE THE LAW

On the sweltering afternoon of 29 September 2011, principal district judge S. Kumarguru began to hand out sentences. There was a hushed silence in the packed courtroom in Dharmapuri, Tamil Nadu. He began at 3.30 p.m. but could not finish until 4.40 p.m. because he had to read aloud punishments awarded to 215 government officials. Among those convicted were 126 forest officials, eighty-four policemen and five revenue officials. Seventeen were convicted of rape and they received prison sentence from seven to seventeen years; others received from one to three years on counts of torture, unlawful restraint, looting and misuse of office. Had fifty-four of the accused not died in the meantime, the sentencing would have taken longer.

Nineteen years earlier, in 1992, four teams of government officials had descended in the early hours of a June morning on the adivasi hamlet of Vachathi. Perched picturesquely in the foothills of Sitheri Hills, the village is situated near the Sathyamangalam forest, home to the dreaded brigand Veerappan. The government party assembled the villagers beneath a neem tree and let loose a reign of terror. They searched house to house for smuggled sandalwood. When they found nothing, they accused the villagers of harbouring Veerappan. They shouted at and slapped the villagers repeatedly. Then they picked up eighteen teenage girls and dragged them into the forest, where they stripped and raped them repeatedly. They kept the girls for a whole day and brought them back only at nine that night. Claiming a haul of sandalwood from the riverbed, the officials arrested 133 villagers and incarcerated them in the local jail in the neighbouring town.

After the court read out the sentences on the officials, a reporter went up to the seniormost official. Even two decades after the event the convicted official was not contrite. M. Harikrishnan, the retired conservator of forests, claimed that the officials had been wrongly punished. 'They had only been doing their duty,' he said. The judge had awarded him three years in jail 'for causing evidence to disappear' and another three years of rigorous imprisonment under Section 3(2)(1) of the Scheduled Castes and Scheduled Tribes (Prevention of Atrocities) Act, 1989. During the trial the judge had reminded him that the Nazis who were tried at Nuremberg for killing millions of Jews had also claimed in their defence that they had been doing their duty. He had added that Harikrishnan's duty was to catch the outlaw, Veerappan, and to stop the smuggling of sandalwood. It was not to rape, assault and pillage a village.

Sixty-five-year-old Angammal, whose daughter had been raped nineteen years ago, said that she felt relieved after the sentencing. 'It is sweet revenge for us,' she added, 'seeing those who raped our daughters being sent to jail.' Angammal watched as the officials who had been sentenced turned over their cell phones, their wallets and other valuables to their relatives. Soon they were herded into a bus for their onward journey to the prison in Vellore.

Angammal's friend admonished her, 'This is not the time to speak of revenge!' A man standing nearby counselled Angammal. 'Only the state is allowed to take revenge in a civilized society, and it is called the judge's punishment,' he told her. But Angammal continued saying that she had 'thirsted for revenge' all these years. In defence of her sentiments she said, 'If a good person suffers, then the bad person should suffer even more.'

The Vachathi case was 'one of the worst examples of the abuse of power in sixty years of independent India', said P. Shanmugam, who had waged a campaign for justice for almost two decades and is a hero of this story.

As president of the Tamil Tribal People's Association, he had worked tirelessly to bring justice to this village of innocent tribal people. He refused to celebrate when the judgement was passed. 'How can I be happy when men in power could subvert justice year after year for so many years?' he said.

What is the human mind to make of this soul-numbing news? My reaction was one of horror when I first heard in the early 1990s about the rape of teenage girls by men in uniform. Almost two decades later I experienced a sense of relief, almost a feeling of catharsis, when punishment was finally meted out to these powerful officials. The third emotion was outrage against those who had allowed the case to drag on for nineteen years. Being powerful officials, these men had used every means at their command to cover up and delay the judicial process. Fourth, I was moved by Angammal's artless feelings of vengeance. And finally, I asked myself, how does one prevent similar abuses of power in the future?

Even after the officials had been convicted and sentenced, Shanmugam thought he detected in Harikrishnan and other high functionaries a firm belief that they were somehow above the law. This belief, I felt, had been punctured that September afternoon. The best feature of the court judgement was that senior officials had been punished for crimes committed by their juniors. It was the judge's way of saying to the mighty that no one was above the law. It was an unusual achievement by the Indian state where too often officials are complicit in shielding the guilty.

'Cultural change has to begin at the top,' said Shanmugam as the guilty officials were getting into the bus to go to jail. He was watching as one official told a reporter that he was planning to appeal the verdict in the high court. 'You think he is contrite?' asked Shanmugam. 'He is already planning his strategy for the appeal. Instead of finding ways to delay the law, his interest now lies in speeding up the law.'

I was inclined to dismiss the Vachathi horror as a 'one-off thing' and not typical of the Indian state. Over time, however, I have reluctantly come to believe that this is how the police and government officials behave towards the vulnerable, especially in remote rural areas. Although brazen lawlessness prevails only in pockets—such as the badlands of Uttar Pradesh and Bihar, where it is called goonda raj, 'rule of thugs'—weak enforcement is a universal problem across the country. In the tribal areas it has given rise to the Maoist movement, presenting the Indian state with one of its most serious challenges—as serious, perhaps, as imported jehadi terrorism from Pakistan.

Cities are also the victims of a weak rule of law as any newspaper will testify daily. A number of well-publicized cases between 2005 and 2010 involving powerful people shook the nation. The most celebrated was the murder of an attractive model, Jessica Lal, who was killed for refusing to serve liquor to Manu Sharma, the son of a powerful minister in the Haryana government. He did not get away in the end because of middle-class uproar, supported by an unrelenting media. But what caught my notice, in particular, was the case of Ruchika Girhotra, who burst into our lives at the end of 2009—and I shall recount her story briefly at the end of this chapter. What is significant here is not the erosion of the rule of law in the weak Indian state but that a new countervailing force has emerged in the form of a strong civil society which is increasingly enforcing accountability on a decrepit system.

At least in these cases justice did catch up—albeit after nineteen years in Vachathi's and Ruchika's cases—but in the day-to-day experience of the marginalized and the powerless there is mostly no redress. Katherine Boo's recent description is convincing in *Behind the Beautiful Forevers: Life, Death, and Hope in a Mumbai Undercity.* A grim chain of events in a slum in India's financial capital drives the precarious lives of her characters into the brutal and malignant world of authority. After Fatima falsely accuses Abdul's family of trying to burn her, the police get involved because crimes provide a chance for extortion. The family is soon plunged into the cruelty and petty corruption of the police and the lower courts, a world in which 'the most wretched tried to punish the slightly less wretched by turning to a justice system so malign it sank them all'.

WHY IS THERE A CRISIS?

There is a profound crisis in the rule of law in contemporary India. The police are a tool in the hands of political leadership in the states, and often used to settle scores against rivals. The lower judiciary is mostly corrupt, and the chance of obtaining justice from it is less than 50 per cent. Judicial delay is the commonest form of injustice. L.N. Mishra, Cabinet minister of railways and right-hand man of Indira Gandhi, was murdered in 1975. The case against the accused dragged on for thirty-seven years; he had been twenty-seven years old at the time of the murder and was sixty-four and ailing in 2012. Meanwhile, thirty-one of the thirty-nine witnesses for the defence had died, gravely prejudicing the case against him. No less than twenty-two different judges had heard the case over the years. The trial was still going on in 2012.

In another example, the former telecom minister Sukh Ram was found guilty after sixteen years in 2011, when he was eighty-five years old and in hospital. Meanwhile, his co-accused had died during the trial. He was granted bail in January 2012, but will probably not live to hear the verdict of the Supreme Court. If this happened in the case of Cabinet ministers, where was the hope of justice for an ordinary person? But former chief justice of the Supreme Court J.S. Verma had a different take. He claimed that although Article 21 of the Constitution guaranteed a speedy trial to every citizen, in reality the status of the person did matter. A powerful person with connections or money could speed up or delay the justice system to suit his needs. More damaging is the collusion between judges, lawyers and politicians at the lower levels of the judiciary, which undermines the integrity of the process and the legitimacy of the rule of law.

The 'rule of law' is an old idea in the West; it has existed ever since Aristotle wrote, 'The law should govern.' As a legal maxim it became popular only in the nineteenth century thanks to the British jurist A.V. Dicey, suggesting that no one is above the law, not even the ruler, by 'divine right'. Some think that the rule of law has frayed in contemporary India because it is a western import which came on the coat-tails of a remarkable ruling elite from Britain; it rubbed off on a small group of privileged Indians who learned English, discovered western liberal ideas and went on to create a liberal Constitution when the British departed. Thus, it was something alien, imposed from above. Since it was 'skin deep' and had not evolved organically, India has gradually shed it and presumably reverted to its old self. This position has been put forth stylishly by Sunil Khilnani in his book *The Idea of India*. He concludes that 'India's constitutional democracy was created in a fit of absentmindedness', and hence 'liberalism was bound to fail in this culture'.

The issue is whether the institutions and values of the liberal West are universal or whether they represent the outgrowth of cultural habits of a certain part of the northern European world. My grandfather and father belonged to the modern middle class but like many in their generation they lived in a 'commuter culture', leading two separate lives. During the day they wore western clothes, spoke English and observed liberal, rational norms demanded by their professional lives. In the evening, they reverted to loose-fitting kurtas and dhotis, spoke in their mother tongue and dealt with their friends and family according to the norms of their traditions. Since the two lives did not mix, western, liberal values remained skin deep.

I think this explanation too runs skin deep. To believe that a liberal rule of law was 'imposed from above' underestimates the Indian experience of more than a hundred years prior to Independence, in which people absorbed the liberal idea in different ways and used it to reform society and went on to wage a non-violent struggle for political freedom. 'The power and influence of liberal ideas in India are hard to overestimate,' writes Chris Bayly in *Recovering Liberties*. He goes on to describe the profound attachment that Indians built for liberal ideas. Beginning with Rammohun Roy, who fought against caste and the rights of women, there were many others: Swami Vivekananda tried to infuse social justice into orthodox Hinduism; Mohandas Gandhi fought against untouchability invoking the liberal idea of sadharana dharma, 'duties incumbent on all human beings'. The Congress movement for freedom was led by liberals from the 1890s who educated people on the values of liberty, equality and the rule of law.

During the British Raj, Indians of all types began to practise the values of the 'liberal state' on the ground. Thousands of lawyers in small and big towns across India, such as my grandfather, employed the Indian Penal Code after the 1860s, and acquired a practical knowledge of rules based on justice and on equality before the law. Millions of Indians participated in sporadic elections to provincial legislatures, the most significant being the ones held after the 1935 Act, which gave a degree of autonomy to the provinces. To the diverse group of Indians of all castes, languages and backgrounds that met in the constituent assembly from 1946 to 1949 to debate and create the Constitution, civil liberties mattered. The assembly was not a moment of 'distracted forgetfulness'; it was a culmination of their history.

What accounts then for the present crisis in the rule of law? Rajeev Bhargava, a political scientist, offers another explanation: 'The current crisis of liberal democracy is due in large part to its own success. The introduction of civil liberties [in the Indian Constitution] gave voice to the mute.' After Independence, India went on to become a passionately political society that both divided and integrated the nation. Competitive politics in which 'the winner takes all' threw up a new generation of political actors who had fewer inhibitions and less awareness of liberal restraints. Popular pressures burst forth as an evolving Indian society tried to cope with a contradiction that B.R. Ambedkar had pointed to in his closing speech in the constituent assembly. 'In politics we will have equality and in social and economic life we will have inequality,' he had said. 'In politics we will be recognizing the principle of one man one vote and one vote one value. In our social and economic life, we shall . . . deny the principle of one man one value. How long shall we continue to live this life of contradictions?'

Nehru's great contribution was in state building. He adopted and nurtured the institutions that the British had put in place for almost a century. He brought stability to a new nation after the transfer of power and relentlessly subjected the new state to the principles of law and democratic procedure as laid down in the Constitution.

However, the British system had been designed for colonial control and revenue collection. That system was not modernized after Independence. Nehru or his successors should have enhanced the capacity of institutions—especially the lower courts and the police—to meet the growing needs of a developing country. But in his ambition to create a socialist society, as I have mentioned, Nehru expanded the scope and the responsibilities of the state and this left a dangerous gap, weakening the state and, in particular, the rule of law.

Barely a decade after Nehru's death in 1964, his daughter, Indira Gandhi, began to transform the nation from a 'constitutional' to a 'populist democracy', as André Béteille and others have observed. She regarded the Constitution as an obstacle and did not hesitate to bend it. Once this manipulation started, India's historically strong society began to assert itself and the state increasingly began to run into the politics of identity, sometimes violently so, as in Bihar and Uttar Pradesh. Indira Gandhi did not respect the rights of the individual states, and usurped their powers. She declared President's Rule more than seventy times in different states, sending elected governments packing. By nakedly exploiting religious sentiment and the money power inherent in her 'licence raj', she further diminished the institutions of the rule of law.

RULE OF LAW ORIGINATES IN RELIGION

Western liberal law may be an alien import but Indians have always had a traditional rule of law that is surprisingly liberal in some ways. Since ancient times it has existed as dharma, a shared norm of just behaviour which has given coherence and predictability to people's lives over the centuries and prevented a state of anarchy. Dharma is part of nature, an immutable structure embedded in the 'order of things' and its laws also apply to human beings. There is a long-held consensus in Indian society that the laws of dharma are prior to and above the ruler and are meant to restrain him. Early in the first millennium BCE, the *Brihadaranyaka Upanishad* famously called dharma 'sovereignty of sovereignty'. That is to say, the ruler is not sovereign, it is dharma that is sovereign. The ruler acquires legitimacy because he observes dharma. To ensure that a ruler acts in the common interest and 'protects all creatures', the dharma texts provide elaborate restraints in the form of duties; these are called raj dharma, the 'dharma of the king'. The epics, the Puranas and other literary texts reinforced the centrality of dharma in the people's imagination.

The rule of law originated in religion almost everywhere. In the West it originated with Christian and Judaic notions of law. This seems odd to us moderns because modernity has so completely separated the state and religion from our secular minds. A number of scholars have traced this transition. The Hebrew tradition of prophets insisted that the kings were under the law. Long before the modern European state came into being, popes in Rome, such as Gregory I, had established laws for marriage and the inheritance of property, asserting in effect the same authority that Brahmins had always done in India. The

Church rediscovered the old Justinian code in the eleventh century, the *Corpus Luris Civilis*, and incorporated the sensible ideas of the Romans. This became the basis of civil law in continental Europe and prevails till today. Most countries now have written constitutions, of course. However, the modern rule of law had its origins in timeless and universal principles, as Abraham Lincoln observed. Because these truths were articulated by religion, it gave the rule of law a higher legitimacy in the eyes of rulers and subjects. Hence, as the jurist Frederic Maitland stated, no English king ever believed that he was above the law. Indian kings had the same conviction about dharma.

FROM STATUS TO CONTRACT

A significant change in the law has come about as societies have progressed from tradition to modernity. Sir Henry Maine, jurist and historian who played an important role in developing statutory laws for India, wrote a legal bestseller, *Ancient Law*, before he came to India in 1862. In it he observed that as society makes the transition to modernity, the law also changes 'from status to contract'. In traditional society individuals are tightly bound by status to groups; in modern society individuals are autonomous agents, free to make legal contracts and form associations. In India 'modern law' preceded the modernization of a traditional society. While still conservative in many ways, India's society is now undergoing rapid change with the rapid rise of the middle class.

Unlike western juridical systems that are based on the concept of legality, pre-modern law in India was based on authority. Dharma texts, or precepts of smriti, were that authority, and their starting point was the notion of dharma, which as we have noted was a code of conduct supported by the general conscience of the people. But in administering justice, custom was equally important and often prevailed over the texts. The appearance of commentaries and digests, however, was a great turning point in India and this is when true juridical science began to be established in the country. Robert Lingat explains in *Classical Law of India* that Bharuci and Medhatithi, the oldest commentators on the *Manusmriti*, 'do not rest content with commenting upon the text of Manu; they compare the verses of Manu with material taken from other smriti works to which they attach the same authority, and, where it is appropriate, they reconcile the propositions. All other commentators do the same.' Todar Mal, during Akbar's time, composed one such digest. Some commentaries even had an imperative character of positive law in the modern sense of the word, as the great scholar P.V. Kane has observed.

When the English came to India they had to cope with the difference in the two legal systems—one based on legality and the other on authority. In 1772, Warren Hastings, the governor general and head of the East India Company, believed that Indians should be governed by Indian laws. He laid the base for the civil courts of the Diwani of Bengal, Bihar and Orissa that had been granted to the company by the Mughal emperor Shah Alam II.

Hindus and Muslims remained under their respective laws. Only the judicial mechanism changed from a qadi (kazi) to an English judge, who applied the Dharmashastras to the Hindus, Islamic law to the Muslims and some version of English 'justice, equality, and good conscience' to others. In the case of 'Hindu' law, the English judge assumed that the dharma texts were to the Hindus what the Church laws had been in Europe, and he began to apply them uniformly with the help of a pandit who was attached to each court.

Hastings also introduced the notion of legality, meaning that each judgement became a precedent. Whereas the Hindu judge had only wanted to settle a dispute, the English judge created case law through law-in-action. But English judges were befuddled when they discovered that their pandit advisers tended to apply dharma contextually and differently in different parts of India. Moreover, achara, 'custom' or 'usage', often seemed to matter more than the authority of the texts. Nevertheless, they found practical ways to cope until the Crown took over the government of India in 1858. The legislative council then removed the uncertainty through codification. The first codes to be issued were the Code of Civil Procedure (1859), the Penal Code (1860) and the Code of Criminal Procedure (1861). There was a rupture at that point. The British Empire in India became a legislating state. However, the attempt to fit religious, communal and personal codes created huge potential for contestation. This led to too many court cases, as Tirthankar Roy points out in 'Empire, Law, and Economic Growth'. India became a litigious society and too much litigation is not good for economic growth.

The traditional Hindu and Muslim laws (except some areas of personal law) did not survive modernization partly because India and the Muslim countries did not produce someone like Gratian, the Italian law teacher who rationalized the traditional Church laws in Europe. Gratian in his *Decretum* had taken the whole body of religious edicts and made them internally consistent, and this helped to pave the way for their application in the European nation states. No one did the same with dharma texts and their commentaries, nor with Sunni Muslim law. No one produced something like the Justinian Code. Nor did the Hindu or the Muslim traditions achieve autonomy between religion and the state. This independence was crucial to the way that the modern institutions of the rule of law developed in the West.

Many think that the fusion of Church and state is intrinsic to Islam while being foreign to the West. This is not true. Law played the same role in the Muslim countries as it did in the Christian ones. There were periods when it successfully deterred political rulers, sometimes more successfully than at other times. 'Rule of law is basic to Muslim civilization,' says Fukuyama. He shows many similarities between the rule of law in India and in the Middle East before they were colonized. In both cases a complex body of case law was created over the centuries by religious judges—pandits in the Indian case and kadis in the Muslim—which political rulers were, theoretically at least, only authorized or deputized to carry out.

The West, however, took a different turn in the modern period. It was able to separate its religious establishment from the state even though the link between its traditional rule of law and the state continued. India and the Muslim nations were unable to do this on their own and were forced to do so by colonial rule. Despite the rupture in the 1860s, when the British colonial government changed the way law and order was implemented in India, the ideal of a ruler guided by dharma exists in the Indian imagination even today. Although the word is infrequently used in the English press, 'dharma' is ubiquitous in regional newspapers.

ENFORCEMENT IS AT THE HEART

Dharma needs to be enforced by the power of the state. This is the central duty of a king, according to the dharma texts. In the West as well, the modern concept of the state originated in society's need for an institution with a 'monopoly of force', which was a key insight of political theorists like Jean Bodin and Thomas Hobbes, and it went on to become the pillar of an absolute monarchy. Max Weber, who has deeply influenced our understanding of the modern state, defined the state as 'a human community that (successfully) claims the monopoly of the legitimate use of physical force within a given territory'. In other words, the essence of being a state is enforcement. This is a lesson that has been forgotten by contemporary India's democracy in which it takes decades to gain justice and hundreds of thousands languish in jail awaiting trial.

The feeling of injustice born of delay defeats the human spirit and is one reason Indians despair over their 'soft state'. Judges are happy to give adjournments because they do not want to be unpopular. Almost no one is hauled up for perjury; court costs are so low that there is hardly a penalty for losing a case or mounting frivolous litigation. Indians have long despaired over judicial delays, but they did not know how bad things were until Bibek Debroy, an economist who headed a project in the ministry of finance in the 1990s, discovered that the backlog in the legal system was more than 25 million cases. It takes up to twenty years to settle a dispute, and it would need 324 years to dispose of the backlog at the current disposal rate. He also concluded that 1500 out of 3500 central laws were obsolete and needed to be scrapped, and half the 30,000 state laws as well.

What shocked the nation's conscience was that the main culprit behind judicial delay was the government, which appealed all judgements automatically and proceeded to lose them again in the higher courts. This crowded out the private individual. The problem lay in the fact that the decision to litigate was made at the lowest level in the bureaucracy but the decision not to litigate was made at the highest level. If this process were simply reversed, government litigation would come down.

According to the *Arthashastra*, the classic manual of statecraft, every society needs a sovereign power wielding kshatra, 'power of command', to maintain order and 'protect creatures'. Hence danda-niti, 'the science of punishment', has been at the core of the instruction of kings since ancient times. Literally meaning a mace or a sceptre in the royal context, 'danda' in common usage signifies a rod or a stick. Bhishma teaches this science to King Yudhishthira in Book XII of the *Mahabharata*. He says, 'If the rod of force did not exist in this world, beings would be nasty and brutish to each other. Because they fear punishment, they do not kill each other. As they are preserved by the rod of force day after day, the subjects make the king grow greater; therefore the rod of force puts this world into a stable order, O king.'

So important is retributive justice in protecting creatures that danda is presented in the form of a god, a powerful deity who was born of Brahma himself. 'If the king fails to administer danda tirelessly on those who deserve to be punished,' says Manu, 'the stronger would grill the weak like fish on a spit.' Both Manu and Narada claim in celebrated verses in their dharma texts that fear of the rod is necessary to get human beings to observe dharma. This Hobbesian view of human nature is not pessimistic—it is an expression of the role of deterrence and punishment in a civilized society to 'protect creatures' which is the duty of the ruler. Thomas Hobbes, the seventeenth-century English thinker, argued that the state was given a monopoly of legitimate power to allow individuals to escape a state of nature which consisted of a 'war of every man against every man'.

Given the central role of enforcement in all dharma texts, it is surprising that enforcement of the rule of law has become the soft underbelly of India's polity. Instead of giving the weak and the poor protection, or as Yajnavalkya puts it, abhaya-dana, 'the guarantee of security', the enforcers of the law have become its chief oppressors. They have forgotten that when the king is unjust in applying danda, he wounds his raj dharma, and he will be ruined, as Manu puts it. Vachathi's story above and Ruchika's below are examples of a widespread crisis. Weak enforcement is at the heart of a weak state in which the most vulnerable and the weakest are its chief victims.

The policeman and the judge in contemporary India need to hear once again Bhishma's message to Yudhishthira in the *Mahabharata*: 'Listen, scion of Kuru, to what the rod of punishment is and how it is judicially prescribed: for punishment is the one thing in this world upon which everything depends. Great king, judicial process (vyavahara) is one of the names of Dharma. The very proceeding of judicial process is directed to this end.'

Thinkers of the liberal tradition in the West all believed in the legitimacy of retributive justice. Even an absolute moralist like Kant felt that imposing a just punishment showed respect for the criminal's human autonomy. The utilitarians justified punishment on the grounds of social control: it was a deterrent, offering an incentive to comply with the laws; it helped reduce crime and thus maximized human welfare. Others think that punishment is supposed to correct an injustice, protect the individual rights of the innocent, and restore moral equality between the offender and victim. To fail to impose a penalty is as much an injustice since it makes the offender superior to the victim; hence, perpetrators must be punished to reaffirm human equality. According to the political philosopher Jean

Hampton, the aim of punishment is not to avenge wrongdoing or to inflict pain and injury on the offender but 'to annul the offender's claim of superiority'.

Bhishma's point in the epic is that retributive justice protects the innocent, and indeed danda is the source of civilized behaviour. In the end the reluctant king Yudhishthira voices agreement: 'O lord, the rod of punishment that reaches everywhere with its tremendous fiery energy is the best thing for all living beings.'

RUCHIKA DID NOT DIE IN VAIN

It was from my friend Shashi Kumar (more on him in Chapter Six) that I first heard about Ruchika Girhotra. I had seen a brief report in December 2009 in the inside pages of my newspaper about a police official who had been sentenced to six months in jail for molesting a teenager. But I had dismissed it until Shashi Kumar phoned me. He said that he had known her family; he was clearly upset. I recall feeling helpless, wanting to alleviate his suffering, but unable to do much.

In the following days, the story shot to the front page and stayed there for almost six weeks. An ugly tale unfolded about the former director general of police Shambhu Pratap Singh Rathore, the highest police official in Haryana, who had molested fourteen-year-old Ruchika Girhotra in 1990. She was a tennis player and he was chief of the local tennis association. He had called her into his office on the pretext of offering her coaching advice and had then groped her. Another young girl had witnessed the assault.

From that moment onward, the story changed to a finely tuned account of a powerful official's ability to use influence and manipulate the system. Ruchika's family complained to the police but the officer at the police station, in fear of his superior, did not register the case. To intimidate the family and discourage them from pursuing the case, Rathore had her brother arrested falsely and allegedly tortured in jail. The police continued to harass her family, and this forced them to go into hiding. Seeing their plight, Ruchika committed suicide in 1993.

Ruchika's friend—the one who witnessed the act—and the Girhotra family did not give up. They continued to pursue the case in the court, but Rathore repeatedly used his influence and managed to scuttle or delay the legal proceedings. Years passed. In December 2009, a six-month sentence was finally announced. And that too was followed by a quick approval of Rathore's bail application.

Rathore left the courtroom smiling. A camera caught that insolent smile, and it stirred the nation, setting off an angry debate in both print and electronic media over the handling of the case. Shashi Kumar also saw the smirk in the newspaper photograph and phoned me to say that he was outraged by the leniency of the punishment. In subsequent months, relentless media pressure forced the government and the judiciary to act. The privileged official in genteel retirement had his bail revoked and his sentence was reviewed and raised to eighteen months in prison. The picture of the smiling police official was replaced by a new image of a mighty official incarcerated behind police bars. Rathore was also booked for an attempt to murder, supervising torture in custody, and under numerous sections of the Indian Penal Code pertaining to conspiracy, forgery and fabricating police records. Other officials in positions of authority who had subverted the law also faced inquiries. The school principal, who had succumbed to pressure from officials and had thrown Ruchika out of school, was in trouble. New trials were expected and there was talk in the government of amending certain laws.

Rathore was granted bail by the Supreme Court on 11 November 2010, after spending close to six months in Burail jail while serving the sentence of eighteen months. But there was little progress on other cases or inquiries. On 26 April 2012, there was a tiny item in the *Times of India* on page 15 with the headline 'Tainted cop SPS Rathore gifts wife Rs 9 lakhs licence plate'. Rathore had won an auction from among eighteen bidders to obtain a special number for a new Mercedes-Benz that he had bought for his lawyer wife. He had paid Rs 905,001 for the fancy number CH 01 AM. 'My wife is number one after all,' he said.

The media may have gone overboard on Ruchika's behalf, but Shashi Kumar's reaction reminded me about the connection between the outcry over Ruchika's case and the Anna Hazare movement, which began to gather strength some months later. Shashi's modest turn to political activism was one direct result. Even if the subsequent trials in her case did not go as everyone hoped, I felt that Ruchika Girhotra had not died in vain. She had energized the moral imagination of a new and confident India, disproving the lazy, unthinking belief that the middle class is purely self-centred. It said something about India's assertive media and its changing society. What had been seen as a minor incident went on to become a source of relentless outrage and provided the nation with intense emotional release, a catharsis decades after the event.

Ruchika Girhotra's story had the unmistakable echoes of Jessica Lal's murder in 1999 (and several others that hit the front pages around that time). Again, the significant aspect of Jessica's case was not the crime itself, but the acquittal of the wealthy and powerful murderer and his accomplices seven years later in 2006. Again, the acquittal released pent-up frustration in the middle class against a blundering, corrupt enforcement machinery, and brought to the fore a deep disgust at the way the rich and powerful could manipulate the system to their advantage. There were numerous protest campaigns, including rallies and candlelight vigils across the country. A sting operation by the newsmagazine *Tehelka* showed that witnesses had been bribed by the politically powerful father of the accused and coerced into retracting their initial testimony.

Following intense media and public pressure, the prosecution appealed Jessica Lal's case. The Delhi High Court conducted proceedings on a fast track and the judgement of the trial court was overturned. Manu Sharma was sentenced to life imprisonment. His father, a Cabinet minister in the Haryana state government, was forced to resign.

THE RULE OF LAW BRINGS PREDICTABILITY

Citizens in a civilized society look to the state to make their lives more predictable. A robust rule of law is the chief means by which the state ensures civic peace. It also gives comfort to investors who take huge risks with their capital—it offers them recourse in case things go wrong. Economists sometimes wonder why, despite the reforms, India has not succeeded in attracting foreign investment commensurate with its economy's potential and attractiveness. China and even smaller countries in Asia have done far better. One reason is the perception of an obstructive and negative bureaucracy—an image from the 'licence raj' that refuses to go away. Even a bribe in India can be inefficient because it may not guarantee predictable results. Hence, many foreign investors still prefer a less than optimal way of doing business in India, which is to engage a local partner, and this sometimes leads to 'crony capitalism'.

The other side of a weak rule of law is, in fact, 'crony capitalism' which became rampant in the first decade of the twenty-first century in the unreformed sectors of the Indian economy. These were real estate, mining, power, oil and gas, telecom spectrum and all government purchases—in short, all the sectors where politicians and officials still had too much discretion. Crony capitalism creates huge uncertainty in the minds of honest investors. In bidding for infrastructure projects the crony of the politician has an unfair advantage over a more competent investor. The reforms in 1991 took away some of that discretion, wiping out the earlier cronyism of the 'licence raj' and replacing it with 'rules-based capitalism'. But it continues to flourish in the dark alleys of unreformed India, alongside the ugly 'inspector raj'. A power plant in 2012 needed 118 approvals. This created 118 opportunities for corruption and a rational businessman used them to weaken competitors while gratifying politicians and officials.

Nevertheless, India's investment rate rose in the first decade of the twenty-first century to an enviable 38 per cent—among the highest in the world—as a result of strong fundamentals in the reformed sectors of the economy. But a spate of government actions, partly in response to scams between 2009 and 2011, undermined that confidence. The Supreme Court cancelled licences of companies involved in the government's 2008 corrupt sale of mobile phone spectrum. Norway's Telenor was one of the three foreign companies affected. It had invested more than $2 billion in rolling out its network and it claimed to be the unwitting victim of the court's decision based on the alleged bribery by its partner before it had invested in the joint venture. It threatened international arbitration against the government, claiming $14 billion in damages.

In another example, Cairn, India's largest producer of petroleum, suddenly faced the prospect of an 80 per cent tax increase in the government's 2012 budget proposal; it was the only private company affected by the change as other private companies' taxes were contractually capped at about $18 a ton. Cairn had been patiently awaiting approval for more than a year for its $6 billion investment in order to double production at its largest oilfield, in Rajasthan—bizarre indeed, when India desperately needed energy and needed to reduce the cost of expensive imported crude.

In the same budget proposal, the government announced a decision to retroactively tax any international transaction dating as far back as 1962 in which any significant Indian asset was transferred. That proposal stemmed from the government's desire to collect more than $2 billion in taxes from the 2007 deal by the UK-based Vodafone Group after the Supreme Court had ruled that Vodafone did not owe any taxes on the deal. At the same time, the budget proposals included a plan to amend the laws in nineteen other cases where the government had lost in either higher courts or appellate tax tribunals. Such a blatant challenge to the courts and the rule of law by the finance ministry had not been seen since the Emergency in the 1970s.

All this came on top of the environment ministry's decisions in the previous two years to reopen cases where permissions by the government had already been granted. In many cases, investments had already been made, and this badly dented India's image. Equally disheartening was the experience of private entrepreneurs in dealing with the railway ministry—encouraged to invest in freight movement, investors discovered formidable hurdles placed in their way. A government which was meant to create order had become the source of uncertainty. Risk can be quantified by entrepreneurs, as the economist Frank Knight wrote in *Risk, Uncertainty and Profit*. Uncertainty, on the other hand, cannot be measured and therefore presents a true barrier to prosperity.

Indian civilization has always understood the role of the state in mitigating risk. The theme of risk and uncertainty appears in the *Mahabharata*, where a famous game of dice is the metaphor for the uncertain, vulnerable human condition. The epic looks to the ruler and his dharma to bring predictability to the lives of people. Indians today look to regulators and the modern rule of law to reduce uncertainty. But the rule of law sometimes collides with the 'rule of life'.

RULE OF LAW VS RULE OF LIFE

Justice V.R. Krishna Iyer, a former judge of India's Supreme Court, once made a distinction between the 'rule of law' and the 'rule of life'. In a judgement in 1975, he used this distinction to uphold the election of a Muslim candidate who had won his election partly by appealing to his Hindu constituents that his mother was Hindu. This was a sectarian appeal and contrary to the law. But Justice Iyer went on to give greater weight to the primordial, irrational realities of social relations in ordinary life, in what he called 'the social inside in the raw'. In his mind, this sometimes trumped the higher, rational ideals embodied in the rule of law and the Constitution. To do otherwise, he felt, would be to not listen to the voice of the people.

Justice Iyer was wrong—it is dangerous for a judge not

to uphold the rule of law. While the Constitution created strong incentives to behave impersonally in public life, the fact is that the rational 'rule of law' sometimes gives way to the irrational and parochial 'rule of life'. The tension between the two is at the heart of democracy, according to the historian David Gilmartin in a seminal essay, 'Rule of Law, Rule of Life: Caste, Democracy, and the Courts in India'. No one understood this paradox better than B.R. Ambedkar, who was the chief framer of the Constitution. He struggled when he advocated reservations for Dalits, for this upheld the 'rule of life' against his attachment to the Constitution's ideal of equal treatment for all. Gilmartin equates the 'rule of life' to svadharma, duties to one's family, one's caste and community. In contrast, the rule of law is akin to sadharana dharma, duties which reflect the higher, universal ideals of the Constitution. Democracy, he argues, emerges from the contradiction between these two duties.

Other founding fathers of the Constitution also faced the same tension as Ambedkar. They wrestled in their souls as they tried to reimagine the ideals of a new nation based on the universal ideals of sadharana dharma compared to the frustrating reality on the ground of divisions, diverse identities and conflicting interests of svadharma. In this mental struggle they were inspired by the two tallest in the freedom movement. Mohandas Gandhi had made them realize how much moral courage was required to resist the sentiment of partiality towards one's own. His moral leadership had popularized the image of the ideal Indian citizen as a person of conscience and self-discipline, who was in tune with the moral order of dharma, and who could achieve personal self-realization through non-violent satyagraha.

On the other hand, Jawaharlal Nehru, the second tallest, was deeply influenced by modernity and British legal thinking. Like Ambedkar, his attachment to the rule of law and a strong state rested on the rational and secular self (of the European Enlightenment). He had an intellectual's contempt for the parochial and primordial passions of India's 'rule of life'. As a result of their moral leadership, the universal and rational sadharana dharma triumphed in the end. They created a sovereign nation founded on self-restrained citizenship as a single moral entity that operated under an impersonal rule of law.

HABITS OF THE HEART

In the West the rule of law pre-dated modern democracy by many centuries. This gave people time to internalize certain values and habits which became deeply embedded in western society. The coming of the capitalist economy reinforced the importance of a rules-based order as commercial contracts had to be enforced on a day-to-day basis. By the time democracy came around, people had got used to the idea that civilized life required an autonomous legal establishment. Visible institutions reminded them daily that their political rulers were subject to the rule of law. A coherent and clearly stated body of rules had been put in place to limit arbitrary behaviour by the executive authority. The legal profession retained a strong influence over its own recruitment and promotion, set its own professional standards, trained its own lawyers and judges, and was granted genuine power to interpret the law without interference from political authority.

Alexis de Tocqueville, a French aristocrat, visited America in the 1830s and wrote *Democracy in America*, which I consider the greatest book on democracy. In it he spoke about the common confusion between 'might' and 'right', and this distinction is at the heart of the crisis of public dharma in India. The norms and values meant to constrain public officials are increasingly absent. Instead of the minimal restraints of the rule of law, people observe the high-handedness of the police, the impunity of politicians, the greed of bureaucrats and the temptations of judges.

Tocqueville observed that a moral core underlay American democracy. Its success, he felt, lay in this moral consensus which was expressed daily in 'habits of the heart'. The habits reflected a deep commitment, for example, in the individual's conscience to human liberty and to an instinctive sense of equality before the law (values that obviously did not extend to the blacks). But these habits, he felt, were absent in the France of his time, and until the French acquired them, they would not become a successful democracy. This was ironical given that the French had articulated these values half a century earlier in a powerful cry—'*Liberté, égalité, fraternité*'—that ushered their famous revolution and was heard around the world.

India too, it seems to me, will have to rediscover a moral

core in order to come to grips with its present crisis of the rule of law and become a mature democracy. 'Rediscover', I say, because a universal ideal of 'public dharma' lives in people's hearts if not in their practice, thanks to the extraordinary continuity of the Indian civilization. For some, especially the English-speaking elite, the recovery of dharma may appear bizarre. Innocent of their tradition, they associate it only with the caste system and its attendant ills. And they are right in condemning its social injustices. But by hollowing their inheritance of its ethical core, they may find to their regret that they have thrown the baby out with the bathwater.

Edmund Burke, who spent two decades managing Indian affairs as an MP in the British Parliament in the eighteenth century, issued a stern warning to his countrymen. He cautioned them not to tamper too much with Indian ways as India had a rich 'law of nature and of nations'. He was referring to dharma. In the trial of Warren Hastings, he condemned Britain's colonial rule as arbitrary, and contended that the English must learn to respect India's rich traditions. When it came to the application of law, he insisted that the colonial government follow precedents of Indian society. The irony is that Hastings was one of the few governors-general who had been deeply respectful of Indian traditions.

The diffidence of India's English-speaking elite may be due to two reasons. The first is that while dharma resonates with over 80 per cent of the people, it may exclude the minorities, especially Muslims and Christians (while it does resonate with Buddhists and Sikhs). It would have been ideal if there had been a more inclusive, non-western term that conveyed 'civic virtue' and appealed to all. The second reason lies in the confusion in the meaning of the word 'dharma'. The concept of dharma evolved over time, its meaning shifting from a 'ritual ethics of deeds' to a more personal virtue based on one's conscience. In Vedic times dharma essentially meant following the rituals and sacrifices enjoined by the Brahmin and endorsed by society, and Sanskrit scholars generally translate this early dharma as 'merit'. Often these deeds were specific to one's caste, and so evolved the concept of svadharma. With the rise of yoga sects, and of Buddhism and Jainism in the middle of the first millennium BCE, the meaning of dharma gradually changed to a sense of harmony through the cultivation of an inner, ethical self and to actions required of all castes. In this sense, dharma had universal appeal and was called sadharana dharma. It had to do with basic traits rather than specific deeds, and the classical dharma texts articulated some of these character traits as not harming others (ahimsa), being truthful (satya), not getting angry (krodha), etc. While there were still visible deeds which accumulated good karma, they became inner traits or attitudes which determined one's character. This marked a change in the way society thought about dharma and karma. The driving force of the *Mahabharata* is a continuous tension between the social svadharma and the personal but universal sadharana dharma.

For the majority, dharma has continued to mean 'moral well-being', something that gives coherence to one's life, reducing uncertainty and providing self-restraint. Muslim travellers such as Alberuni understood this meaning but in nineteenth-century Bengal, Christian missionaries claimed that 'Jesus's path is the true dharma'. For the first time, 'dharma' was used to mean 'religion'. Orthodox Hindus countered this challenge, claiming theirs was sanatana, 'eternal', dharma, and present-day discourse in India reflects this confusion. Despite this muddle, the traditional Indians can easily distinguish the different usages without feeling any confusion. The ordinary person continues to believe in dharma as duty, virtue and righteousness. In judging a failure of conscience—for example ahimsa, satya—he or she will employ the usage of sadharana dharma. In a social or caste context, she will comfortably switch to the social meaning of svadharma. The *Manusmriti* distinguishes clearly between the two, and even elaborates the specific duties of sadharana dharma, which are incumbent on all persons. But it is clearly more interested in svadharma. Buddhist texts are obviously more interested in sadharana dharma.

Could this universal dharma be invoked and revived today and become that moral core, in Tocqueville's sense, to energize the liberal rule of law? Mohandas Gandhi, as we have noted, did precisely that during the struggle for freedom in the twentieth century. Since sadharana dharma is no 'respecter of persons', it is consistent with the ideal of modern justice which is shown blindfolded in pictures. For this reason, the founding fathers sometimes invoked dharma in their speeches. Brajeshwar Prasad, a member of the constituent assembly, stated on 24 November 1949 that 'dharma is in consonance with the fundamental principles of democracy, and a state based on dharma will not tolerate economic inequality or social injustice'. The founders were not nostalgic revivalists, unlike today's members of the Sangh Parivar, who are content to extol the glory and the wonder that was India. They were hard-headed men and women concerned with writing a Constitution for a strong, liberal state.

Liberal restraints to power, as I have said, existed in the form of raj dharma in pre-modern India—dharma was above the ruler and it was his duty to uphold it. An ethic of enforcement, danda-niti, which is at the heart of the crisis in the rule of law today, was the central expectation from raj dharma. The scholar and jurist P.V. Kane called India's Constitution a 'dharma text'. The creators of the nation were so committed to dharma that they chose to place the wheel of dharma in the centre of the new nation's flag so as to remind future generations to do the right thing. Kane went on to win the Bharat Ratna, but the project he had in mind remains unfinished to this day. In calling the Constitution a dharma text, he had wished it to be a living entity, which would fuse the ideals of modern constitutionalism with the pre-modern ideal of sadharana dharma.

When the vast majority on the subcontinent is deeply religious, and when the religious traditions of both Hindus and Muslims contain liberal ideas about the rule of law, it does make sense to turn to tradition in the quest for that moral core in order to reinvigorate India's democracy. Such a project will not risk undermining the secular commitment. As Tocqueville clarifies, 'habits of the heart' are civic in nature, not sacred or profane, even though their original inspiration may have been religious. Mohandas Gandhi understood this when he fought against untouchability, inspired by sadharana dharma.

The timing for the recovery of dharma is also right. There are intimations of an imperceptible but profound change under way in India's strong society. Chapter Six elaborates further the awakening in the Indian middle class. Its response to the cases of Ruchika Girhotra, Jessica Lal and others is a beginning. The extraordinary support garnered by Anna Hazare's movement is another sign that India's state is capable of being challenged, albeit imperfectly, and brought to some sort of accountability by civil society. The newly assertive middle class will no longer accept a civic life shaped by who is powerful or by who stands to lose and gain. True, the methods adopted by Anna Hazare were not in the spirit of the Constitution, but his moral discourse against corruption was, and the new middle class may well be ready to engage with the polity. The next step is to do what Gandhi did in the fight for freedom—translate the liberal values of the Constitution into the language of sadharana dharma so that they become habits of the Indian heart. No easy task, but it can be done.

4

A FLAILING STATE

For forms of government let fools contest;
Whate'er is best administer'd is best.

—Alexander Pope,
'Essay on Man', 1733

Seeing Gurgaon's stupendous rise, a young Indian might well ask, 'If India can grow at night, why do we need a bloated government with corrupt politicians and unresponsive bureaucrats?' Some Internet activists in Bangalore have argued that the power of the state, in any case, is being undermined around the world by new information technologies, making it difficult to enforce traditional rules of the state and to police its borders. Their financial counterparts in Mumbai fantasize about a global capitalist economy which will replace governments by sovereignty of the market. They claim that if the bond market in India were liberalized and states and cities were able to issue bonds as in the United States, a state legislature that votes for a bad policy will get punished quickly by the capital markets and will be forced to adopt sensible policies.

Dreams of statelessness are not new. Throughout history people have had fantasies about a world without a state. The most famous was of Karl Marx, who prophesied that the 'state would wither away' once the proletarian revolution won power, abolished private property and achieved the communist utopia. There were many anarchists in the nineteenth century who wanted to destroy the old structures of power but they did not have a clear idea about what would replace them.

Mohandas Gandhi was also ambivalent about the power of the modern state. He dreamt of an India of autonomous village republics, and when the nation became free he did not join the government and wanted to disband the Congress party. His followers after Independence kept his dreams alive through many 'small is beautiful' policies, some of which turned out to be disastrous. One of these, legislated during the Janata government's rule in the 1970s, reserved 800 products for the small-scale sector, which made Indian industry uncompetitive for decades, and prevented India from becoming an exporting nation. Supporters of Jayaprakash Narayan in the 1970s and Anna Hazare in 2011 had similar Gandhian fantasies in which a mobilized civil society would take the place of traditional political parties and a centralized government.

Not having a state is worse than having a dysfunctional

one. Even in the age of globalization when it is fashionable to speak of the end of the nation state, it is difficult to imagine a world order without something that has the essential traits of a state. It is facile to expect a nation to grow economically without the help of the state. Markets depend at a minimum on government institutions to enforce property rights and contracts, provide security of life and secure liberty. A state is a precondition for a flourishing capitalist economy, and indeed, India's economic rise in the twenty-first century has been facilitated, as I have already explained, by the invisible hand of the state. If India had had more independent and tough regulators, it would have done even better.

I have already pointed out that a strong, liberal state is based on three pillars: first, the power to act independently and resolutely; second, a rule of law which constrains political power and limits corruption; and third, democracy and accountability which allow the people to change their rulers when they start behaving badly. A successful state combines these three elements in a balance that Fukuyama says is 'the miracle of modern politics'. The nations of Scandinavia come closest to this miracle.

The phrase 'strong state' has a bad odour because of the unhappy history of the twentieth century. Hitler's Germany, Stalin's Russia and Mao's China tyrannized their people and committed aggressions against their neighbours. These totalitarian dictatorships were strong, unaccountable and opaque—the very opposite of a strong, liberal state. The classical conception of a liberal state was a limited one that focused on its core functions. The

German sociologist and economist Alexander Ruestow coined the term 'small but strong state' in opposition to a 'big but weak state'. The big state was supposedly weak because it tried to do too much. In Jeremy Bentham's words, the big state overstepped its 'agenda' and wandered aimlessly in 'non-agenda' territory. But the decisive issue may not be that of the American 'big' versus 'small' government. Some European states, especially in Scandinavia, have shown the capacity to manage an extensive welfare state extraordinarily well while remaining strong and liberal.

A strong, liberal state is not an intrusive or a meddling one, the sort that Indians experienced during the 'licence raj'. It has a light, invisible touch over its citizens' lives and yet is tough on corruption. The trick is to strike the right balance. On the one hand, the raw power of the state must be domesticated to ensure that it will not confiscate private property and abuse the rights of its citizens; it will only use that power to protect property and human rights, and provide public safety. On the other, the state must control its tendency to expand its activities and become inflated; it should only do what others—civil society or the market—cannot do. This is how a state becomes effective, legitimate and accountable. Let us see how India measures up.

CHECK NAKA BLUES

Vachathi is a dramatic example of the Indian state's failure. But there are dramatic examples of its success too. The green revolution was ushered in by the state and made the country self-sufficient in food. It created pockets of excellence in higher education institutions, such as the Indian Institutes of Technology and the Indian Institutes of Management (IIMs), which helped fuel the liberalized economy after 1991. Elections involving hundreds of millions are conducted routinely to exceptionally high standards. The Right to Information Act is an outstanding achievement which is already beginning to hold the government more accountable. The Delhi Metro was built in record time and to world standards. Both the great revolutions of the early 1990s—economic reforms and local democracy—were engineered by the state. The Kumbh Mela, attended by tens of millions, is invariably managed with quiet efficiency. Postal remittances work for migratory workers. There are other examples as well. For this reason, Lloyd and Susanne Rudolph use the infelicitous term 'weak-strong' to describe the Indian state in their book *In Pursuit of Lakshmi: The Political Economy of the Indian State*. It is strong when it wants to be, as some of its successes mentioned above testify. It is weak for the reasons I have given, in particular extremely poor implementation capability at the lower levels and the lack of accountability of officials. The Rudolphs too cite the battering Indira Gandhi gave to state institutions as a serious cause of governance decline. I believe the successes fade quickly in the face of the quiet, humdrum disappointments of each day. For me they seemed to come together like an army in January 2007. After attending the literary festival in Jaipur, I went by road to Ajmer. The six-lane highway was a beauty and the potholed India of the Public Works

Department (PWD) had soon become a distant memory. The wondrous colours of Rajasthan deepened as I moved south, and for an instant I thought I may be witnessing a paradise of sorts, which combined modernity and tradition, and world-class infrastructure with the ineffable loveliness of an older India.

My enjoyment was boosted somewhat by the knowledge that the Jaipur–Kishangarh segment of the Golden Quadrilateral had been built as a public–private partnership, through which the private sector had built the road under the stringent eye of a regulator and would recover its costs through tolls. This model of infrastructure development was based on the recognition of the limited capacity of the state. The Golden Quadrilateral was the name given by the previous government of Prime Minister Vajpayee, who had initiated this bold programme to connect with highways the four metros of Delhi, Mumbai, Chennai and Kolkata.

The key to the success of this public–private partnership lay in transparent contracts which tried to get around the ever-present danger of crony capitalism. The contract for this one was based on a template drawn by my friend Gajendra Haldea, an unusual economist-lawyer at the Planning Commission. Such contracts had helped create a level of trust and enabled the country to access funds, skills and technologies from the best companies in the world to build and operate new roads, ports, bridges, airports and container trains, which were then transferred back to the state in fifteen to thirty years. As a result, Haldea was one of the most hated men in Delhi's infrastructure ministries. He had demolished opportunities for corruption. The ministry would have preferred building the highway through its own contractors and earning a cut on every substandard kilometre.

Soon my wondrous journey hit a bump of reality. There was an interminable line of unhappy trucks parked on one side of the road. Since I was not in a hurry, and it was time to take a break anyway, I decided to stop. I pulled up alongside an idle truck driver, and asked him what was going on. He had been waiting at the revenue check naka for four hours, he said. He was afraid that the bribe on this occasion was going to be double because the Check Sahib's daughter was getting married. There would be more than half a dozen checkposts like this on his journey from Delhi to Mumbai. There would also be police posts to bribe, and a journey of twenty-four hours would take forty-four, half the time lost in queues and in negotiating bribes.

Here was another irony. While the speed of trucks had risen 50 per cent thanks to four- and six-lane highways, truckers were still mired in the old inefficiencies. While the economy was becoming globally competitive, octroi posts were preventing the nation from becoming a common market. Many municipalities in India continued to levy octroi because this medieval tax was their only source of revenue. Meanwhile, checkposts not only slowed the nation down but they also destroyed its moral character. Transparency International reported in 2006 that India's trucking industry had paid Rs 22,200 crore in bribes in the previous year. This is roughly equal to what India's truck drivers earn annually by way of salaries. How would a truck driver explain this to his children?

Soon after octroi was introduced in the mid-nineteenth century, efforts began to get rid of it for the very reasons I have just cited—corruption and inefficiency. But for 150 years no one has heeded the cry of the municipalities: 'Give us another source of revenue!' Vijay Kelkar, adviser to the finance ministry, held out the hope of eliminating octroi in 2002–03 when he introduced the sensible idea of merging all indirect taxes into a single, national goods and services tax (GST). From this tax, municipalities would be compensated for the loss from octroi. By 2010 it looked like it was about to happen, but the GST has kept getting postponed, despite everybody realizing that it is the most important reform in India's fiscal history, not least because it will transform India into a common market.

I was still suffering from 'check naka blues' when I arrived the next day at my friend Navin Parikh's factory near Ajmer. I was proud of him. He made the most sophisticated parts and equipment for the suppliers to the world's defence industries. To my dismay, it took an hour and a quarter to travel eight kilometres on the PWD road to his factory; the road was full of potholes and filth. It was another reminder of private success amid public failure. What dismayed me particularly, however, was his never-ending saga of government inspectors.

'Not a week goes by,' Navin said, 'without an inspector from some department or the other coming for his hafta vasooli, "weekly bribe". Labour, excise, fire, police, octroi, sales tax, boilers and more—we have to keep them all happy. Otherwise, they make life hell. More than 10 per cent of my costs are in "managing the system".' I was not surprised. This is how the police and the municipal and sales tax inspectors routinely treated shopkeepers and 'roadside vendors' in my neighbourhood.

A FLAILING STATE

Petty corruption is not a special feature of the Indian state. It is a symptom of a weak state that finds it difficult to implement its own laws. At a higher level, corruption is a result of public officials enjoying too many discretionary powers, particularly in the unreformed sectors of India's economy. At the lower level it is a function of a continuing 'inspector raj', as I have already pointed out. This leads to arbitrariness and uncertainty in citizens' lives. The latter aspect, in particular, touches the day-to-day life of the ordinary person, bringing anxiety and misery, as when a truck driver struggles at a check naka or Navin Parikh with hafta vasooli.

The Nobel Prize winning economist and philosopher Friedrich A. Hayek wrote in *The Road to Serfdom* that 'nothing distinguishes more clearly conditions in a free country from those in a country under arbitrary government than the observance in the former of the great principles known as the Rule of Law'. This means, he added, that 'government in all its actions is bound by rules fixed and announced beforehand—rules which make it possible to foresee with fair certainty how the authority will use its coercive powers in given circumstances and to plan one's individual affairs on the basis of this knowledge'.

A rules-based system destroys administrative discretion. India discovered this in 1991 when discretion was replaced with market outcomes. Competition between rivals rather than officials began to decide what would be produced, at what price and of what quality. 'Rules-based capitalism' gradually replaced 'crony capitalism' in many sectors. But those working in the unreformed sectors remained un-free. Hayek's other point is that discretion also reduces the freedom of citizens. John Locke, the father of classical liberalism who had a profound influence on both India's and America's founding fathers, made the same point. He wrote in the *Second Treatise of Civil Government*, 'The end of law is not to abolish or restrain, but to preserve and enlarge freedom ... where there is no law, there is no freedom.'

Another irony: Indians are rightly proud of their ability to dissent in a vigorous democracy; but they often do not enjoy the freedoms of democracy when they interface with the state. Corruption sometimes begins right when you are born—your parents have to bribe someone to get a birth certificate—and ends when you die—your children are forced to 'buy' your death certificate. In between is a dreary life of civic unvirtue—of rishwat and sifarish, 'bribery' and 'influence'. Transparency International ranks India among the most corrupt nations in the world. In 2005, of the eleven public services it surveyed, India's police were found to be the most corrupt, with 80 per cent of the citizens admitting that they had had to bribe someone in the police to get their work done. Forty per cent had paid a bribe to influence the legal system. When an official can slam the window on a citizen arbitrarily, there is loss of freedom.

In the midst of a booming private economy, Indians despair over the simplest services. Lant Pritchett of Harvard's Kennedy School calls India a 'flailing state' and claims that its crisis of governance is 'one of the world's ten biggest problems'. Where the state is desperately needed—in ensuring the citizen's basic needs, security, law and order, education, health and drinking water—it performs appallingly. Where it is not needed, it is hyperactive in tying the citizen in miles of red tape and harassing him through the 'inspector raj'. Pritchett asks this question: if everyone across India's ideological spectrum is agreed that child immunization is a priority, why have only 43.5 per cent of India's children between twelve and twenty-three months received the complete recommended vaccinations? In this, India lags behind Bangladesh (73.1 per cent), Cambodia (66 per cent) and Pakistan (47.3 per cent).

Contemporary India is thus a puzzle. How is it that one of the world's most stable, vigorous democracies with an enviable record of economic growth has among the worst records in human development? Bangladesh and other third world countries score better in infant mortality. India's child malnutrition levels are among the highest. Learning achievements in government primary schools are among the worst—on a par with Ghana. The stubborn persistence of child malnutrition is particularly tragic. In sub-Saharan Africa only 30 per cent of children are malnourished, versus 50 per cent in India. One-third of the babies in India are born with low birthweight compared to one-sixth in sub-Saharan Africa. For more than twenty years, India has 'sustained the greatest effort in history to improve nutritional standards'. It has obviously not delivered.

How does one explain the discrepancy between the government's commitment to universal elementary education, health care and sanitation and the fact that more and more people are embracing private solutions? One answer is that the Indian bureaucratic and political establishments are caught in a time warp, clinging to the belief that only the state must meet people's needs. The Indian state generates fewer and poorer public goods. Instead, it creates private benefits for those who control the state. Consequently, it has got so 'riddled with perverse incentives ... that accountability is almost impossible', says the political scientist Pratap Bhanu Mehta.

NOT AN ORIENTAL DESPOTISM

One of the explanations for today's 'flailing state' is historical. The Indian state was always weak, and pre-modern India was never an 'Oriental despotism', a phrase coined by the ancient Greeks to refer contemptuously to their enemy, the Persian Empire, where 'the king owned all and everyone was his slave'. By characterizing all Asians in this manner, the Greeks were flattering themselves—contrasting their own status as free citizens to Asia's slavery. The Frenchman François Bernier, physician to the

Mughal emperor Aurangzeb between 1656 and 1668, created some of the confusion when he described life in India through the lens of Oriental despotism. Visiting the Mughal court at a time when the imperial Mughal state was already in crisis, he interpreted the reality of the Indian state in terms of the European image of the despotic Ottoman Empire. Montesquieu employed the vision of an Oriental despot in his *Persian Letters* to criticize the French absolutist despot, Louis XIV. Marx took up the idea of Oriental despotism, calling it the 'Asiatic mode of production' to explain why 'Asia fell asleep in history'. The Asiatic mode referred in particular to the agrarian empires of ancient Egypt and China, where an absolute ruler farmed out the right to collect tribute from peasants to a hierarchy of petty officials, and where extorting tribute from village communities became the mode of enrichment for the ruling nobility. When the British came to India they initially believed that India too was under 'Oriental despotism', and made wrong decisions about land tenure.

Unlike many societies Indians did not subscribe to the notion of the 'divine right of kings'. Also alien to them was the notion of 'divine origin of kingship'. Although some Vedic texts hint at a celestial beginning of kingship, later dharma texts clarify that divinity refers not to the person of the king but to his office—to ensure obedience to the state. To make up for the reality of a weak state, the texts insist on the need for a sovereign power with kshatra, 'power of command', to maintain order, protect creatures and avoid anarchy. Hence, the king had to be anointed (abhishikta) in a religious coronation to invest him with supreme power. A society without a king (a-rajaka) is not viable as the big fish will eat the small fish and matsyanyaya, the 'law of the fish', will prevail.

As already noted, the classical texts provide elaborate restraints on the king in the form of raj dharma, 'dharma of the king', to ensure that he acts in the common interest. While kshatra, or pure power, gives him independence, dharma places controls on his power. The smriti texts, in fact, calculate the exact amount of demerit that falls on a king who does not observe raj dharma. 'A king who protects his subjects acquires a sixth of their spiritual merit; if he does not protect them, he gains a sixth of their demerit,' says Manu. One-sixth, shad-bhagin, was the king's normal share of the produce of the land, or the legitimate tax rate. The king had two main privileges: the right to punish and the right to tax. When it comes to tax, the dharma texts are tough on the king and correlate the right to tax with his duty to protect. Narada treats it as though it were a contract—a salary given to him for providing a service. If the king fails to protect, he loses the legitimacy of taxation. Worse, if he fails in raj dharma, he is punished in the afterlife.

The king in pre-modern India did not own the kingdom as he did in some societies, and this placed another limitation on state power. He had a bhaga, 'share', and there was a separation of the individual's property from the king's. The notion of bhaga refers to possession and use, not ownership; to ensure that a householder feels secure about his possession, the king is told not to interfere: 'A house and a field are two fundamentals of a householder's existence—let not the king upset either of them,' says the *Naradasmriti*. Madhava, the eminent jurist, emphatically warns the king that the land is not his but the 'common wealth of all living beings'. Thus, there were plenty of checks on the pre-modern state. As a result, the king in India was a 'distant figure'. Politics was relegated to the realm of ceremony, spectacle and periodic wars between competing kingdoms.

ARRIVAL OF THE MODERN STATE

A major change occurred in the 1860s after the British Crown took over power from the East India Company. The British defined power in political terms and decided to fashion India into a centralized state based on the modern institutions of a strong bureaucracy, police and an impartial judiciary. But even they were careful not to take on India's traditionally strong society. British colonialism succeeded in creating durable institutions in other colonies as well—for example, it was the adoption of the British legal system by Singapore and Hong Kong that laid the foundations for their economic miracles after their independence.

The British inheritance also included, ironically, the idea of self-rule. Educated Indians quickly learned this lesson from nineteenth-century liberal thinkers. Democracy in England did not come about because the English were inherently inclined to democracy, the so-called germ theory of constitutional development. English kings from the eleventh to the thirteenth centuries wanted the people to govern themselves, as James Muldoon shows in a recent essay, 'The Roots of Democratic Self-Government'. Invoking the research of a nineteenth-century American scholar, Muldoon shows that the vehicle for self-rule was the jury system. It was economical—the king did not have to pay the sheriff to deliver justice—and it also checked the powers of the nobles. The people themselves found the duties of self-rule burdensome 'but the long discipline did much to make modern self-government possible' after the Glorious Revolution in 1689.

At Independence, India inherited a small but efficient government from the British. Ruled by the meritocratic Indian Civil Service—sometimes described as a 'platonic guardian' or a 'steel frame'—India had the enviable reputation of being well governed—even better than Britain, some said. In 1938, eighty-one civil servants ran the central government and a thousand officers ruled an undivided India of 300 million people. But, of course, the colonial state's agenda was limited, and only after 1947 did India become a developmental state. Sunil Khilnani describes the ambition vividly in *The Idea of India*: 'The state was enlarged, its ambitions inflated, and it was transformed from a distant, alien object into one that aspired to infiltrate the everyday lives of Indians, proclaiming itself responsible for everything they could desire: jobs, ration cards, educational places, security, cultural recognition.'

But the ambition did not match capacity, as I have

pointed out. India's leaders did not modernize or expand the capability of its institutions. They forgot that western democracies had taken more than a hundred years of economic growth and capacity building to achieve the welfare state. On the contrary, after Nehru's death, Indira Gandhi expanded the ambition and promised a 'mai-baap sarkar', practically a limitless state, and this made it worse. She also had in mind an absolutist state, and in its pursuit she bent constitutional norms and weakened institutions. Hence, there was poor implementation, and quality suffered. One reason for today's weak state is the mismatch between ambition and capacity. The more transactions expanded with the state, the more the perception grew that India was a soft, corrupt state. While Indians were proud that one branch of the state could check others, they did not realize that this could also lead to paralysis in decision-making and poor enforcement. Courts could be used to frustrate state action, and prolonged judicial appeals could bog down everything, including critical infrastructure projects.

Thus, sixty-five years after Independence, India has become a 'flailing state' and faces a crisis in the rule of law. There is profound discontent everywhere. Too many transactions of the citizen with the state are morally flawed. The ideal of a state guided by raj dharma born during the freedom struggle has receded far in the Indian imagination. During the incessant scandals that beset the government in 2011 and led to the Anna Hazare movement, it was not uncommon to read in the vernacular press the question: 'Where is raj dharma?'

RED TAPE IS THE KILLER

Gathered in an elegant room in Chicago in May 2004 were fifteen soft-spoken individuals whose collective net worth exceeded one hundred billion dollars. The group, known informally as the Billionaire's Club, had been brought together by the investment firm Goldman Sachs. The firm's economist, Jim O'Neill, had proposed the now famous BRIC thesis which argued that Brazil, Russia, India and China would become the four most dominant economies of the world by 2050. The billionaires had sufficiently large investments in China but not in India. I was invited to make a pitch for India on this occasion.

At the end of my talk, I asked the billionaires why they preferred to invest in China rather than in India. One of them gently corrected me, 'Forget China, we have made far greater investments in much smaller countries—places like Thailand, Malaysia and Vietnam—than in India.'

I asked, 'Why? Don't you like us?'

'We love India, but we hate your red tape,' he replied.

Over the next thirty sobering minutes I bit the dust. One horror story tumbled out after another about India's officialdom and red tape. The owner of one of the world's largest hotel chains described how it took five years to get a road to access his hotel in Mumbai. Another spoke about his humiliation by the Reserve Bank. 'In other countries we deal with banks, but we are not forced to deal with the central bank like in India.' A third described almost in a whisper how his factory was delayed by months together because he refused to pay a bribe to get a 'completion certificate'. A fourth complained about the ham-handedness of central excise and customs officials. Still another, a foreign institutional investor who had a considerable portfolio of investments on the Bombay Stock Exchange, explained why portfolio investors preferred taking the Mauritius route. 'It is not to avoid Indian taxes—we do it to avoid dealing with your tax officials.' To drive the point home, the group contrasted the welcoming behaviour of Chinese officials, who they said were also corrupt but created a more predictable and friendly environment.

'Face it, Indians are a great people, but your red tape is the killer.' This was the conclusion of the meeting. I tried to put up a brave front but as I trudged back to my hotel, I had a sickening feeling. I consoled myself thinking, what does it matter to India's poor what fifteen rich Americans think? But I knew in my heart that it did matter—if these men invested in India, others would follow. And this would create jobs, bring technology, make India competitive, and bring revenues to the government, which would be invested in village primary schools and health centres.

THE RISE AND FALL OF THE BABU

Coming as I do from a family of government officials, I was not surprised when a senior official of the Indian Administrative Service (IAS), an old friend of the family, dropped in one evening for a cup of tea. What came as a surprise was that his college-going son was ashamed of him. The father was almost in tears as he told us about a conversation with his son about potential careers. When the possibility of joining the elite civil service came up, the son shot back, 'Dad, only corrupt and inefficient people join the IAS.'

It was a devastating verdict. The provocation in this case was the manner in which the government had treated applications of Fulbright scholars. Himself a Fulbright candidate, the son was appalled at the way the Indian bureaucracy arbitrarily rejected research proposals of some US Fulbright scholars, delayed visa applications of others from six to twenty months and even asked a few to change their subject. I too had heard that visas of foreign scholars were routinely delayed; some foreign professors even advised their students, 'Don't bother with India—choose another country.'

The problem went back to the dark days of Indira Gandhi's rule when every American was considered a CIA spy. The story went that one of her ministers had been denied a US visa, and he had tightened India's visa rules to take revenge on 'all American scholars'. Academic black humour had it that Megasthenes, Hiuen Tsang and Alberuni would all have been denied visas today. The Peace Corps was disinvited for the same reason. Visas evidently were delayed because the scholars' files were sent to the much burdened Intelligence Bureau (IB). Since the files were not an intelligence priority, the IB sat on them for months. Meanwhile, the applicants' careers went for a toss. But the scandal is that no official bothered to ask in the past thirty years why the IB should be involved at all. Wouldn't it have been easier for a terrorist to come in as a tourist rather than as a student?

After the Fulbright scandal broke in the media in 2007, the government finally instituted a red and a green channel, which has helped in clearing the backlog. That it took thirty years to fix a leaking pipe is what bothered the son. Now, we cannot have our children being ashamed of our highest civil servants. We must treat the civil service with some possessiveness. It cannot be demonized in the daily discourse of the land. When I put this to my niece, she said, 'Have they not treated us badly all these years?'

No single institution has disappointed Indians more than the bureaucracy. In the 1950s, we bought the sensible idea of Jawaharlal Nehru's that India's outstanding professional bureaucracy would provide stability and continuity to the new nation. It would keep a diverse country together. It has done that. The disappointment comes from its inability to cope with change. The folks of Nehru's time had a touching faith in the state's ability to solve people's problems through the bureaucracy. That faith was called 'high bureaucratic modernism' by the political scientist James C. Scott. The bureaucracy was asked to do more and more without enhancing its capabilities. It failed to cope. Nehru, the socialist, asked the civil service to give him a regulatory framework for his 'mixed economy'. It gave him the 'licence raj'. In the holy name of socialism, the political masters and the senior policymaking officials created dozens of controls, which in the end may have killed India's industrial revolution. In my thirty years in active business, I hardly met a single official who really understood my business, yet he had the power to ruin it. Hence, I believe that India's failures have been as much due to bad management as to ideology. Even the public sector could have performed better had it been given more autonomy and been made accountable. Today, the bureaucracy has become an obstacle to development, blocking economic reforms instead of shepherding them.

Consider this: it takes eighty-nine days to start a business in India, because of red tape. The same process takes less than two days in Scandinavia, the United States, Canada or Singapore. Because so many officials are able to close a window on the citizen, Indians may, in fact, be less free in this respect than citizens of some dictatorships. No wonder India ranks 116th out of 145 nations on the Freedom Index. What do the poor do in these circumstances? They simply start a business without approval and are forced into an informal, black economy. Every Indian city is a hive of feverish, informal activity. The vast majority of Indians are, in fact, self-employed entrepreneurs in the informal economy who cannot enter the formal economy because of formidable barriers of red tape and bribery. The lack of formal, enforceable property rights reduces their investment horizons and prevents small businesses from becoming bigger. The poor, thus, have houses but no titles; crops but no deeds; and business without licences. The informal economy is people's spontaneous response to state failure. India had the distinction of being 134th in a list of 180 countries in the World Bank's ranking of 'the ease of doing business' in 2011.

After 1991, the reformers pushed for independent market regulators to replace the old ministerial style of decision-making by government departments. Their assumption was that regulatory decisions, which were often extremely complex, would be better informed and based on expertise; they would also be more insulated from political pressure. Twenty years later, in 2012, T.N. Ninan, a respected editor and publisher, took a good hard look at the experience with market regulators. His verdict, which he expressed in his famous Saturday column in *Business Standard*, was one of disappointment, far more negative than mine. Ninan laid the blame partly on the civil service, calling it a 'powerful trade union, which has progressively engineered a monopoly on virtually every regulator's job, including the governorship of the Reserve Bank of India ... The electricity regulator's job was once kept vacant for several months so that a particular IAS officer could retire and step into what he must have seen as a sinecure. Being such a regulator is the babu's dream—absolute power with no retribution for wrong decisions, no ministerial oversight, no substantive answerability to Parliament, a guaranteed tenure of three to five years, and all of it post-retirement.'

The Indian bureaucracy still attracts some of the brightest who are admitted on the basis of merit and an examination. Despite their high IQs, they have failed to cut red tape and bribery. One reason is a perverse incentive system which values seniority above performance. They have been unable to change a system whereby a typical file moves from a dealing assistant to a section officer, deputy secretary, undersecretary, joint secretary and secretary to a minister and then back down the long ladder before orders can be issued. And if other ministries or departments are involved, the file has to repeat this up and down process many times. No one has been able to modify this in the age of computers. It is too easy to push the decision upwards. This is what happened during the terrorist attack on Mumbai on 26 November 2008. There was a well-laid-out drill in which the Cabinet secretary was expected to take charge in such an emergency. He did not. He pushed the matter up to an ineffectual home minister and as a result precious hours, lives, and the credibility of the state were lost.

This is a surprisingly negative verdict on the nation's premier service. India's higher bureaucracy is still considered by many to be a solid institution compared to that of other third world countries. It is selected on merit, is trained and has helped maintain a steady course of the ship of state in a climate of political wrangling. When it comes to maintaining stability and the status quo, the bureaucracy seems to perform well. There are innumerable quiet examples of outstanding, selfless performance by officials, but they are now the exception. Moreover, no one anticipated that politicians in India's democracy might gradually 'capture' the bureaucracy and use the system to create jobs and rents for their friends and supporters. Ronald Herring introduces the notion of 'embedded bureaucracy' to explain why officials fail to protect the weak and the disadvantaged. He argues that the official is not a neutral player implementing policy—he is part of the elite who is also 'captured' by the local landowners and the bourgeoisie. But the question arises: why has the bureaucracy not been captured by politicians in Japan, Korea or Taiwan? Is it because the basic values of the elite running their bureaucracies have prevented them from falling into a rent-seeking trap? Whatever the reason, the truth is that the Indian bureaucracy now is not the kind that can propel India to the next level as a global power.

THE HOPE OF LOCAL DEMOCRACY

In 1947, the founding fathers of our Constitution faced two possible directions for the successor state to the British Raj. One was to continue the centralized authoritarian rule of British India; the other was to become a decentralized, federal, parliamentary state. Muhammad Ali Jinnah, Pakistan's founder, chose the first option. India could only select the second and became a parliamentary government in a federal system. These were momentous choices. Generals and authoritarian bureaucrats went on to rule Pakistan for almost half its history. India reinforced the federal character of its Constitution in 1956 by sweeping reorganization that redrew the boundaries of its states on the basis of language. Mohandas Gandhi had set the stage for this in the 1920s, when he reformed the Indian National Congress by creating twenty provincial Congress committees based on regional languages. Jinnah, on the other hand, declared Urdu as the only official language of Pakistan when less than 10 per cent of the people spoke Urdu but 56 per cent spoke Bengali. Thus, he sowed the seeds for Bangladesh.

The hope for India's democracy may well lie in today's fierce competition between the states for investment and resources. Power has been devolving insistently from the Centre to the states for more than a generation after Indira Gandhi. The trickling down of power has made India more difficult to rule with fractured verdicts and weak coalition governments, but it has also brought democracy closer to the people and made the state more accountable. Paradoxically, this gradual enhancement of accountability may be leading India towards a stronger liberal state, even though the big picture might look messy today, and the Centre might be weaker. No one fears any longer that India will break up as a consequence of devolution. Many states seem to act far more decisively than governments in New Delhi because chief ministers seem to have the power and inclination to act far more resolutely than the prime minister in New Delhi. I return to this theme in Chapter Nine in my discussion of the 'new federalism'.

It is essential now that power goes down further and more vigorously to the village panchayats and municipalities in towns. John Stuart Mill, like Tocqueville, laid great emphasis on local government and influenced the reform of chaotic and corrupt local administrations in nineteenth-century England. In India, Prime Minister Rajiv Gandhi took up the cudgels on behalf of local democracy, and his efforts eventually culminated in two constitutional amendments in 1992 ushering in 'panchayati raj'. This was the second great revolution of the early 1990s—the first being economic liberalization in 1991. Both these revolutions are incomplete, however. The second generation of economic reforms are awaited. Most states, sensing a loss of power, have resisted giving financial independence to panchayats and municipalities. Strong mayors with independent resources could make a huge difference to the quality of life in a town or city.

The word 'panchayat' literally means an 'assembly of five', who traditionally settled disputes in the village. The modern panchayat is not to be confused with the old unelected khap, or 'caste panchayats', which still operate in some parts of India. Since the time of the Rig Veda (circa 1500 BCE) Indian villages seem to have had self-governing sabhas, 'assemblies'. However, this form of local governance declined over time and was disrupted during the Mughal and British empires. Gradually, in the twentieth century, the British colonial government came around to the idea of restoring local self-government, and the Montague–Chelmsford reforms (1919) were a first step. By 1925 eight provinces had established village panchayats. The Government of India Act, 1935 took this process further. During the freedom struggle, Mohandas Gandhi advocated a return to decentralized governance (gram swaraj) as the foundation of India's political system, where each village would be responsible for its own affairs. But B.R. Ambedkar, a leader of the Dalits and chair of the drafting committee of the Constitution, vehemently opposed the idea, arguing that the village represented a source of oppression. He prevailed, and local democracy was delayed for a half a century.

Since 1993 panchayat elections have been held

periodically in most states and there are more than 3 million local legislators, of which 1 million are women. By law, one-third of the legislators are women—a third again as heads of these local councils. This was raised to a 50 per cent reservation for women in 2009. It may well be the greatest change in the Indian village in a thousand years and a grand affirmation of women's freedom. Basanti Bai's is one of thousands of testimonials. In the summer of 1994, Basanti Bai, a Dalit, made history by becoming the first woman sarpanch, 'head', of Barkhedi gram panchayat in Sehore district in Madhya Pradesh. However, her family remembers that upper-caste villagers repeatedly threatened her and registered fake complaints with the police. After she resigned no one in the village gave her work and she had to look for it outside. Eventually the village realized its mistake—she had been an excellent sarpanch—and they voted her back at the next election. Today, the village hand pump is a testimonial to her leadership. I have been reading stories such as Basanti Bai's with much pleasure in the regular Panchayati Raj Updates of the Institute of Social Sciences over the last two decades.

Studies show that women are increasingly exercising a benign influence over local affairs and many panchayats headed by them outperform those run by men. They also contradict the common belief that women representatives belong to influential families with political connections. Susheela Kaushik's study of six states confirms that women representatives are mostly from the backward castes, with 40 per cent belonging to families below the poverty line. Other studies show that women leaders perform better because they focus on the right priorities: installing water pumps and wells, and constructing toilets, village roads, and schoolhouses—with good teachers. The women themselves report that they now receive a new kind of respect from their families.

Where panchayati raj has taken off, communities report lower teacher and student absenteeism and better-run poverty programmes. There may not be less corruption overall but it is now a corruption of those in the village who can be identified, shamed or removed at the next election. In a few places where gram sabha, 'the assembly of all adults in the village', has become the norm, it is not local officials or sarpanches who decide who will be the beneficiaries of the projects to be executed under the rural employment scheme. It is the gram sabha. Men and women assemble, vote for what asset they want to create in the village—a water tank, a school building, a road. Those who want to work in exchange for food come forward in the assembly. Although the panchayat executes the poverty project, the gram sabha meets to ratify the panchayat's accounts.

Overall the verdict is mixed, however. Despite the legal sanction for panchayati raj for two decades, states are reluctant to push funds and power downwards. There is not enough pressure to hold regular gram sabhas in most villages and they remain the exception. Only a few in India's political class are enthusiastic about village democracy, and they have urged the Centre to push the funds for centrally sponsored rural schemes directly to the villages, thus bypassing the states. Politicians and bureaucrats in the states oppose it because they will lose power. Villagers themselves lack confidence and education. Only in a few states—among them West Bengal, Kerala, Karnataka and Madhya Pradesh—has vigorous local democracy emerged. As for mohalla sabhas in towns, the new middle class is too occupied with upward mobility to push for them.

History teaches that real democracy lies at the grassroots. As already noted, modern democracy in England originated in medieval English juries in the villages. Self-government in the colonies in North America is an even better example. The colonists governed themselves through a charter without royal supervision. In Massachusetts, the governor called the colonists together once a month to deliberate on their public affairs. The American Revolution, thus, did not bring democracy to America but only upheld the tradition of self-rule which was established in the colonial period. Ancient India too had a long and rich tradition of democratic republics, but these were forgotten as kingship gradually prevailed and become the norm. The lesson for contemporary India is that successful democracies are based on customs and habits acquired and perfected over a long period of time. The sight of the colonists in Massachusetts deliberating every month should be an inspiration for our panchayati raj. Anna Hazare's movement has also highlighted the importance of the gram and mohalla sabhas. Its energetic pursuit is the key to embedding moral habits in the hearts and minds of Indians, thus strengthening the rule of law and reducing corruption.

WHAT WILL IT TAKE—A KURUKSHETRA?

The conundrum of Indian democracy is this: why have honest and regular elections, socially inclusive politics, a rising economy and a growing middle class not led to a better government that provides effective service? According to classical modernization theory, political, economic and social development were supposed to go together. But in India a rising economy and society have not been able to stem political decay of the state.

When he took office in May 2004, Prime Minister Manmohan Singh proclaimed that administrative reform was his top priority. A year later, he announced a new system to evaluate the IAS officer. It was based on a performance-based report card, and meant to be the first in a series of administrative reforms that could begin to cure a sick bureaucracy. Replacing the present ineffective and subjective annual confidential report, it held the potential of making officers accountable, motivating the honest and punishing the lazy and corrupt. The idea was to link good performance with faster promotions and to punish bad officers with delayed or no promotions. A similar system had helped improve the performance of private and public sector bureaucracies in many countries.

Eight years later Manmohan Singh had given up. A senior official in the prime minister's office revealed that the bureaucracy had sabotaged his well-meaning efforts at administrative reform. When I asked naively how it could have defied its own boss, the prime minister, I was told that it had done it cleverly with the collusion of the political class.

So, what will it take to reform the Indian state? The solutions are well known—for example, transforming the bureaucracy from a system based on seniority to one which rewards good performance and punishes poor outcomes. There are excellent proposals for speeding up the judicial system too, and for freeing the police from the clutches of chief ministers. There have been many commissions for reform in the past fifty years. Most have repeated the same sensible recommendations, but they have not been acted upon. Given a powerful vested interest—more than 20 million employees of the state—reforming state institutions is not going to be easy. Yet the reform of the institutions of the state—the bureaucracy, the police and the judiciary—is even more important today than economic reform.

To its credit, the government was able to push through the Right to Information Act, and this has begun to open up the bureaucracy to public scrutiny. Another success has been to jettison the dogma of 'bureaucratic high modernism' and pragmatically create public–private partnerships to augment the limited capacity and resources of the state in the building of infrastructure. There has been some success in this regard in building roads and highways. Some of the new airports, such as the one in Delhi, are another example. Far more could have been achieved in other infrastructure areas. There is an ever-present danger in public–private partnerships of 'crony capitalism', but successful countries have been able to overcome it through a transparent process in partner selection and through rigorous legal contracts.

Eliminating unwanted laws or simplifying them is another simple idea for improving governance. When Manmohan Singh was finance minister in the early 1990s, he set up a group under the economist Bibek Debroy to precisely examine this. The group made an exhaustive study of central laws and concluded that 1500 out of 3500 laws of the central government were obsolete. They concluded that if these were scrapped or significantly modified the citizens' life would improve. Arun Jaitley, when he was law minister, scrapped 350 of these laws. When Manmohan Singh became prime minister in 2004, many expected him to follow through with this but he did not.

Our framework of government services is still based on the Whitehall model of the mid-nineteenth century and remains unchanged. Meanwhile, Britain has moved on and transformed its own civil service in the past twenty-five years, making it far more accountable to ordinary citizens—it had 40 per cent less people working in the government in 2005 than in 1979, and this had not only saved more than a billion pounds a year, but governance too had improved. Australia and New Zealand have done an even better job of administrative reform.

If it is lucky, India might throw up a strong leader who is also a reformer—a Deng or a Thatcher. Since there is no guarantee of this happening, though, the next best hope may lie in the recent rise of a young middle class—a class that has found its voice via an aggressive electronic media, which was reflected recently in the Anna Hazare movement. History teaches that states will reform institutions only when they are pushed to the wall or if there is a crisis, such as the one that India faced in 1991. With the present crisis of corruption and confidence, India may have begun to generate demand for such a reform.

In the *Mahabharata*, the state at Hastinapur was a repository of crisis, 'a world whose karmic dominoes of human weakness reach into past and future horizons until bounded by creation and apocalypse', according to David Gitomar. Hastinapur had problems also with the self-destructive Kshatriya institutions of its time, and it had to wage a civil war at Kurukshetra to cleanse them. It is tempting to compare crisis-ridden Hastinapur with today's flailing Indian state. Equally luring is to liken its deteriorated Kshatriya institutions to our corrupt governance institutions. The impatient clamour on the street for a Lokpal made this connection, but the last thing India needs is a civil war like Kurukshetra. Reforming government institutions is never easy, but it has to be done. If citizens do not see leaders up to the task, they will go beyond street protests at Ramlila Maidan. But it would be a shame if they undermined our finely crafted constitutional system that has made India's democracy, warts and all, the envy of the developing world.

5

THE DHARMA OF
CAPITALISM

*It is difficult but not impossible to
conduct business honestly.*

—Mohandas K. Gandhi,
Non-Violence in Peace and War, 2.127

Ever since the Indian Premier League of cricket was
born in the spring of 2008, it has stood for a non-stop
party that lasts for a couple of months each year to which
everyone is invited, provided they want to have fun. A
heady cocktail of cricket and Bollywood, chatter and
glamour, high-rolling betting, tomfoolery and unrequited
sensuality, it has brought magical evenings to millions
across India. IPL is a metaphor for a new India—crass,

brash and razzmatazz. The cricket league is also symbolic of Indian capitalism with its red-blooded firms, creative and energetic, that compete brutally and innovate fiercely as they stomp onto the world stage.

When the timing of the IPL clashed with the elections in its second season, the IPL did not sit back and wait for a grumpy government to sort things out. It played off the English and South African cricket boards to get the best deal and the result was an amazing sight—Delhi playing Hyderabad in Cape Town, and Mumbai playing Chennai in Johannesburg. With bold ambition, quick thinking, meticulous planning and brilliant execution—all the skills that are making Indian companies successful—the IPL filled stadiums, shuttled tens of thousands of Indians to South Africa and enticed millions to their TVs back home. It took a hundred years for Major League Baseball in America to hold its first game outside the United States and fifty for the American Football League to play outside. The IPL went global in its second year.

The IPL is a work of entrepreneurship, and the guiding entrepreneurial spirit behind its rise was Lalit Modi. He had undoubted ability to take big risks and he valued novelty, characteristics that are not common in a traditional society. Within three years the IPL achieved a brand value of a staggering Rs 19,600 crore, and it had paid almost Rs 600 crore to the government in service and income taxes. It gave an unprecedented opportunity to young, talented cricketers to showcase their talents. Even Modi's critics admitted that the IPL would not have been born had he not possessed a rare talent for execution. If he had not snatched autonomy from the babus at the Board of Control for Cricket in India (BCCI), the regulator and owner of the IPL, the league would have ended up as a pale copy of the amateurish Ranji Trophy that no one watched. But Modi was also flawed and soon he stumbled, almost bringing the house down with him. The regulator also failed—partly because it was the owner. Of this, more later.

RISING ON THE BACK OF FREE MARKETS

That India is rising in the twenty-first century on the back of free markets is not surprising. It has a long tradition of encouraging and promoting markets. Since ancient times the merchant has been a respected member of society, one of the 'twice-born', a high caste in the social hierarchy. Merchants and bazaars, however, emerged even earlier as centres of exchange in the towns of the Indus Valley (3300–1500 BCE) or even in the Neolithic age, soon after Indians first engaged in agriculture and there was a surplus. As Jean-Jacques Rousseau has taught us, inequality also had its origins with the birth of agriculture because with it was born private property.

There was purpose to economic activity and the ancients were acutely aware of it when they posited artha, 'material well-being', as one of the goals of life. They believed that the pursuit of money is justified to the extent that it leads to the good life. That good life also had other goals, in particular, dharma, 'moral well-being', which was higher than artha. This meant that there was a right and a wrong way to pursue wealth, something that Lalit Modi forgot. Moreover, the pursuit of artha was meant to make the world a better place. In today's language we might interpret this to mean that business has a purpose—for example, to take a society from poverty to prosperity, a goal that many contemporary Indian entrepreneurs subscribe to.

Because the state was historically weak, regulation in India was generally light. An exception to this was the heavily regulated state in the political economy text *Arthashastra*. The king's dharma, we are told in the *Mahabharata*, was to nurture the productive forces in society, including the market: 'The king, O Bharata, should always act in such a way towards the Vaishyas [merchants, commoners] so that their productive powers may be enhanced. Vaishyas increase the strength of a kingdom, improve its agriculture and develop its trade. A wise king levies mild taxes upon them' (*Mahabharata*, XII.87). Practical advice indeed—otherwise, the epic goes on to suggest, Vaishyas will shift to neighbouring kingdoms and the king will lose his tax base.

The merchant was generally well thought of. He is often the hero in the animal and human stories of the *Panchatantra*, the *Kathasaritsagara* and other texts, where he is sometimes a figure of sympathy and at other times of fun. The *Mahabharata* speaks of Tuladhara, a respected trader of spices and juices in Varanasi, who surprisingly instructs a high Brahmin about dharma and how to live. Speaking modestly, he compares his life as a merchant to a 'twig borne along in a stream that randomly joins up with some other pieces of wood, and from here and there, with straw, wood and refuse, from time to time'.

The analogy of the twig brings to mind the picture of a real-life trader who has multiple suppliers and buyers, and whose gains and losses are not in his control but depend on the impersonal forces of the market. A classical liberal in the eighteenth century, Adam Smith, taught the same lesson. He observed in *The Wealth of Nations* that a businessman was at the mercy of an 'invisible hand' of the market, which determined his prices and profits. In a competitive market, an entrepreneur is more like Tuladhara's twig randomly swept along the flow, not an oligarchic 'crony capitalist'.

Despite a general sympathy for the merchant, commerce in India had a bad odour at times, not unlike in other societies. The Vaishya, after all, is third in the caste hierarchy, and somewhat suspect in the minds of the ruling castes. This is typical of all agrarian societies. Even in Babylon of the sixth century BCE, Jean Baechler, the great economic historian, tells us that firms took in money deposits, issued cheques, gave loans at interest and invested in agricultural and industrial enterprises. Yet they were looked down upon and commercial activities were universally held in low esteem.

In India the negative image scaled a peak during its socialist decades between 1950 and 1990 when the state was placed at the 'commanding heights of the economy'. 'Nehru the Brahmin' combined with 'Nehru the aristocratic Fabian socialist' and this deadly blend set a tone for the rest of society in its view of the businessman. That image has gradually changed after 1991, but even today when there is the wondrous spectacle of thousands of young

Indians starting business ventures, the idea that their struggle for personal gain might actually promote the common good is still too fantastic for people to accept. This prejudice is partially behind the animus against the commercial nature of the IPL. Even sophisticated Indians continue to distrust the market—perhaps because no one is in charge. This is also why market-based reforms are hard to sell during elections. No wonder Samuel Johnson used to say, 'There is nothing which requires more to be illustrated by philosophy than trade does.'

CAPITALISM, INDIAN STYLE

Freed of the shackles of the 'licence raj', in the 1990s Indian entrepreneurs responded beyond the most optimistic hopes of the reformers. Within two decades, by 2010, there were over 150 Indian companies with a market capitalization of over a billion dollars; foreigners had invested in over a thousand Indian companies via the stock market; 750 international companies had research and development centres in India—a testament to its human capital; 390 of the Fortune 500 companies had outsourced software development or business processes to India. High-tech manufacturing had taken off even though labour-intensive low-tech manufacturing was lagging. All these changes had disciplined the banking sector, whose bad loans in 2008 accounted for less than 2 per cent of all loans (compared to 20 per cent in China) even though India's shoddy state-owned banks had not been privatized.

Today, approximately twenty-five Indian companies are

globally competitive; another twenty are on their way. There has been a churning—only nine out of thirty companies which made up the 1990 Sensex of the Bombay Stock Exchange were still around in the 2010 Sensex, as Swaminathan Aiyar reminded us in one of his incomparable Sunday columns. This is testimony, indeed, to the new dynamic, competitive and innovative climate. The nine survivors were Reliance Industries, three Tata companies— in steel, autos and power—the Mahindras, Hindalco, L&T, Hindustan Lever and ITC. Outstanding new entrepreneurs have come up in telecom, airlines, health care, IT and auto components.

Some flabby business houses have decayed but many have defended themselves surprisingly well. The protectionist rhetoric of the 'Bombay Club' died by the end of the last century as firms began to benchmark with the best in the world. The distractions of family feuds also receded in the competitive battles when survival was at stake. A surprise was the nimbleness and ambition shown by the old house of Tatas as it led the charge in acquiring companies abroad. Despite all this, Indian capitalism in 2012 is still skewed overall towards the state and business houses. Government companies, hugely inefficient, continue to dominate energy and finance. Although a drag and a bottleneck, they account for 40 per cent of stock market profits.

In the private sector, the family still continues to loom large and institutional capitalism has not yet arrived. Because the Indian state is weak and relatively incompetent in its ability to build infrastructure and regulatory capacity, companies must build their own infrastructure. This is a major weakness when you are competing globally. In the unreformed sectors, crony capitalism has become a real problem. In real estate, power and infrastructure, India is now dominated by a handful of business oligarchs, many of whom flourish because of their political connections. Generally, India's firms have thrived despite a weak state, but in the unreformed sectors, they are thriving because of it. This is a dangerous thing, and there is an urgent need for reform, as already pointed out.

Newcomers have kept zooming into the top ranks of Indian business with relentless regularity. K. Dhargalkar and R. Desai's study shows that first-generation companies on Bombay Stock Exchange's blue chip Section A had risen from nine in 1991 to sixty-two by 2011. Of the latter, thirty-two had exited Section A mostly because they had been acquired. One of these successful entrepreneurs, Gautam Adani, began life as a trader. One day an opportunity came his way and he took it fearlessly. As a supplier of electricity, he faced relentless obstacles and red tape, especially in obtaining coal for his power plants. He finally solved the problem innovatively and with panache. Instead of depending on Indian coal, he bought coal mines in Indonesia and Australia, a cargo ship in Korea and a port in Australia. He also built the now-famous Mundra port in Gujarat, along with its own railway spur. Not only did he go around the government, he went around a subcontinent, and began to generate power reliably and competitively via imported coal. Although Gujarat is, perhaps, the least corrupt of the

Indian states, Adani's proximity to the chief minister helped. Adani is now India's sixth richest person with a fortune valued at $10 billion, and his rise reflects another aspect of Indian capitalism: the private sector is playing a significant role in areas which were once controlled by the state such as power, telecommunications, ports and airports. The future of Indian business lies both with business innovators like Adani and the vast pool of scientists and engineers employed by the research and development centres of multinational companies, who are doing cutting-edge research in India.

LALIT MODI'S TROUBLES

Nothing is quite perfect in the world and certainly not human beings. In the IPL's third year, Lalit Modi, its founding spirit and commissioner, got into deep trouble. What began as a trifling spat on Twitter ended with the resignation of a Union minister of state. A few weeks later, Modi was himself sacked, going from public hero to enemy within a month. Coming on the heels of the troubles on Wall Street and the global financial crisis, the legitimacy of the market was once again in question in a country where capitalism was trying to find a comfortable home.

Lalit Modi's problems began in March 2010 when the IPL decided to expand from eight to ten teams. The winning bids came from the Sahara group for Pune and the Rendezvous consortium from Kochi. The affair came out in the open on 11 April when Modi revealed in a tweet that among the shareholders of the Kochi group was

Sunanda Pushkar from Dubai, who had allegedly received Rs 70 crore in 'sweat equity'. She had been seen prominently in public with the charming and elegant minister of state Shashi Tharoor. There was public clamour. Who was the lady? And why did she receive stock options worth Rs 70 crore? And was this, in fact, the minister's share; if so, what had he done to deserve it?

Tharoor tweeted back accusing Modi of sour grapes because the teams he had backed had lost the auction. He claimed that he himself was merely mentor to the Kochi franchise and denied having any financial interest. Pushkar explained that she was an events manager in Dubai who had planned to promote the Kochi team and it was common for professionals to get 'sweat equity' instead of salary at the start. Neither the Opposition nor the government was convinced in Parliament and consequently Tharoor resigned as minister. In three weeks Modi was sacked as the IPL's commissioner. Soon Sunanda Pushkar and Shashi Tharoor were married.

More serious allegations of corruption came in shortly that undermined Modi's neutrality as a commissioner. He was accused of being a shareholder in the Rajasthan team behind certain 'front names'; his relatives were said to have a stake in the Punjab and Kolkata teams; $80 million had allegedly been paid to him via a 'facilitation fee' from Sony/MSM to the World Sports Group—the money had supposedly gone into Modi's dubious bank accounts. Lalit Modi's extravagant lifestyle did not help matters—a private jet, a yacht, a fleet of Mercedes-Benzes and BMWs. However, his friends claimed in his defence that he had always been a high roller. They recalled that his father had given him $5000 to buy a car when he was a student in America, but the young man had instead spent the money on a down payment for a Mercedes-Benz. He had also been convicted in a drugs case, it was rumoured.

Modi retorted that he came from a wealthy family, and besides what had his lifestyle to do with his running the IPL? Since he was an impatient man who did not suffer fools, he had made plenty of enemies, especially among the 'small men' at the BCCI. There were too many who were consumed with envy at his success. But even his critics admitted that the IPL would not have been born if the flawed Lalit Modi had not possessed a rare talent for execution.

Shashi Tharoor has been a friend of mine for a dozen years and I did not believe the allegations against him. He claimed he was innocent and many were inclined to believe him, unlike Modi, who was branded a crook. Ms Pushkar announced that she had renounced her claim to the sweat equity. The BCCI declared that it would prosecute Modi in the courts, but nothing had happened till mid-2012. Meanwhile, Modi had left the country and was living in exile in London. But the cricket league, loved by millions in India, is in safe hands, managed by capable people—and continues to bring joy to huge audiences.

One explanation for the minister's presumed gains is that businessmen in India still seem to place great faith in the power of politicians to influence outcomes, and in this case 4.5 per cent equity was the price they were willing to pay to ensure that their bid won. The losing consortia might also have had their political mentors. To me it was a reminder of the ever-present danger of crony capitalism in a free-market democracy. It reinforced the need for tough, independent regulators, and India's record on this has been mixed at best.

A COMFORTABLE HOME FOR CAPITALISM

The most strident critics of Lalit Modi were in the Parliament, and they demanded a probe by a joint parliamentary committee. The socialist political parties called for nationalizing the IPL. Lalu Prasad Yadav, Mulayam Singh Yadav and Sharad Yadav insisted on banning it. The Janata Dal (United) member Shivanand Tiwari demanded that funds of the IPL and the BCCI be confiscated. The communist leader Gurudas Dasgupta criticized the Twenty20 game format, saying it was a 'caricature' of cricket in which players were bought like 'vegetables'. The deputy leader of the Opposition, Gopinath Munde, asked that if bar girls in Mumbai had been barred from performing, why should cheerleading girls be allowed in the IPL? Mulayam Singh Yadav called cricket a 'foreign game' and wanted it replaced by a desi sport.

A prominent leftist member of the Rajya Sabha blamed the IPL for commercializing cricket. He complained that the real evil in the IPL was a 'foreign import called the market'. He traced it to the East India Company and was much applauded when he concluded his speech saying that the 'market was immoral'. Around the country, journalists and academics took up this refrain and criticized the IPL's capitalist ideology. Theirs was a more intelligent assessment. Aside from the dangers of crony capitalism, they reflected on capitalism's other defects—for example, its dependence on greed in motivating human action, its tendency towards inequality and the poor state of board governance where 'independent board members' were really ineffectual. When a reporter went around asking the critics of the market what should replace it, hardly anyone wanted Marx's utopia, state ownership of the means of production—the predictable exceptions being the members of the Communist Party of India-Marxist (CPM). The conclusion seemed to be that capitalism was not perfect but there was nothing else to replace it. I felt that India had come a long way from 1991 and its mindset had changed.

This change is palpable in the minds of ordinary persons, particularly in the new middle class. A worldwide survey on the popular perception of capitalism revealed at the end of the last decade that 67 per cent of the Chinese strongly support their variety of capitalism. (It is charming how China has emerged as one of the strongest supporters of capitalism in the world.) By comparison, in the United States only 43 per cent feel positively about it. Expectedly, in France, the support is the lowest at 37 per cent. The survey did not have Indian figures but I would not be surprised if India is at the top of the charts. Both India and China have accepted the capitalist road to prosperity, but in the end, capitalism is more comfortable in a democracy which fosters entrepreneurs naturally. A state enterprise can never be as innovative or nimble, and this is why some Chinese envy India's private companies.

Capitalism depends on the right to property, which is one of India's advantages, but it needs to do more to strengthen that right. There was an assault on the right to property in the 1970s by the socialist state, which weakened the right through an amendment to the Constitution. However, after 1991, the judiciary has interpreted this right in a stronger way in its judgements. Only in 2007–08 during a controversy relating to the land acquired by the state on behalf of the Tatas for manufacturing the Nano car at Singur in Bengal did the left-leaning establishment realize that even the poor have property. One of the best ways to help the poor is to give them titles to their property, as De Soto has suggested, so that they can collateralize it.

Indubitably the 1991 reforms have unleashed business enterprise and this has done a lot of good in lifting millions out of poverty and into the middle class. But it has also given greater freedom to 'robber barons', as it did in the United States at the turn of the nineteenth century. A very real example of India's poor governance is the too cosy relationship among business houses, civil servants and politicians. I have been sufficiently critical of the latter in this book, but this is the place to bring some balance and also hold business houses accountable. Collusive corruption, as I point out in Chapter Eight, has both a giver and a taker of bribes, and both need to be punished. Because many sectors of the economy have not yet been reformed India has increasingly moved to a disturbing situation where large business groups enjoy excessive power. The country is in transition, and this is the time to unleash reforms in the sectors already identified, bring in strong regulators and keener enforcement of competition, but without killing the animal spirit of the likes of Lalit Modi.

THE DHARMA OF CAPITALISM

Although two decades have passed since Indians began their love affair with free markets, capitalism is still trying to find a comfortable home in India. Indians, like most people, believe that the market is efficient but not moral. The market is also not bothered with inequality. A lesson from Lalit Modi's morality tale is that human beings may be immoral and will behave badly whether in a socialist or a capitalist society, but the institution of the market itself is neither moral nor immoral. Hence, the honourable members of Parliament got it wrong. At the heart of the market system is the idea of exchange between ordinary, self-interested human beings, who seek to advance their interests peacefully in the marketplace. The reason that strangers are able to trust each other in the market is, in part, due to dharma, which represents the underlying norms that are shared by members of a society. The belief that the average person acts according to dharma—that he or she wants to do the right thing—gives people a sense of safety when they cooperate and transact.

The idea that an ancient Indian idea might offer insight into the nature of the market is, on the face of it, bizarre. Dharma, as I have already explained, can mean many things but it is chiefly concerned with doing the right thing. It is commonly believed that when individuals behave in accordance with dharma, there is order and harmony in society. Moreover, dharma is especially useful for public policy because it is a pragmatic concept and does not seek moral perfection; it views men to be sociable but imperfect, with strong passions that need to be restrained.

Dharma thus provides the underlying norms of a society and gives people the confidence to cooperate with strangers. It creates obligations for citizens and rulers. In the marketplace, it places restraints on buyers and sellers. Because we share a common dharma I readily accept a cheque from you. Millions of transactions in the global economy are conducted daily based on trust without resorting to contracts. For example, a taxi driver stops and takes me in as a passenger because he knows that the restraint of dharma will ensure that I will pay him at the journey's end.

Similarly, I trust my fruit vendor who claims that her mangoes are expensive this week because of their higher quality. If the mangoes turn out to be bad, I will punish her by buying mangoes the next time from her competitor. She not only loses my custom but that of others as word of mouth spreads—she comes to be known as a person of low dharma. Suppliers will not trust her; she will not be able to attract good employees. On the other hand, a person of high dharma will be rewarded with a good reputation; she will be highly regarded by her customers, suppliers and employees. Thus, dharma sends the right signals in the marketplace, while it punishes bad behaviour and rewards good behaviour. Smart businessmen know this and work incessantly to improve their reputation.

The market system depends ultimately not on laws but on the self-restraint of individuals. A sense of dharma provides that restraint for the vast majority of people who tend to behave with mutual respect in most societies. However, there are also crooks in all societies who do not feel bound by dharma; hence law and enforcement are necessary. It is in man's nature to want more, and dharma seeks to give coherence to our desires by containing them within an ordered existence. Since no amount of regulation will catch all the crooks, self-restraint is needed on the part of each actor in the marketplace in order to achieve dharma within society.

Dharma's approach, as already mentioned, is not to seek moral perfection, which leads inevitably to theocracy or dictatorship. It offers a modestly coherent world that is also close to our everyday one, and hence suited to understand exchanges in the marketplace. We also know that beyond a certain point increased wealth does not appear to make people happier, and they seek other goals. Successes of capitalism produce over time enervating influences when a generation committed to saving is replaced by one devoted to spending. This creates its own problems as India and China will discover soon. Ferocious competition is another feature of the free market and it can be corrosive. But competition is also an economic stimulant that promotes human welfare. The choice for policymakers is not between unregulated free markets and central planning but in getting the right mix of regulation. What is right may vary from society to society depending on people's disposition and the state's capability. Except for a small minority of communists, hardly anyone in India wants state ownership of production, where the absence of competition corrodes the citizen's character even more. We know this too well from the dark days of the 'licence raj'.

6

MIDDLE-CLASS DIGNITY

Who is it that exercises social power today?
Who imposes the forms of his own mind on the period?
Without doubt, the middle class.

—Jose Ortega y Gasset,
The Revolt of the Masses, 1930

A SENSE OF POSSIBILITIES

I first met Shashi Kumar in early 2000. He was twenty-two and had just joined a business process outsourcing (BPO) call centre in Gurgaon. He came from a tiny village in Bihar; many of his friends at work did not know that his grandfather had been a low-caste sharecropper in good times and a day labourer in hard ones. They had been so poor that on some nights they had nothing to eat.

Somehow his father had escaped from bondage and found a job in a transport company in Darbhanga. Since they could not manage on his father's salary, his mother had gone to work. She taught in a tiny school in their neighbourhood where she earned Rs 400 a month, and she would take him with her to the school, where he was educated for free under her watchful eye. Determined that her son should escape the indignities of Bihar, she tutored him at night and got him into college. When he finished, she presented him with a railway ticket to Delhi.

Ten years later Shashi Kumar had risen to a middle manager position, and exuded the self-assurance of a young man with a future. He earned Rs 65,000 a month and spoke confidently in English to customers in America. He lived in a two-bedroom flat, which he had bought four years ago with a mortgage from a private bank. He drove a nice car and sent his daughter to an expensive private school. He had just returned from an assignment in Boston where his company had sent him for training at their customer's office.

'It's a good time to be alive,' said his mother, who has been living with him in Gurgaon ever since her husband died. 'I don't know how he managed it. I just saved a few paise each day and gave him a railway ticket. He did the rest.'

Shashi Kumar had turned out to be an affable, diligent young man. What made his life different from those of the previous generations was a real sense of life's possibilities. He was a product of the new middle class, the fastest growing segment of Indian society. Had his grandfather dared to dream of another kind of life he would have been beaten up by his landlord in Bihar.

Shashi Kumar's story goes back to 1991 when India opened its economy and the first reforms in the telecom sector made it possible for a company in America to 'outsource' its back office jobs to India. It was the engineers in information technology who showed that they could write software at a fraction of the cost, and during their day hours while America slept; in the morning, the American companies would have IT solutions waiting for them. They provided a valuable activity to their customers for which they were richly rewarded. Gradually the customers realized that they could also send other back office jobs to India, jobs that could be attended to via the telephone. For many of these low-end jobs, you did not have to be an engineer. All that was needed was a modest knowledge of English and familiarity with computers. The jobs involved customer service, and the time slots for these were America's daytime hours—India's night-time—when customers called the helpline. These jobs had never migrated before, but India's companies were ready when the opportunity came. Gradually, they also hired accountants, lawyers, scientists and advertising professionals as outsourcing moved up the knowledge chain. If the government had not liberalized and had remained closed, Shashi Kumar would not have got a break. This is how several million youngsters found jobs in glass-enclosed office towers in places like Gurgaon.

Before 1991, there had been little possibility of upward movement. The only way to break into the middle class was to get a government job, which was not easy. So, if you got educated and did not get a job, you faced a nightmare that was called 'educated unemployment'.

'Now anyone can make it. All it takes is basic education, computer skills and some English,' said Shashi Kumar.

'But why have these jobs not come to Bihar?' asks his mother mournfully. Her son had the answer.

'I am a Yadav, and so was Lalu,' he said, referring to Lalu Prasad, the former chief minister of Bihar who was apparently of the same caste. 'You educated me but Lalu did not educate Bihar. He dismissed computers as toys of the rich and kept his people backward. Eventually, he realized his mistake. By then it was too late.'

AN UNLIKELY BAND OF REVOLUTIONARIES

Last year I ran into Shashi Kumar on the spanking new platform of the Guru Dronacharya station of the Delhi Metro. I was surprised to see him in a Gandhi cap. He was surrounded by friends from his middle-class neighbourhood in Gurgaon and he introduced them enthusiastically. They also wore the same cap. All winners in India's economic rise, they were headed for the Ramlila ground where Anna Hazare was holding another anti-corruption rally. They looked an unlikely band of revolutionaries. With good jobs and nice families, they lived in comfortable flats in Gurgaon, drove cars and sent their children to good schools. What were they doing waving flags on a platform of the Metro line between Gurgaon and Delhi?

Shashi and his friends belonged to the new middle class,

which voted daily in the bazaar but hardly ever at election time. India's middle class had great economic clout in the marketplace but that did not seem to affect the nation's political life where the countryside still determined the outcome of elections. The power to consume had got divorced from political power, and looking at them I wondered if this was about to change after Anna Hazare.

Shashi Kumar explained that his modest turn to political activism began with Ruchika Girhotra, whose tale I have recounted in Chapter Three. He was acquainted with her family—they had come from Chandigarh on a visit to his neighbour's home. He was vaguely aware that her case had languished in the courts for almost two decades. When the verdict finally came, and he saw it on television, he was outraged and he wanted to do something.

The train came and we squeezed in. A young man got up and made a place for me. I smiled at him, happy that some of the old courtesies of the road persisted in the razzmatazz of a rising India. The young men found places near me. One of Shashi Kumar's friends explained that all these years they had been intent on their careers and had had no time for anything else until Anna Hazare roused them.

'We hate politics and politicians,' added Shashi Kumar. 'They remind me of everything ugly in Bihar. So I never vote. It wouldn't matter anyway.'

'But why Anna?' I asked.

'What has attracted me to Anna-ji,' answered his friend, 'is his belief in dharma-centred leadership. To make a political revolution you have to first make a moral revolution within yourself. When citizens are moral they can make their government listen to their demands.'

I was moved by these Gandhian chords in the speeding Metro train.

'I don't know if anything will change, but at least I will be able to tell my grandchildren that I was there when history was taking place,' Shashi said.

I rose to leave as my station was approaching. Shashi and his friends were continuing towards Ramlila Maidan. We agreed to meet the following weekend when they were planning to attend another Anna Hazare rally.

'Anna-ji woke us up,' shouted Shashi from the train.

Anna Hazare had also woken up India's political establishment. No one could remember a time when so many powerful political figures were in jail. Some of the credit belonged to Anna's anti-corruption crusade. Shashi Kumar and his friends were on their way to support his second hunger strike in August, which he staged in Ramlila Maidan. It drew tens of thousands of supporters and this show of strength forced the government to reconsider a stronger version of the Lokpal bill—a considerable victory, since politicians of all parties had stonewalled the creation of an anti-corruption agency for forty years.

BOURGEOIS DIGNITY:
THE KEY TO AN INDIAN PUZZLE

Most people were taken by surprise at the strength of the support for Hazare from the urban middle class. They had not realized how rapid economic growth was multiplying this class. 'Middle class' has always been frustrating to define, and Max Weber, the sociologist, famously called it the group in the middle between the working and the upper classes—in old Europe, this meant between the nobility and the peasantry. In argumentative India, definitions are especially contentious and the size of the middle class depends on how you define it. Some economists place India's middle class at roughly a third of its entire population. That is roughly consistent with the generous way the *Economist* defined it in February 2009— as beginning at the point where people have a third of their income left for discretionary spending after paying for basic food and shelter; this allowed them to provide for their children's education, health care and some consumer goods.

On this basis, the weekly announced that half the world's population belonged to the middle class as a result of rapid economic growth in emerging countries during the first decade of the new century. Some consumer multinationals placed the cut-off at the level of annual family (not per capita) income at a purchase price parity of $20,000, and this too was in harmony with the *Economist*. More modest estimates were made by the Organisation for Economic Co-operation and Development (OECD) and the Brookings Institution, where Homi Kharas calculated that only by 2020 would half the world become middle class, up from 30 per cent now. The *Economist* stated that middle-class persons in Asia already exceeded those in the West and that more than half of China was already middle class. I felt this must be a scooter-owning middle class, as in India, not a car-owning one—although its attitudes were probably the same.

What this means is that a significant number of Indians had experienced a palpable betterment in their lives. Everyone was not better off and there were still vast areas of horrible deprivation; but a large enough number had begun to notice a difference in their lives. As a result, the discourse of the nation had also begun to change. More and more people had begun to believe that their future was open, not predetermined, and could be altered by their own actions. The same thing had happened in the West after 1800. In her book *Bourgeois Dignity: Why Economics Can't Explain the Modern World*, Deirdre McCloskey argues that the West rose after 1800 not only because of economic factors but because the discourse about markets, enterprise and innovation changed. People became enthusiastic and encouraging of entrepreneurs. The development of the West is explained not so much by colonialism and imperialism; not by Marx's theory of classes; not by Max Weber and his Protestant ethic; not even by Douglass North and the central role of institutions. It has as much to do with how people's perceptions and expectations changed. Merchants, tinkerers and practical persons seeking profit in the marketplace came to be respected, and even admired. This 'bourgeois revaluation' gave further impetus to innovation, which has produced our present-day capitalist society.

Robert Lucas, the Nobel Prize winner, says that 'for income growth to occur in a society, a large fraction of people must experience changes in the possible lives they imagine for themselves and their children ... In other words ... economic development requires a million mutinies.' And for the first time in India's history, dignity is being bestowed on the Indian middle-class's dreams: everyone, it seems, is getting an MBA and aspires to become a CEO. Ordinary conversations over chai and chaat are about markets and innovation. And about how while the private sector provides cutting-edge services and products to the world, the roads outside are potholed, electricity is patchy and the water supply erratic. The difference between the two worlds is brazenly obvious to the middle class, whose private life is governed by accountability as I have already noted—if you don't work, you don't eat. In contrast, government jobs are effectively for life with little answerability.

Dignity is a sociological fact while liberty is an economic and political concept. Middle-class Indians won some dignity when they won political independence in 1947; they gained some more when they attained economic liberty in 1991; but only now, twenty years later, have they begun to feel the full meaning of dignity after the economic rise of India. The strong response to Anna Hazare's movement is a testimony to this achievement. Underlying bourgeois dignity is what Adam Smith called a 'natural system of liberty'. This means that when free individuals pursue their own interests peacefully in an open, transparent and competitive market, an 'invisible hand' helps to gradually lift them into a dignified, middle-class life and raises living standards all around. Liberty without dignity is self-despising; dignity without liberty makes for status without hope.

India's modern middle class rose in the nineteenth century under British rule, with the introduction of western education and the English language. Educated professionals were needed to man the jobs required to run a country on a nationwide scale—clerks, lawyers, teachers, engineers, doctors, bureaucrats and so on. However, it had its beginnings even earlier. Chris Bayly traces its origins to the eighteenth century after the waning of Mughal rule. He writes that 'between the revenue bearing state and the mass of the peasant society, there existed a range of intermediate entities from which were recruited the middle class'. These were a mobile class of merchants and a locally rooted service gentry that provided a host of services to the rulers of the various successor states to the Mughal Empire.

But even a hundred years after its first rise, the middle class in India remained small. In 1950, it was estimated to be less than 2 per cent of the population and by 1980 it had grown to only 8 per cent. It still consisted largely of those who had a job with the government. Then it began to expand rapidly as economic growth rose in the 1980s and accelerated after 1991. The middle class of today is qualitatively different from the old middle class that I wrote about in *India Unbound*. That consisted mainly of civil servants who lived in government housing and sent their children to government schools. Its heroes were Mahatma Gandhi and Jawaharlal Nehru. Today's new middle class is a creature of the economic reforms and is connected to rapid growth in the private sector. Its heroes are business captains. Its success is celebrated in Bollywood movies and on more than 400 television channels in different Indian languages.

The lesson from the modest success of Anna Hazare's movement is that the new middle class, having attained a degree of dignity, will no longer allow itself to be humiliated by officials and politicians as it had done for the past sixty years. As the social anthropologist Shiv Viswanathan says, 'The consumer revolution that we have experienced in the past two decades has told the citizen that he can expect a higher quality of governance.' Social media and technology are now strong instruments in the hands of the middle class as it mobilizes itself in its quest for accountability of the state. But so far, it has behaved apathetically towards electoral politics. However, if Shashi Kumar's response to Anna is representative, things are set to change.

SMILES AND KOESTLER

Samuel Smiles would have approved of Shashi Kumar and his age of great expectations. I had arrived almost an hour early by mistake at the Café Coffee Day near Scindia House. But I had two books to keep me company. One of them, Smiles's classic *Self-Help*, I intended to present to Shashi Kumar and his friends. No one reads Smiles any more but he was the Victorian age's bestselling author and 'superstar', whose sales were only beaten by the Bible. When he died in 1904, his funeral cortège was shorter than only Queen Victoria's. Emperor Meiji, who also lived in an age of expectations, promulgated that his book be issued across Tokyo's school system and eventually every prefecture in Japan followed suit. The emperor believed that the Japanese men of commerce could learn something about the plain virtues of honesty, punctuality, diligence and energy from Smiles.

Smiles gives better advice than most MBA courses. While extolling the virtues of entrepreneurship, he focuses on opportunities, risks, knowledge of the market and philanthropy. Above all he dwells on 'character' and the ethical dimension of doing business. Shashi Kumar, with his concern for 'dharma', would respond to it, I thought. Smiles had little time for politicians and their taste for expensive blunders. He would share my anguish over the ruling coalition in New Delhi which came to power in 2009 and drove India's fiscal deficit to the same disastrous levels as in 1991. Karl Marx was Smiles's contemporary but ironically he had endured while Smiles had not. For Marx all the answers lay with the state; for Smiles they were to be found in the character and quiet diligence of the daily work life of the people.

The young man at the cafe's counter came up to me and suggested another cup from the 'best coffee beans'. He proudly informed me that his cafe was one in a chain of 1096 Café Coffee Days in India. This was impressive in a nation of tea drinkers. It made sense, however. The young and the upwardly mobile middle class needed a public place 'to hang out', to see and to be seen. The women especially needed a place where they felt safe, and everyone needed clean toilets. I ordered a black coffee and while I waited I turned to my other book, Arthur Koestler's *The God That Failed*. No one reads Koestler any more either.

My friend Philip Oldenburg had directed me to it in order to cure me of some of my triumphalism about the middle class.

The middle-class commitment to a clean and just society as we are witnessing in the India of today would have to be balanced by the example of Weimar Germany, a stellar 'middle-class' polity in the 1920s and 1930s. When that class was pushed against the wall as their life savings were destroyed by inflation, it turned to fascism. This is how Arthur Koestler describes the economic and social conditions in the Weimar Republic just before its collapse: 'This disintegration of the middle strata of society started the fatal process of polarization ... The pauperized bourgeois became rebels of the Right or Left ... Those who refused to admit that they had become déclassé, who clung to the empty shell of gentility, joined the Nazis and found comfort in blaming their fate on Versailles and the Jews ... With one-third of its wage-earners unemployed, Germany lived in a state of latent civil war and if one wasn't prepared to be swept along as a passive victim by the approaching hurricane it became imperative to take sides.'

FROM THE BEST COFFEE BEANS

A sobering thought, indeed, as I sipped my coffee from the 'best coffee beans'. I looked around and saw tables filled with romantic college-going couples. This was where the upwardly mobile middle class met. India did not have the traditional culture of public squares and sidewalk cafes of the Mediterranean cities, and social life was confined mostly to private homes and the bazaar. When I was young it was to the bazaar you went to 'take the air' with a desperate hope of meeting the girl next door.

The first Café Coffee Day opened in Bangalore in the mid-1990s, soon after the reforms. Around the same time my friend Amit Judge had started a competitor cafe called Barista, now owned by the Italian coffee company Lavazza. Café Coffee Day overtook Barista in a few years and rapidly became the leader. It had the benefit of growing its own coffee. Part of a well-known South Indian group, Amalgamated Bean Coffee Trading Company, it grew arabica coffee beans over 10,000 acres. It was puny, however, compared to the formidable Starbucks, which had 19,000 outlets worldwide, and had announced a joint venture in India with the Tatas. Once it arrives, Café Coffee Day will have a real fight on its hands.

India had mentally come a long way. The strident criticism against American fast food had almost died. Hardly anyone worried about cultural imperialism or a standardized, homogenized consumer world. McDonald's and others were quietly expanding but not as rapidly as in other Asian countries. This could be due to the strong hold of Indian street food. On a recent visit to McDonald's in Panipat, two hours from Delhi, I felt that it was gradually moving away from its American roots and evolving into a local institution for the new Indian middle class. Rather than fast food for the masses, it was for the upwardly mobile. It had become a leisurely place to hang out in, for courting a girl, for hosting a birthday party. The menu had vegetarian McNuggets, Maharaja Macs, McTikkis and other Indian touches.

Fast food is not a new idea. Indians have dhabas and similar places for pao-bhaji and idli-dosa; Chinese commuters hurrying home have their deft noodle cutters; the British their fish and chips; the Turks döner kebabs; and the Japanese their station eki bento boxes. The American innovation is reliability—in the way the food is hygienically prepared and served in a clean place with a clean toilet. Indeed, local eateries everywhere complained that they had to invest in new bathrooms when American fast food franchises arrived on their street. In India, the queue is the other innovation much appreciated—civic virtue does not come naturally to human beings. Women, used to waiting on men, note the fact that customers and employees both stand when ordering (rather than the customer sitting and the employee waiting on him). Working women especially like American fast food outlets as a friendly, alcohol-less place to meet their friends.

ENGAGE WITH POLITICS?

My random musings on fast food soon came to an end as Shashi Kumar and his friends burst in. I heard them order lattes and cappuccinos, and marvelled at the ease with which habits changed when you became middle class. Until a few years ago some of these young men would have never seen coffee. They had grown up after 1991 without having to pay a bribe for a telephone or a gas connection. This explained their impatience with corruption in other areas.

But the mood in the group was decidedly down this week. The campaign against corruption wasn't going anywhere. I felt they had lost some of their confidence. There were divisions in Anna Hazare's team. 'The government is trying to divide and smear our movement,' said Shashi. Kiran Bedi, a former police official, had come under attack for misusing her travel expenses. Anna had distanced himself from Prashant Bhushan over the latter's comments on Kashmir. Some had accused Anna of harbouring sympathies for right-wing Hindu groups.

One member of the group announced that they had made a pledge not to pay bribes any more. Another added that all citizens were free to choose: whether to bribe or not. This belief, he felt, was the foundation of a dharma-based citizenship. If everyone thought like this, it would lead to a dharma revolution and political change would come on its own. Listening to them reminded me again that the appeal of Anna Hazare was fundamentally a moral one. Indians would have to recover a moral core in order to come to grips with their contemporary political crisis. They would have to decode and begin to practise the values of the Constitution so that they became enduring 'habits of the heart'. This had been Gandhi's project in the freedom movement. But no one since had attempted such a dharma project. Anna Hazare, alas, was probably not the right person to do it.

'What should we do?' asked Shashi Kumar.

'Yes, we want your advice,' said another, more despairingly.

There was a long pause and they looked at me expectantly. I did not like this moral burden.

'Well, you must engage with politics,' I replied hesitantly.

'But we have jobs and families to raise!' wailed Shashi.

'Don't give up your jobs. Start working part-time in your neighbourhood in Gurgaon. Work for the municipal councillor in your ward—someone like Nisha Singh in Ward 30. I don't know her but she has an impressive website. Start by making your own neighbourhood corruption free. That is where you might find your dharma.'

There was a long silence.

'So, will you at least vote the next time?' I asked.

More silence.

Slowly one of them nodded. Another said, 'Yes, I will vote.'

Their eyes told me that they would.

As we rose to leave, I felt that injustices would continue in the world but as long as Shashi Kumar and his friends were around, there would be people to correct them. They disproved the common view held by my intellectual friends that the middle class was only self-absorbed, consumerist and callous. I was content seeing in it a new-found bourgeois dignity.

A GLOBAL REVOLT

Another friend of mine, Moisés Naím, who lives on another continent, believes that India's middle-class upsurge is part of a global story. A seminal thinker from Latin America, Naím says that the middle class is the fastest growing segment in the world and it will be the main cause of coming conflicts. It will not be clashes with other civilizations such as Islam—the instability will come from anger generated by unfulfilled expectations of a middle class that is declining in rich countries and booming in the poor countries.

In the Far East, rising incomes had already brought a demand for greater democratic rights and accountability in the government. The new middle class had helped to topple authoritarian governments in South Korea and Taiwan. In India, China and other third world countries, the rise of the new middle class held politically dangerous possibilities. While it had increased its consumption of food, clothing and housing, it was now demanding better schools, cleaner water, better hospitals and more convenient transportation. Chile, says Naím, is one of the most economically successful and politically stable countries with a rapidly growing middle class, but it is filled with street protests insisting on better public education. Chileans do not want more schools, they want better schools. In India too, the middle class is discovering that it is far easier to build a school than to improve the quality of teaching. In China, there are thousands of demonstrations calling for more and better public services. No government can adequately meet these new demands.

Meanwhile, in the countries of Europe and North America the status of the middle class has fallen. In 2007, 43 per cent of Americans claimed that their salaries were just about enough to make ends meet; in 2011, this had risen to 61 per cent. The fall in living standards is behind movements like Occupy Wall Street, which was ineffectual, but the next one may be more serious. Inevitably, many in the West blame their decline on the rise of China, India or Brazil, but I agree with Naím that these accusations are mostly unfounded—data shows that lower wages or job losses in developed countries are mostly due to technological change or anaemic productivity.

THE IDEA OF MIDDLE-CLASS SUCCESS

Shashi Kumar's mother was impassive the next time we met. She had decided to return to Bihar. She had had enough of glittering and glamorous Gurgaon. Her son had to live here, naturally, but she wanted to spend her remaining days among her neighbours, relatives and friends in Darbhanga. Shashi was devastated. He felt he had failed somehow in his duty as a son. After his father died he was determined to keep her with him and to make the rest of her years happy. His wife had willingly agreed. Now he felt defeated. He wondered if his hospitality was wanting in some ways.

I was at the Kumars' home that morning because Shashi hoped that I might be able to get her to change her mind. But I quickly realized that it was like pushing water uphill. She had made up her mind. Gurgaon, it seems, had changed her conception of success. This had happened gradually over her stay of eighteen months. She had not spoken of it to her son or daughter-in-law, and so her decision came as a shock. She didn't say much that day but I could tell from the few sentences she spoke that she and her son had drifted apart, not emotionally but in their view of the world.

John Steinbeck's famous lines came to my mind and I recited them to console her son: 'The things we admire in men, kindness and generosity, openness, honesty, understanding and feeling, are the concomitants of failure in our system. And those traits we detest, sharpness, greed, acquisitiveness, meanness, egotism and self-interest, are the traits of success. And while men admire the quality of the first they love the produce of the second.'

These sentiments of Steinbeck also have something to do with India's present crisis in public morality. What is at stake, both then and now, is the middle-class conception of success. Of particular interest is the case of Andimuthu Raja, the former minister of telecommunications, who was in jail for more than a year, awaiting trial in the 2G scam. He caused discomfort among the middle class because he undermined this conception. He not only committed a huge fraud in the way he distributed telecom spectrum, but he got caught and was not contrite.

Shashi Kumar's mother said to me that she had watched Raja time and again on TV after the scandal broke. He grew up in a middle-class Dalit home in Perambalur, a small town in Tamil Nadu. He had risen from below and become a successful lawyer. Then he went on to become an even more successful politician.

'He had everything!' she said.

'Yes, he must have been the toast of the town and a huge success in the world's eyes—he had power, money and status,' I said.

'Why did he have to do it?' she asked sadly.

Steinbeck raises many thorny questions for the newly

awakened middle class: What price are we willing to pay for worldly success? Is it possible to be both successful and good? Why cannot high status be conferred on a person who is honest and kind?

There are no easy answers.

7

POLITICS OF ASPIRATION

Not failure, but low aim is the crime.

—James Russell Lowell,
Under the Willows and Other Poems, 1868

Nothing quite captured the growing gap between a rising economy and a falling polity more than a hapless Rahul Gandhi, prime-minister-in-waiting, campaigning in Uttar Pradesh in February 2012. Rahul Gandhi was speaking about how only the Congress party, and his family going back to Jawaharlal Nehru, understood the relentless poverty, oppression and unfairness of life in village India. The village migrant, who had received India's 89,36,95,668th cell phone connection during that month, was not impressed by Gandhi's downbeat message which was aimed at a starving, shirtless, landless labourer toiling relentlessly in the sun without any hope. The migrant did not see himself as that victim and this may be one of the reasons for the Congress's resounding defeat in the state election.

Democracy, with all its weaknesses, has a way of correcting its excesses. The 2012 elections in five Indian states showed that the politicians of the two leading national parties of India—the Indian National Congress and the Bharatiya Janata Party—were dangerously close to becoming obsolete, left behind by the voters, who in the case of Uttar Pradesh, India's largest state and one of the poorest, had experienced 7 per cent growth during the previous five years. Many regional party leaders—for example, Akhilesh Yadav of the Samajwadi Party in Uttar Pradesh and Sukhbir Badal of the Shiromani Akali Dal in Punjab—had spoken a different language in their campaigns. Akhilesh won a resounding victory against Rahul Gandhi by turning the traditional socialist message of the Samajwadi Party on its head—he had appealed to the young and aspiring by promising them free computers. He also defeated the powerful incumbent Mayawati of the Bahujan Samaj Party, who had stuck to the old appeal of victimhood to the low-born Dalits.

The results of the 2012 elections brought cheering news to a 'strong democracy' but jeering news to a 'weak' state. The regional parties had won in many states and their victory showed that power was continuing to devolve to the states which were growing stronger at the expense of the Centre. No one worried any more about it weakening the unity of India, as they would have in the early years of the republic. They worried if India was becoming less governable as a result of regionalism. It did not help that the country was being presided over by one of its weakest prime ministers, whose government had been paralysed for years, partly by its inability to control its coalition partners from the regions.

There was a risk that the parts might dominate over the whole, and the Centre might weaken further. Yogendra Yadav, the election analyst, argued otherwise. He believed that strong states were the 'foundations of India's unity' based on a 'thick' idea of nationhood in which regional cultures and parties ought to prevail. I agree with Yadav but I also worry that India might be reverting to a historical norm. As indicated in Chapter Two, India's history is one of warring regional kingdoms; empires, with a strong central authority, were the exception. Certainly history seemed to be on Yogendra Yadav's side. I have argued in support of federalism but there is a cost to it. One of these we have seen in recent years—the delay in the imposition of the GST because states have not yet given their assent. The tax holds the promise of consolidating the country into a 'common market', removing huge inefficiencies in the way of doing business, lowering transaction costs and consumer prices while dramatically raising revenues of the government.

There are two spaces in the politics of India and one of them is largely empty. They reflect the classic division between those who look ahead and aspire versus those who look back and complain. India's political parties still tend to cater to the second—to the victim in us—through their politics of grievance. A very few reflect the spirit of a rapidly growing India. No one thinks big, when it actually is criminal to think small in India. Until this space is filled, India's politics will not be whole.

The Congress appeals to the victim in its policies for the aam aadmi, 'ordinary person', with an ever-expanding menu of job guarantees, food security and subsidies for gas, diesel, kerosene, fertilizers and more. The BJP panders to the successors of the sufferers of historical Muslim misrule and the Congress's minority vote-bank politics. Mayawati and the caste parties focus on the historical injustice to Dalits and Other Backward Classes (OBCs). The Shiv Sena gratifies the injured pride of the 'Marathi manoos'. All this is about the politics of grievance and injustice. While grievance admittedly can be a powerful motivator to action, it is surprising that India's electoral politics do not cater to the aspiring middle class. This also explains the middle class's apathy to politics. Every party treats the voter as a victim.

With high economic growth, mobility and a demographic revolution of the young, the number of Indians who aspire is also growing rapidly and will overtake within a decade those who see themselves as victims. Pew surveys show that the majority of Indians believe that they are better off than their parents and that their children will do even better. China's politicians have done a far better job of tapping into the aspirational spirits of its young. While Indians debate if growth is pro-poor, China talks about growing rich. It understands that performance is a function of expectations. Those with higher expectations get higher performance. China has stopped thinking of itself as a third world country and is challenging America today. In India, only a few politicians—Nitish Kumar, Sheila Dikshit and Narendra Modi among them—appeal to aspirers. They speak the language of governance, good roads and schools.

The political dichotomy, which Rahul Gandhi reflected in the Uttar Pradesh election, was between an India that was 'shining' and one that was 'whining'. These are the mental constructs of the two coalition governments, the National Democratic Alliance (NDA) and the United Progressive Alliance (UPA), which have ruled India during the first decade of the twenty-first century. 'India Shining' was the slogan of the Vajpayee-led NDA government, which was defeated by the Congress-led UPA in 2004. Although economic growth accelerated to almost 9 per cent over the next five years—as a cumulative result of the reforms of the previous thirteen years—the Congress continued to believe that the common man was whining. So it stopped economic reform and expanded subsidies. While India enjoyed the best years of its economic history, the ruling political formation remained focused on poverty and victimhood.

History teaches that expectations drive progress. While policies and institutions help in forming expectations and contribute to progress, the real driver of development is the optimism and expectation of the people. In this sense, political theory is a bit like economic theory. Markets work on expectations, and self-fulfilling prophecies are all too common. The world is witnessing a dramatic example of this in Europe at the beginning of the twenty-first century's second decade. Europe's economy seems to be unravelling. It is not the result of political classes not doing the right thing, but of not inspiring confidence. Thus in 2011–12, capital was leaving the Greek banking system in droves, and the problem was spreading to Spanish and Italian banks. India too was witnessing a similar loss in confidence mainly because of its politics. India's economic outlook was clouded by a feedback loop of negative expectations which drove negative outcomes, including a frightening drop in the value of the currency.

The politics of aspiration in India came to an end in 1964 with the death of Jawaharlal Nehru. There was a short period of hope in the mid-1980s when Rajiv Gandhi was prime minister, but he was not able to mobilize people on the basis of his modern ambition. Even during the extraordinary years in the early 1990s when P.V. Narasimha Rao, supported ably by Manmohan Singh, revolutionized the economy, Congress politicians were not up to the task of selling economic freedom and liberalization to the people. They were not of the same mettle or stature as Deng, Thatcher or Reagan, and thus they implemented reforms 'by stealth'. Aspiration asserted itself in 2003–04 with the slogan 'India Shining' towards the end of Atal Bihari Vajpayee's NDA government's tenure. The NDA lost and the theme of 'India Shining' was discredited along with it (even though the aspiration had nothing to do with the defeat).

The age of the politics of aspiration in India began from 1909 with the publication of Mohandas Gandhi's *Hind*

Swaraj. The entry of Gandhi in the movement for India's freedom from colonial rule electrified the Indian National Congress, which had hitherto been a debating society. To feel that palpable sense of hope and expectation, one must read the writings of Gandhi, Nehru, Dadabhai Naoroji, Gopalkrishna Gokhale, Bal Gangadhar Tilak, B.R. Ambedkar, the early Aurobindo Ghosh, Surendranath Banerjee, Maulana Abul Kalam Azad, C. Rajagopalachari and others. Jawaharlal Nehru's *Letters to Chief Ministers* is the closest thing to the famous Federalist Papers written at the birth of the American republic. Politicians of today could learn much from India's 'golden age of aspiration'. But even teachers in contemporary India's colleges and schools have not mastered this body of national treasure and are unable to inspire their students.

The politics of the 'golden age' culminated in the writing of an inspiring Constitution which was democratically debated in the constituent assembly in the late 1940s. That assembly was inspired by the ideals of swaraj, 'self-rule', satyagraha, 'force of truth', ek-praja, 'one nation', sarvodaya, 'service to the downtrodden', and of course sadharana dharma, 'doing the right thing'. In contrast to the politics of aspiration of those days is today's reality of the politics of family dynasties, criminals in Parliament, the promise of free electricity and other freebies at the polls. As a start to address today's political malaise, there is a need for two great books in the language of the people. One would translate the ideals of the Constitution into the language of dharma in order to inculcate liberal 'habits of the heart'. Another would narrate the story of

India's golden age of the politics of aspiration from 1909 to 1964, in order to bring back some hope into politics.

'India Shining' was a nice expression and it is a pity that it got mixed up with politics. Before relegating it to the dustbin of history, it is good to remember that the slogan did succeed in one respect: it helped to raise the ambitions of millions of young people who have joined the middle class since the 1991 reforms. When I put this to a Congress politician, he gruffly dismissed the thought, declaring that 'India Shining' had died with the 2004 election. I gently reminded him that twenty years of high growth had lifted 200 million people out of poverty and raised another 300 million into the middle class. This was half a billion people surely worth fighting for. 'Ah, but there are still half a billion whiners!' he said, 'and their votes are more reliable than the shiners'!' Since poverty was not going to magically disappear soon, he felt that the Congress party would continue to have a reason to exist.

NOT ASPIRATIONS BUT GIVEAWAYS

Instead of the politics of aspiration, Indian politicians prefer to bribe voters. In Tamil Nadu, the Dravida Munnetra Kazhagam (DMK) was convinced that it had won the election of 2007 because it promised free television sets to the electorate. To promise is one thing, but the DMK went ahead and gave away millions of TV sets— paid not by party funds but by the state treasury. In the next election, there was a scramble by all political parties who offered a menu of gifts to choose from: electric fans, mixies, laptops and four grams of gold for a bride's mangalsutra. Some taxpayers in Tamil Nadu were outraged, but Kanimozhi, daughter of the DMK boss and a member of the Rajya Sabha, asked, 'What is wrong in giving people what they need?'

Populist giveaways have always been a great temptation. Roman politicians devised a plan in 140 BCE to win votes of the poor by offering cheap food and entertainment—they called it 'bread and circuses'. Punjab's politicians gave away free electricity and water to farmers, and destroyed the state's finances as well as the soil (as farmers over-pumped water); hence, Haryana supplanted Punjab as the nation's leader in per capita income. There are many other examples, the most common one being the distribution of liquor.

The idea of free TVs is morally troubling but is not illegal. When the Election Commission was asked to stop this practice, it pleaded helplessness, saying that freebies only contravene the law when they are distributed before an election. It claimed that if citizens could accept state spending on roads, why not TVs? But roads, parks, hospitals and schools are public goods in the way TV sets are not. Similarly, it is legitimate for the state to equip schools and public libraries with computers, but not to give free laptops to a section of the voters. By the same logic, the Supreme Court absolved Mayawati of erecting statues of herself with public money. It argued that the people of Uttar Pradesh had elected her and could remove her at the next election if they objected to her statues.

Nothing quite explains India's politics so much as the

fact that it embraced democracy before capitalism. As I have mentioned, the rest of the world did it the other way around. India became a full-fledged democracy in 1950 with universal suffrage and extensive human rights, but it was not until 1991 that it opened up to the accountability of market forces. This curious historic inversion means that generations of Indians learned about their rights before their duties. In the marketplace, one has to produce before one consumes; one must earn a salary before one can buy a TV. In the same way, elections enforce accountability in competitive politics. A voter is expected to vote on the basis of performance but in a populist democracy, the voter is too often tempted by free giveaways.

It is ironic that Tamil Nadu should be ahead of the pack in freebies because it is a state well known for high literacy with a reputation for being one of the best governed and most prosperous. It has had a succession of good administrations no matter which party was in power—food rations in the state actually reach shops that distribute subsidized food (under the public distribution system) and wages are actually paid to beneficiaries of the job guarantee programmes (under the National Rural Employment Guarantee Act, NREGA). However, it is officials rather than politicians who are responsible for this success. One day, the Tamil voter will also understand the trade-off. Free TVs mean less money for investing in the future—in roads, ports and schools. Without that investment, growth will slow down. Free TVs mean that children will have a poorer future. But in the world of democratic politics the future is far away.

AMORAL FAMILISM

The lack of aspiration is compounded by 'tyranny of the cousins' in a strong society. Indian politics is held hostage to the primordial problem of partiality to one's kin, and this weakens the state further. Nepotism comes naturally to human beings, although many Indians think it a peculiarly Indian disease. It is a universal flaw, deeply ingrained within our genes, going back to the evolution of our species. Human beings will act partially to their relatives in direct proportion to the genes they share. It is thus natural to favour relatives. The children of rulers at the end of the Han dynasty in China filled offices in the bureaucracy; offspring of the Ancien Régime in France sold offices of the state as heritable property. Today, children of Indian politicians routinely inherit the mantle in political parties. The Indian state has decayed partly because political parties have become family firms. This is happening ironically at a time when competitive demands of the market are weakening kinship bonds in business enterprises.

A democracy with a rule of law is based on the principle of impartiality and the idea that no one is above the law. This was the great achievement of the modern state: it created strong incentives to behave impersonally in institutions like the bureaucracy, the judiciary and the police. These institutions were introduced in India in the second half of the nineteenth century, as we have seen. They took root quickly and began to flourish under the bright Indian sun. Although they may have weakened in recent years, the principle of impartiality still applies at the time of selection and career advancement. What undermines impartiality is relatives inside political parties. Since there is no inner-party democracy in any of the parties, there is a huge temptation for the inheritors to behave like feudal chiefs. They find it easy to trespass the hard-fought impersonal principle in the institutions. Political power does not solve the problem of kinship. It merely relocates it up the chain of power, a phenomenon all too common in human history.

The mischief in India goes back to Indira Gandhi, although some trace the hereditary principle to her father, Jawaharlal Nehru, and his allowing his daughter to become president of the ruling Congress party for a year in 1959. There is no evidence that he was seeking to found a dynasty but that single, unwitting move embedded 'family politics' in the country. During her premiership in the 1970s, Indira Gandhi dismantled the structure of the old Congress party, concentrated power in her hands, trusted only her son Sanjay and forced state legislatures to select her nominees. Inner-party democracy disappeared in her party and the space vacated was filled by sycophants. The Congress president Dev Kant Baruah symbolized that transformation when he said, 'Indira is India, and India is Indira.'

The regional parties soon discovered the vast benefits of family enterprise and began to emulate the Congress's example from Kashmir to Tamil Nadu. Farooq Abdullah took over Jammu and Kashmir from his father, Sheikh Abdullah, and was succeeded by his son, Omar, as chief minister in 2009; in Bihar, the Rashtriya Janata Dal (RJD) became a fiefdom of Lalu Prasad's family; the Samajwadi Party became a Mulayam Singh enterprise in Uttar Pradesh, which is now led by his son, Akhilesh; Bal Thackeray's son and nephew fought to inherit the Shiv Sena firm in Maharashtra. Chandrababu Naidu inherited the Telugu Desam Party from his father-in-law. In Tamil Nadu, the DMK became a Karunanidhi family business, while M.G. Ramachandran's companion Jayalalithaa took over the rival All India Anna Dravida Munnetra Kazhagam (AIADMK). And in Karnataka, Deve Gowda's son H.D. Kumaraswamy took over the party's leadership from his father.

In 2009, almost a third of India's parliamentarians had a hereditary connection and it was a darker picture among the younger set. The writer Patrick French portrayed a troubling scene in *India: A Portrait*. Every MP under the age of thirty had inherited a seat; more than two-thirds of the sixty-six MPs under the age of forty were hereditary politicians; every Congress MP under the age of thirty-five was hereditary. 'If the trend continued,' French said, 'most members of the Indian Parliament would be there by heredity alone, and the nation would be back to where it had started before the freedom struggle, with rule by a hereditary monarch and assorted Indian princelings.' It was a devastating slap in the face of those idealists who had proudly created a republic in 1950. Only the three cadre-based parties—Communist Party of India (Marxist), Bhartiya Janata Party and Bahujan Samaj Party—were less affected by this trend.

The brazen way in which political firms use politics to aggrandize the family is infamously exemplified by the Karunanidhi family and the DMK. Ever since its alliance with the Congress party in Delhi, the family has regarded the telecom ministry as its family fief. It got the coalition government to appoint Andimuthu Raja, a party loyalist, telecom minister in 2007. Raja allegedly made a vast fortune on behalf of the Karunanidhi family firm in the corrupt way he distributed the 2G spectrum licences to favoured firms. The fragile administrative system was not strong enough to stop the minister's crooked ways, and the scandal finally blew up in 2010–11. The loss to the government was placed at Rs 1,70,000 crore by the Comptroller and Auditor General, making it the biggest corruption scandal in Indian history. *Time* magazine ranked it the second among the top ten abuses of power in 2011. As a result, the DMK lost power in Tamil Nadu in 2011 despite huge pre-poll spending, and the scandal paralysed the central government for much of 2011. Raja, Kanimozhi, senior civil servants and some CEOs of telecom companies spent a significant period of time in jail, awaiting trial.

Just when India's companies are breaking out of the shackles of the family, as I noted, politics is going the other way. Whereas the best Indian companies are building depth of management, delegating power and becoming professional, political parties are creating family dynasties and beginning to resemble old business houses. No political party is managed professionally, none has depth in organization and none has a clear command structure down to the grass roots. This weakness—the inability to separate the interests of the family from those of the party—explains, in part, why some of the best performing governments fall so easily. When family interests prevail, political parties become weak, governments do not perform and things don't get done. Political families are as big a threat to liberal democratic order as is the crony capitalism of certain business families.

Political dynasties have also existed in other successful democracies. So has money and influence. The United States, the world's oldest 'modern' democracy, had the distinguished Adams family, which produced two presidents and almost a third in the nineteenth century. In the mid-twentieth century it had the glamorous Kennedys and more recently two presidents from the Bush family. But a crucial difference with India is that the impartial institutions of governance in the United States and other western countries—the police, judiciary and bureaucracy— are stronger, more robust and better able to stand up to the power of a family dynasty. India's institutions are fragile; hence, India faces a greater risk of degenerating into a feudal, populist democracy instead of a strong, rules-based, constitutional one. Indians could learn a profound lesson from the significant decline of nepotism and hereditary privilege in parliamentary politics from the history of the British House of Commons.

Some will shrug their shoulders and say what is wrong if a politician's son enters politics? Doesn't a doctor's child want to be a doctor and a film star's daughter yearn for the cinema? Tom Paine, one of the founding fathers of the United States, wrote in *The Rights of Man* (1791): 'I smile when I contemplate the ridiculous depths to which literature and science would sink were they to become hereditary.' The idea of a hereditary ruler is even more ridiculous than a hereditary author or scientist because the interest of the public is at stake. Becoming a film star or an author is primarily a matter of private interest. A politician's son might turn out to be the 'best person' and go on to become a great leader, but the arithmetical odds of this happening are rare. The 'best person' is more likely to be found when you spread the net wide; nature distributes talent, it does not concentrate it. So, one cannot just shrug at the return of bloodlines in political life.

When family interests prevail, political parties become weak and governments do not perform. The result is that things do not get done: reforms slow down, roads and schools are not built. The mentality in a family-run polity is this: 'I don't do what is right, but what serves my family.' Loyalty matters more than performance. In trying to explain why southern Italy keeps failing and northern Italy keeps succeeding, Edward Banfield described, in his 1958 classic *The Moral Basis of a Backward Society*, the mentality of south Italy as 'amoral familism'—an expression that may also apply to family politics of twenty-first-century India. By this he meant a self-interested, family-centric society which sacrificed the public good for the sake of nepotism and the immediate family, its extreme version being the Mafia.

In the end, the truth is that the public seems to respond to dynastic arrangements at the ballot box. There is a redeeming feature, however, and Sukhbir Badal, heir to the Akali Dal leadership, expressed it well. After his party retained power in Punjab in February 2012, he was asked by a reporter about family dynasties. 'Yes, I have lineage and this is a huge plus,' he said, 'but the post is not hereditary. If I fail to deliver, I will be voted out the next time.' It was a significant point—lineage gives you a head start in a democracy but after that you are on your own. Hence, democracy will make it difficult for India's political family firms to become what Napoleon had in mind: 'hereditary asses, imbeciles, and this curse of the nation'. It is important to remember the distinction between 'legacy' and 'dynasty'. India may be feudal in many ways but it is also a vibrant democracy, and democracies have a way of correcting themselves. The party that is able to democratize itself, even with legacy leadership, will remain in touch with the grass roots and will be eventually rewarded in throwing up competent, local leaders.

NOT ASSES BUT CRIMINALS

Max Weber famously defined the state as the owner of a monopoly in violence, and the rule of law is meant to enforce and constrain that monopoly. A private citizen who engages in violence is jailed. But in a weak state like India with a weak rule of law, where the police and judiciary can be influenced, criminals get away. They use force with impunity to settle disputes against their enemies and suddenly they find they are superior to the state. To institutionalize this superiority they join politics—and lo and behold, a lawbreaker has become a lawmaker.

Napoleon may have fretted about hereditary asses but many Indians feel far more anxious about criminals in politics. A weak state and the lack of inner-party democracy in the political parties—especially the lack of transparency in selecting candidates—enables felons to enter politics. Thus, one in five members elected to the Indian Parliament in 2004 had a criminal charge against him. Of the 128 MPs charged, eighty-four were for murder, seventeen for robbery and twenty-eight for theft and extortion. Those charged included 40 per cent of Maharashtra's MPs and 35 per cent of Bihar's. One MP faced seventeen murder charges. This situation had worsened by the time of the election of the President in July 2012. On 13 July 2012, the *Times of India* reported that of the 4896 MLAs and MPs who constituted the electoral college for the presidential votes, 31 per cent had declared in sworn affidavits before the Election Commission that they had criminal cases pending against them. Of these tainted legislators 641 had serious cases—rape, murder, kidnapping, attempt to murder, extortion and robbery—against them.

You would think that political parties would not want to be tainted by criminals. So, why give them tickets? It is generally because they stand a great chance of winning because of their money and muscle power. Criminals join politics in order to shield themselves from the law. They gain enormous influence as legislators, ensuring that cases against them are slowed down or dropped. Delay, as we know, is also a function of a weak state, and it is easy to influence the pace of legal proceedings, especially if one is in power. Parties may nominate these candidates because of their ability to win at the polls, but why do voters elect them? Is it because they are 'outlaw heroes'?

Democracy, as I have said, tends to correct itself slowly. Outraged by criminals in Parliament, a group of professors at the IIMs formed the Association of Democratic Reforms (ADR), which filed a public interest litigation in the Delhi High Court in December 1999 demanding that the Election Commission provide voters with the criminal background of candidates. They won the case. The government appealed, however. The IIM professors finally won in the Supreme Court in May 2002. At this point, twenty-one political parties rose up against the Supreme Court's decision. The government hastily brought in an ordinance, which the Supreme Court again declared illegal. Election candidates are now required to file an affidavit giving details of convictions or pending criminal cases. As a next step, the ADR mobilized 1200 NGOs to form an organization, Election Watch, to publicize the criminality of candidates at election time. This organization has been vigorously publicizing criminal politicians in all elections since 2004. A bill on electoral expenses in 2003 tried to control political expenditure, and the Central Information Commission's verdict now requires that income tax returns of the political parties must be provided under the Right to Information Act.

When criminals give a bad name to the entire political class, why did politicians of all parties unite in preventing a reform that would bar felons? Politicians argue that such a law would lead to frame-ups by rivals. The law today bars only 'convicted' felons, not those who are merely 'charged'. Candidates are expected to disclose cases that have been admitted for trial and where charges have been framed by a judge. The other claim of politicians is that offences are mostly political in nature—related to protests and rallies. Which also begs the question: why should politicians flout the norms of law and order in the first place?

It is true that some candidates will take advantage of a law to file false cases against their rivals so as to bend the competition in their favour. But the greater evil is a lack of transparency. The real worry is that many crimes of politicians are never booked. For the whole political class to unite to prevent disclosure and transparency is an amazing act. One day, perhaps, the cost of harbouring criminals will become intolerable as pressure from civil society is continuing to grow. Meanwhile, one can celebrate the fact that a few determined individuals have been able to achieve a degree of transparency.

Social economists believe that the problem originates in perverse incentives, and suggest institutional change. A few years ago, Swaminathan Aiyar, the economist and commentator, proposed three institutional changes which have much merit. To encourage criminals to leave politics, Swami suggested a law mandating that all cases against elected MPs and MLAs be given top priority, and be heard on a day-by-day basis until completed. Instead of shielding them from the law, it would expedite their trial and conviction, thus making electoral victory 'a curse for criminals'. This could also deter corrupt civil servants from entering politics, if it were extended to them. Swami's second suggestion was to provide judicial incentives to speed up justice. However, research shows that such initiatives in most countries have failed. One institutional change that has worked is the promotion of judges who complete the most cases. Judges have responded to this incentive by eliminating time-wasting procedures, and these are quickly emulated by the whole system. The third suggestion was to shield the police from politicians by having a truly independent Police Commission in each state, similar to the Election Commission, that would investigate and prosecute politicians. All these ideas have been suggested before but they have been stalled by the political class. A strong Lokpal bill might be able to create deterrence, provided that it is able to fast-track judicial proceedings related to politicians. Criminal politicians will only be deterred by the real possibility that they will end up in jail.

NEVER OPPOSE WHAT YOU WOULD DO

The inability of parties to cooperate is a problem in all democracies but the lack of bipartisanship especially hurts in an already weak state like India. In June 2008, Lal Krishna Advani, leader of the BJP, lost the chance of a lifetime to grow in stature from a politician to a statesman. Less than four weeks remained before the historic Indo-US nuclear accord expired. The left allies of the UPA government had refused to go along with the treaty, and without enough votes in Parliament, either the treaty would die or the government would fall. But it could be saved by the leading opposition party, the BJP. Although the BJP had enthusiastically supported the idea when it was in power, it now opposed it mostly because it did not want the ruling Congress party to get the credit.

To many Indians it was inexplicable that the BJP was quibbling over something that was so obviously in India's national self-interest—in terms of both energy and security. If China had been in India's shoes and had been presented with the same opportunity, it would have run with it. But then China is not a democracy. The problem of when to compete and when to cooperate in Parliament afflicts most democracies, but it tends to weaken an already feeble state and leads to a paralysis in decision-taking.

By making a grand gesture of bipartisan statesmanship to save the accord, Advani would have completed a historic process begun by his party colleague Atal Bihari Vajpayee, prime minister of the previous BJP-led government, when he sanctioned the nuclear blast at Pokaran. Jaswant Singh, the BJP's foreign minister, had followed up with strategic dialogues with Strobe Talbott, the US deputy secretary of state, and passed on the baton to India's national security adviser Brajesh Mishra, who had continued the process in talks with Condoleezza Rice, the US secretary of state. The current prime minister had merely crowned this effort by signing an accord with President Bush, thereby striking a strategic partnership with America.

The nuclear treaty would not compromise India's right to another nuclear test, something that worried the BJP. Both China and France had shown that this was possible.

Moreover, India would soon be the world's third largest economy, and 'non-proliferationists' in the Democratic Party, who were critics of India's nuclear bomb, were relieved to see India balance China's power in Asia. It increasingly looked like China would be an overwhelming power in the twenty-first century, flex its muscles and dominate Asia. When that happened, some nations would become its satellites, including its closest ally, Pakistan. At that moment, India would need friends, and it would have a greater chance to hold its own if it had closer ties with western democracies. This nuclear accord was an important step in that direction—a turning point in India's security relations with the West.

It was also easy to imagine a day in the not-too-distant future when oil would run out. While nuclear energy has many drawbacks, those charged with the pursuit of national interest had to protect the nation's options. Signing the deal would not only free India from thirty-five years of nuclear apartheid, allowing it to import uranium, and lift the performance of its seventeen reactors from around 50 per cent to 95 per cent, it was also a measure of prudence, giving the nation flexibility to pursue different options in energy.

In the end, the BJP did not rescue the accord, and it became hostage to tragic politics. The UPA government scrambled to get another ally, forming a cynical alliance with the Samajwadi Party of Uttar Pradesh. But that was not enough and it led to the infamous 'cash-for-votes' scandal in order to get the remaining few votes. It became a low point in the history of the Indian Parliament, when cash was paid for votes to save the Congress-led UPA coalition government from falling over the vote on the nuclear deal. Bipartisan statesmanship on Advani's part could have spared that fate.

Happily, the deal did go through and the negative stand of the BJP and the left against the accord did not help them at the polls. The Congress-led UPA government was re-elected. Partisanship between the two national parties became more bitter over the next few years. Parliament practically ground to a halt during 2011, the infamous year of scandals. Important bills were kept pending as most of Parliament's time was lost in 'walkouts', protests, inter-party wrangling and other unproductive pursuits.

India has paid a huge price over the years in lost time and opportunity because of competitive politics and the inability of the two main political parties to cooperate, many times, over issues of national interest. Parliament took five years to open up the insurance sector, for example, when it should have taken five months. Prior to the opening up, insurance writing had been a monopoly of the Life Insurance Corporation (LIC), the state insurance company, and not surprisingly service had been dreadful. Opening it up to private providers led to the creation of six million new jobs, and with competition, service also improved. No one calculated the price that the nation had paid for retaining a monopoly—in terms of the suffering caused by poor service or in the jobs not created.

Both the main political parties had proposed to open up the insurance sector when they were in power, but had argued against it when in Opposition. When the legislation finally went through, the BJP agreed to limit foreign equity to 26 per cent even though it had earlier killed the same bill because it was against a lower foreign equity of 20 per cent. It has been the same tragic story with regard to the delay in the imposition of the goods and services tax, perhaps the most beneficial change in India's tax history, and all because of the unwillingness of the BJP-governed states to cooperate. This issue is connected with federalism, as I have mentioned, and a lack of trust between the states and the Centre, but a strong central BJP leader would have rallied the states on an issue of paramount importance to the nation. The BJP's support of other reforms, too, would have helped the nation's prosperity—for example, permitting foreign investment in retailing, a sensible move that would have led to the creation of a 'cold chain' and prevented 30 to 40 per cent of the nation's perishable foods from rotting in the fields or godowns. The killing of the railway budget in March 2012 by the quixotic coalition partner Mamata Banerjee is another example of the price extracted by competitive politics.

What is the right balance between competition and cooperation in a democracy? Arun Shourie, a respected writer and a minister in Vajpayee's government, offered a sensible rule: the Opposition should never oppose anything that it would have done had it been in office. To be in the Opposition and not to automatically oppose requires character. Many democratic countries have pursued bipartisan policies when national interest is at stake. In the UK, the Northern Ireland issue was always above politics, and prime ministers invariably kept Opposition leaders informed. The unwieldy US Congress used to have an unwritten rule: 'politics stops at the water's edge', and this bipartisanship did deliver the Marshall Plan to reconstruct Europe after the Second World War, the formation of homeland security after the 9/11 attack and the sub-prime mortgage bailout a few years ago.

Democracy is an inherently weak form of government; yet hardly anyone in India today would agree to substitute it for an autocratic government. Besides, a weak democratic state is suited to India's historical plural temper. But bipartisanship is not India's problem alone. More than two hundred years ago America's founding fathers were warned against this weakness. Periodically these fears have been realized, including a few years ago when Republicans in the US Congress brought Barack Obama, a Democratic president, to his knees on the subject of managing the national debt.

The Federalist Papers, a series of essays arguing for the ratification of the American Constitution, had raised this question in 1787. Federalist Papers Nine and Ten were determined to guard against factions or political parties when they acted in their own interest but 'contrary to the interest of the whole community'. The solution of the authors, Alexander Hamilton and James Madison respectively, was to have a strong central state with a strong executive. Madison worried that excessive partisanship would not only paralyse government but might even endanger individual liberty via a tyranny of the majority. He wrote: 'A pure democracy can admit no cure for the mischief of faction. A common passion or interest will be felt by a majority, and there is nothing to check the inducements to sacrifice the weaker party.'

Influenced by liberal thinkers of the eighteenth-century Enlightenment, particularly Montesquieu and David Hume, Madison despaired that it would not be easy to limit the damage caused by factions, rendering a majority unable to act. He felt, like John Stuart Mill, that suppressing factions or dissenting opinions would destroy liberty and 'liberty is to faction what air is to fire'. The other option—creating a society homogeneous in opinions and interests—was not practical (and is even less so in a diverse, plural society like India's). Besides, he felt that not to have diversity of opinion would wound the very nature of democracy.

Some of the Federalist Papers assume that a lack of cooperation between legislators comes from an excessive concern with self-interest and not enough with the common interest. Hence, they underline the importance of the ruling elite being imbued with a deep commitment to the common good. The ancient Greeks (particularly Aristotle) and Romans were, of course, wedded to this ideal, which is in some ways similar to the ideal of public dharma that some of India's Constitution makers debated in the constituent assembly. Many Indians today would agree with this prescription.

IF GOOD MEN DO NOTHING

It is not healthy for the world's largest democracy to have a poor opinion of its political class. It devalues public life. As it is, political engagement does not come naturally to

Indians because of a bias for other-worldly goals. They are mesmerized by the ideal of the sanyasi, 'renouncer', who stands tall in their imagination, a splendid figure in ochre robes. They may tear into their politicians daily but they feel squeamish at the thought of joining politics. My central critique of the Anna Hazare movement is that it has further devalued politicians and political life, which is the legitimate means to effect change in a democracy.

Curiously enough, western philosophical tradition also tended to devalue political life. Plato was the chief culprit, and in *The Republic*, he describes the world of human affairs in terms of shadows and darkness, and instructs us to turn away from it and pursue the sublime life of contemplation. Aristotle, however, tried to redeem politics. The basic fact of human life, he said, is that we are not alone and must learn to live sensibly with others in society. Attending to civic matters is essential to living a virtuous life. Aristotle's thinking, however, got submerged by the contemplative spirituality of the Christian Middle Ages, until the fourteenth century when Petrarch found merit in politics, and this marked a transition towards the active political life of the Renaissance.

In the twentieth century, Hannah Arendt, the political thinker, attempted the formidable task of rescuing the worldly life from the depredations of philosophy and religion. She confronted Marx, whose politics exalted 'labour' at the expense of an equal commitment to all members of society. She accused the communism of Lenin and Mao of causing untold harm to the idea of a civic life of mutual respect among equals.

In India, Mahatma Gandhi rescued the political life. He discovered to his surprise that India's classical tradition, too, supported active engagement with the world. He latched on to the notion of karma yoga from the ancient Bhagavad Gita to give meaning to the life of the ordinary householder, who has to make a living, look after his family and live as a citizen in society. Gandhi reminded him that it is not necessary to renounce the world to find moksha, 'liberation', from our fragmented, finite and suffering existence. One can find it by living in the world with the right attitude—that is to say, selflessly, with the attitude of a 'renouncer'. The Gita's ideal of a 'secular ascetic' is a fitting reply both to the rituals of the Brahmins and to the renouncer's escapism. Indians today may admire Gandhi and Nehru but good persons are unwilling to enter politics. It is easier to admire vanished heroes of earlier generations than to take the plunge. But the truth is that the practice of democracy requires the same heroic qualities of its citizens daily. Decent Indians need to look into their hearts and act before criminals completely swamp India's politics. 'All that is necessary for evil to triumph is for good men to do nothing,' said Edmund Burke.

But what if none of the political parties pass the test? Does one start a new party? India already has too many parties. The psephologist Dorab Sopariwala says that 177 parties contested the 2004 parliamentary election and ninety-four parties got a combined vote of less than 0.005 per cent; 139 parties did not win a single seat, and twelve parties got one seat each. This would inhibit even the most optimistic from starting a party. India needs a remedy to weed out small, sometimes frivolous, parties. Germany punishes parties that receive less than 5 per cent of the votes by denying them state funding. France has a run-off system that only elects those who receive a majority of votes. Both these measures help in reducing the number of parties. In India, among the 177 parties, it is difficult to think of one that stands single-mindedly for good governance, reform and performance. The Lok Satta Party of Jayaprakash Narayan of Hyderabad might be one, but it has not met with real electoral success so far. Although it stands strongly for the rule of law, I am not sure if it can rescue the nation from the kinship trap.

On a number of occasions Amartya Sen, the Nobel laureate, has suggested to me to help start a classical liberal secular party—a sort of modern-day Swatantra Party—which would be attractive to secular persons in the new middle class. The first time he made this suggestion was at a public function at the launch of my book *India Unbound*, at the Nehru Centre in London. As a leftist, he confessed, he couldn't vote for it but the country desperately needed it to expedite the reforms. I agree with Sen, now that the middle class is growing rapidly and none of the existing parties addresses its needs; the timing is also right as the nation's centre of gravity has shifted to the right. Such a party is needed to transform India into a strong, liberal state, and in Chapter Nine I make an impassioned appeal for it.

The Swatantra Party was such a party—but it failed. Founded in 1959 by the distinguished C. Rajagopalachari and N.G. Ranga, it sought to remind Indians they were in danger of losing their hard-won liberty as a result of Nehru's socialist policies which were leading to a 'licence-permit-quota raj'. The twenty-one principles of its manifesto broadly reflected a classical liberal orientation. By placing the state 'at the commanding heights', it believed that decisions that should legitimately be made by market forces were increasingly being made by bureaucrats.

The party quickly attracted eminent names from across the country: Minoo Masani, an articulate former socialist; respected business leaders Homi Modi and A.D. Shroff; former civil servants H.M. Patel, N. Dandekar and J. Prabhu Lobo; K.M. Munshi, a former Congress veteran; Dahyabhai Patel, the son of Sardar Patel, the former deputy prime minister; and a host of maharajas, as also the beautiful Maharani Gayatri Devi of Jaipur. It performed surprisingly well for a new party, capturing eighteen seats in the 1962 general elections, and became the main Opposition in four states. In 1967, it won forty-four seats and was the single largest Opposition party. But after 1971 it suffered a precipitous decline, particularly after Rajaji's death. The Swatantra Party was ahead of its time as it tried to push water uphill in a socialist age. History shows, however, that it is difficult for a liberal free-market party to succeed in a modern democracy without a conservative social agenda.

What will such a party stand for in the twenty-first century? It will be the party of aspiration for a young India with governance as top priority, advocating relentlessly to reform institutions in order to restore the rule of law and fight corruption. It will trust markets rather than bureaucrats for economic outcomes, bringing momentum to the economic reforms. It will do what no party has done—educate the voter and 'sell' institutional and economic reforms to the citizen. Since most of the reforms are well known it will focus more on the 'how' rather than the 'what', thereby underlining a bias for action and implementation in order to improve the delivery of services to the poor. It will place the human agenda high and work tirelessly to improve the quality and quantity of education and health care (although not necessarily through the public sector). Finally, it will insist on confining religion to the private space.

The idea of a new secular party of governance and reform may seem hopelessly idealistic to the voter, who has grown cynical over time, but isn't it common sense to want politics to satisfy our most basic needs and reflect our aspirations to create a better India?

It is also important to say what this party will not stand for. It will eschew dogma and the utopian politics of the extreme left and right. At both extremes, collectivism increases and freedom decreases. The idea of a perfect world in which all good things exist is not only unattainable but is also dangerous, and those who allow themselves to come under the spell of dogma, religious or secular, become victims of myopia and in the end less human. Spontaneity is the fundamental human quality, and it is not compatible with 'total solutions', as Isaiah Berlin has eloquently argued. Yet, one must do everything one can to reduce hunger and fight against injustice. Talking about equality is cheap in a poor country, and one must avoid it unless one is willing to enact great crimes or suffer great costs. Meanwhile, the best one can do is to work for open markets and rules-based government—that is the only civilized way to lift living standards, reduce environmental destruction and achieve shared prosperity.

8

CONFRONTING CORRUPTION

They say the gods themselves
Are moved by gifts, and gold does more with
men than words.

—Euripides, *Medea*, 431 BCE

'Clear the swamps if you want to tackle malaria,' I said to Arvind Kejriwal as he sat down on a sofa in my study. He looked baffled. I explained that the Lokpal was necessary medicine but you gave it after the sickness appeared. Forty-three-year-old Kejriwal was a leading light in Anna Hazare's movement against corruption and he was unprepared for a harangue on corruption. I added that prevention is better than cure, and to prevent corruption, you had to reform the institutions of governance, eradicate the 'licence raj' and stop the populist policies that created opportunities for corruption. So, good old-fashioned reforms of the 1991 variety would do far more than sending the hounds of the Lokpal after every official who yielded to temptation.

This is not what the soft-spoken Kejriwal wanted to hear on that spring afternoon in 2012. Charming and gentle, he had an endearing manner, but I also sensed illiberal tendencies. He was genuinely interested in what I had to say. He called me a 'management guru' and I sensed that he wanted to talk about managing their movement. When I blithely mentioned that such a guru stood for someone 'Good at Understanding, but Relatively Useless', he laughed. Since he had brought it up, I said that the key to getting things done was to do only a few things, but to do them well. I approved of his movement's single-minded pursuit of an anti-corruption agency, the Lokpal. But it needed to be framed in a broad strategy of reform and a reassurance that their movement stood for upholding, not subverting, the Constitution.

Kejriwal struck me as an unlikely mobilizer of the masses. Born into a Marwari family—the proverbial entrepreneurs of India—he went to IIT Kharagpur to become an engineer and then became an income tax official. But he changed course midway and turned his considerable skills to the cause of social entrepreneurship. He was one of the successful drivers of the Right to Information Act, which has helped bring a degree of transparency in the government, and for this he was rightly awarded the prestigious Ramon Magsaysay Award in 2006. What won me over to him was a report in the newspaper that he had been attacked with a slipper by a Congress supporter in Lucknow. The man had been arrested and sacked from his job, but Kejriwal had gone to great lengths to get his attacker released from jail and restored in his job.

I first heard about Arvind Kejriwal before he became a celebrity. We were on opposite sides. In 2006, I discovered the shocking reality of mismanagement of water in Delhi. But I was even more astonished how a first-class reform to provide water twenty-four hours a day in Delhi had been killed by a well-meaning but ideologically inclined NGO, Parivartan, founded by one Arvind Kejriwal. At the time, I chalked my distress to the downside of democracy. It is a sobering but interesting tale, but since it is not fully germane to my central argument, I have recounted it as a postscript at this chapter's end.

ROOTS OF CORRUPTION

Kejriwal and I spoke about many things that afternoon but we were both too polite to bring up the subject of Delhi's water. We spoke about the human DNA and how it was imprinted with a natural propensity to favour family, friends and fellow members of caste and community. This universal flaw reasserted itself in the absence of strong incentives in favour of impartiality. It triumphed particularly in a country like India where society had been historically strong and the state weak. Even though India was changing into a middle-class society, family bonds remained strong, and trumped the rational recruitment of talent. The individual was loyal first to the family, caste, religious or linguistic group and only then to the nation as a whole. Fragmented loyalties invited a special type of corruption called nepotism, an example of which we encountered in the previous chapter in India's political family firms.

I asked Kejriwal why the Hazare movement had been silent over one of the root causes of corruption. It originated, I felt, in too much discretionary authority with officials and politicians, which bred crony capitalism. The reforms in 1991 took away some of that discretion but many sectors of the economy were still unreformed. Thus, scams happened in the dark alleys of the unreformed sectors such as land transactions, mining and governmental purchases. So, one answer to corruption lay in turning over economic decisions to the impersonal forces in the market. If competition rather than officials decided what is produced, by whom and at what price, corruption would diminish.

Eventually Kejriwal had to leave. After I saw him out and before I settled down at my desk, I noticed John Kenneth Galbraith's *The Affluent Society* on the shelf. I recalled that Galbraith had been concerned with the same problem in the United States fifty years ago as we faced in India today—of public failure and private success. Galbraith had been an éminence grise when I was an undergraduate at Harvard. He was a wonderful writer but a poor teacher. He taught me Eco 1, the elementary class in economics, and on some days he was so bored that it appeared as though he might actually fall asleep on his notes. He almost succeeded in making me lose interest in economics, and perhaps to expiate for his sins he graciously invited me to lunch. By then he was US ambassador in Delhi and I was home from college.

GALBRAITH AND SHENOY

On a hot but fragrant day in June 1963, I found myself walking up the elegant steps of Roosevelt House in Chanakyapuri, Delhi's diplomatic enclave. It was a beautiful white building that had recently been designed by the fine architect Edward Durrell Stone. There were others at the lunch, including Professor B.R. Shenoy, the only major Indian economist at the time who trusted the market, and who had written a note of dissent to the Second Five Year Plan. The subject soon turned, as it always did in those days, to the charms of socialism versus capitalism. Galbraith was full of wit and elegance, and he recounted a meeting a few months earlier with Milton Friedman, the libertarian economist from Chicago, who would go on to win the Nobel Prize. Galbraith did not agree with Friedman's capitalist ideas, but he felt that 'they would do less harm in India than anywhere else'. I was surprised to find him advocating a strong dose of Friedman's free market for India. 'Yes, I think India has gone too far in its suspicion of the market and reliance on the state,' he said.

The most remarkable aspect of the conversation over lunch was a thoughtful discussion on corruption, which was as much in the news in the India of the 1960s. The home minister, Gulzarilal Nanda, had announced at a press conference the previous day that eradicating corruption was his 'main occupation'. Shenoy spoke about the relationship between corruption and state intervention, and wished that India had fewer economists committed to socialism and more to the market. He believed that the only hope for eradicating corruption was a complete U-turn from India's socialist policies. Professor Shenoy had offered a strong critique of central planning in 1931 in the *Quarterly Journal of Economics*, but it had been completely ignored. In post-Independence India, he had become marginalized by India's left-leaning economic establishment.

I met Shenoy again twelve years later. It was in the trading city of Ahmedabad in February 1975. He had just delivered an excellent lecture in which he had argued that state intervention was the root cause of corruption. Corrupt payments arose, he said, because 'a piece of paper which costs nothing acquires immense value when it has the signature of a government official on it'. Government policy at that time insisted on a dozen such papers with official signatures for licences, permits and quotas that were needed before a person could run his business. An official, behaving perfectly rationally, extracted a bribe for each piece of paper on which he placed his signature.

There was much nodding of heads in the audience. Many of those present were either victims of or in collusion with a system in which the government fought inequality by redistributing incomes through tax rates that rose fairly quickly to 97 per cent. It controlled inflation through price controls; it restricted imports via severe licensing, and controlled production of desirable goods through quotas and permits. The result was corruption, shortage of goods, tax evasion, black money and smuggling. Ahmedabad was famous for its enterprise and it had suffered probably more than any other city during the long and sad years of the 'licence raj'.

During 'question hour' following the talk, an elderly man rose. He said he was a follower of Mohandas Gandhi, and he quoted his mentor as follows: 'One should earn bread by the sweat of one's brow—not by the bounty of the state.' He wondered what Gandhi might have made of this peculiar system in which one needed so many licences and permits that it ended in corroding the soul.

LICENCE RAJ

Corruption had become visible early in the life of the new republic. Rajaji, as we have already noted, was the first to describe Nehru's socialist economy as a 'licence-permit-quota raj' in the late 1950s. When a reporter suggested that corruption had increased because Indians, not the British, were ruling, Rajaji had quickly retorted that corruption was less a matter of culture and more about economic incentives. Socialist controls sent out the wrong signals to human beings about how to behave. Yes, culture mattered but culture would quickly change if the incentives changed. By the early 1960s corruption had grown to such a level that the government set up the Santhanam Committee for the prevention of corruption. In its report in 1966, the committee offered fascinating insights into what the 'licence raj' was doing to the behaviour of the civil servant:

> When suspicion of corruption is rampant, a natural protective device is to spread to share the responsibility for decisions to the maximum extent possible . . . To avoid direct responsibility for any major policy decision, efforts are made to get as many departments and officials associated with such decisions as is considered desirable. Again, such consultations must be in writing; otherwise there would be nothing on record. Therefore a file must move—which itself requires some time—from one table to another and from one Ministry to another for comments and it is months before the decision is conveyed to the party concerned . . . Thus, administrative delays are one of the major causes of corruption . . . We have no doubt that quite often delay is deliberately contrived so as to obtain some kind of illicit gratification . . . Generally the bribe giver does not wish, in these cases, to get anything done unlawfully, but wants to speed up the process of the movement of files and communications relating to decisions . . . Certain sections of the staff concerned are reported to have got into the habit of not doing anything . . . Even after an order had been passed, the fact of the passing of such order is communicated to the person concerned and the order itself is kept back till the unfortunate applicant has paid appropriate gratification to the subordinate concerned.

The idea of a Lokpal, an ombudsman, to investigate corruption in high places was an outcome of the Santhanam

Committee. It urged simpler and more precise rules and procedures for political and administrative decisions that affected business enterprises. Its main thrust was to reduce the discretionary powers of officials. It conceded that it was important to safeguard the independent judgement of civil servants, but this should not be a blanket shield to protect the venal and the corrupt. In effect, it indicted 'licence raj', suggesting that more licences meant more corruption.

Over the years the government set up more and more committees for administrative reform but it never acted on their sensible recommendations. To prevent day-to-day corruption, they suggested, India's bureaucracy had to have a transparent decision-making process; discretionary powers ought to be reduced; opportunities to manipulate public rules for private gain should shrink; and there must be a system to penalize delays—the favoured tactic of a corrupt bureaucrat. The civil service needed to be transformed from a system based on seniority to one that rewarded good performance and punished poor outcomes (as we discussed in Chapter Four). Side by side, of course, judicial delay had to be tackled, since there was no point catching crooks in high places if you could not quickly try and sentence them.

The licence raj began to ebb finally after the great liberalization initiative of 1991 when tortuous, bribe-laden procedures for running a business were abolished or pruned. This included freedom from industrial licensing and import restrictions; permissions for technology, capital issues, foreign investment and much else. Some said that these reforms helped only businessmen. In fact, they helped everyone. People no longer had to queue up for years for a telephone, a scooter, or for cement and steel for building a house. They were no longer at the mercy of a government monopoly company for an airline ticket, bus service, telephone, insurance, a television set and more. Reforms ended the perennial scarcity of the days of the 'licence raj'. Lower import duties ended the smuggling of gold, synthetics and consumer electronics. And lower tax rates reduced black money.

After twenty years of economic reforms, you'd have thought that corruption might have disappeared. But it was alive and well in 2012. The problem lay in the incompleteness of reform, as I have pointed out. Entrepreneurs still lacked the freedom to operate in the unreformed areas. This is why many economists relate corruption to the 'freedom to do business', another expression for a liberalized economy where individuals are not at the mercy of politicians and bureaucrats. This freedom is measured annually by the Heritage Foundation, while the 'corruption index' is measured by Transparency International. In 2010, seven of the world's ten 'least corrupt' countries were also ranked among the top ten in 'business freedom'. Among them were New Zealand, Singapore, Denmark, Canada, Sweden, Finland and Iceland. The ten most corrupt countries on the average had a business freedom rank of 154. India's was 167. The Scandinavian countries, from which India had borrowed the concept of the Lokpal, had on the average a 'business freedom' rank of eight.

The worst affected by the lack of freedom and the 'licence raj' was the small entrepreneur who did not have political influence. As we saw in Chapter Four, he faces on an average seventeen inspectors who have the power to close his factory down unless he pays a bribe. The most notorious are those in the excise, sales and income tax departments. Even the poorest person in the informal economy, the ragpicker, suffers from the same lack of business freedom which makes him vulnerable to the depredations of the police and inspectors.

A CODA FOR KODA

There was only one thing wrong at a smart luncheon party I attended in South Delhi in October 2009. It was Madhu Koda, and our celebrity hostess pretended he was not there. Someone whispered to her, 'You do have a talent for picking your guests, my dear!' This did not go down well. The former chief minister of Jharkhand was causing her discomfort because he had undermined her friends' conception of success. Koda had made a triumphant entry into some circles of Delhi's society a few years earlier. He had power, money and status. Then he fell.

Madhu Koda's was a rags-to-riches story. His father, Rasika Koda, had been a small farmer in a tribal area of Singhbhum district in Jharkhand, who wanted his son to live the 'normal life' of a farmer. But Koda got a job as a labourer in a state-owned iron ore mine in Chaibasa. There he saw at first hand corruption in the iron industry, and decided to embark on a career in politics. He fought an election and became an MLA in 2000. Five years later he was minister in charge of the lucrative mines portfolio. In 2006, he won the ultimate prize—he became Jharkhand's chief minister.

Along the way, he amassed almost Rs 4000 crore by giving away mining licences in exchange for bribes, according to the charge sheet of the investigating agency. He turned non-entities into mining barons, gifting 11,100 acres of land to dubious companies. A close associate told a reporter, 'He shared his wealth with his friends and made everyone happy.' He was arrested in November 2009, two days after the luncheon party where we had met.

Mining stands for all that is wrong with unreformed India—the nexus among politicians, officials, police and big business, a powerful labour mafia, disenfranchisement of local residents, damage to the environment and massive corruption. Two chief ministers were brought down in mining scandals in recent years—Madhu Koda in 2009 and then B.S. Yeddyurappa, chief minister of Karnataka, in 2011. Like defence contracts, mining is prone to corruption. Extracting resources from the ground does not lend itself to the usual rules of market competition. A mine is a natural monopoly and the state, which gives the right to mining, is also a monopoly. When the two come together in the backroom, you get crony capitalism.

The mess in mining had its roots in half a century of terrible governance, going back to the 1957 Mines and Minerals Development and Regulation (MMDR) Act. This law was typical of laws enacted during the 'licence raj'. For an honest businessman it was a nightmare. With overlapping authority between the central and state governments, an honest mine operator was bounced around from office to office for years. It was a perfect recipe for corrupt politicians, officials and businessman to get together and manipulate the system, resulting in huge losses to the government, excessive exports of unprocessed ores and unauthorized production and smuggling. Royalties were levied, not based on the price of the commodity but on arbitrary, administered rates. With vigorous lobbying, these rates were kept artificially low, and ended in depriving the government treasury of thousands of crores in revenue over the years.

In the first decade of the twenty-first century, there was a surge in the prices of commodities. High prices and easy profits attracted more unscrupulous operators who were even more adept at colluding with corrupt politicians and officials. Since legitimate ways to operate were too cumbersome and involved years of wrangling, the few honest operators were forced to exit. There was a sharp rise in unreported production and smuggling. The Lokayukta of Karnataka brought to light a scam by politicians, bureaucrats and businessmen worth Rs 12,000 crore, and the Supreme Court stepped in and banned the movement of iron ore in Bellary district of Karnataka.

Oddly enough, the ban penalized most companies which had done nothing wrong. Over 40 per cent of India's iron ore deposits were in Bellary. Twenty thousand people were employed by its ore mining industry. The ore fed the steel industry, which in turn supplied the automobile and many other industries. As a result, lakhs of jobs were affected by the Supreme Court's blanket ban. The government lost Rs 10,000 crore in revenues and commercial banks suffered an asset deterioration of Rs 50,000 crore.

Clearly, a ban on mining was not the answer. The environmentalists who had provoked the ban did not care that a developing nation needed steel, aluminium and power, all of which depended on raw materials from the mines. Environmentally conscious countries like the United States and Australia operated their mines responsibly, without scandals. Since a mine was a natural monopoly, the answer lay in simulating competition. This meant having open, transparent bidding or an auction under a firm regulator. The regulator would evaluate the quantity and quality of coal in a mine, set a minimum price (to keep out frivolous bidders and cartels) and offer the mine to the highest bidder. This would replace the present corrupt system of leases and licences, monitoring production at each mine, and checking each truck to ensure the operator did not clear 100 trucks and record only thirty.

The word 'coda' means the concluding passage in a composition of western classical music. The coda in Madhu Koda's story would hopefully see a speedy trial and a deterrent sentence for the guilty. But a truly satisfactory coda would be the reform of the mining sector along the lines of the Hoda Committee report. The government did make several attempts in this direction but the vested interests turned out to be very strong. The latest, in 2010, was an amendment to the 1957 MMDR Act, which provided for auctioning of new coal blocks. But there was more to be done, and a new 2011 MMDR Act was pending. The laws for land acquisition and environmental compliance needed to be revamped. It was also important to break the monopoly of Coal India and denationalize coal mines which had been nationalized by Indira Gandhi in 1973. India was the third largest producer of coal in the world but the coal industry had suffered gravely from the lack of competition. 'Power plant shut down because of lack of coal' was a headline as frequently found in 2012 as in 1973. Madhu Koda was a creation of this system and efforts to undo it—like the Coal Mines (Nationalisation) Amendment Act, 2000—remained stuck because politicians in the mining states did not want it.

DON'T BE SILENT, MR PRIME MINISTER

If liberalization is the answer to corruption, why did the biggest corruption scandal occur in telecommunications? After all, telecom was the biggest success story of the reforms. As a result of market competition, India had the lowest tariffs and the second largest number of mobile phones in the world. How did one explain the 2G scam? The one thing that the market did not control in telecom was the radio spectrum. The state controlled it and no one reckoned with a devious minister who created artificial scarcity in the 2G spectrum and then gave it away in driblets to those who allegedly bribed him. The scam could have been avoided had the licences been awarded via open, transparent bidding on the Internet.

By January 2011 there was plenty of rage over 2G across the land, and at its heart was the problem of silence. The public was furious with the prime minister. His telecom minister, Andimuthu Raja, had announced a policy to distribute radio spectrum to companies in September 2007. Manmohan Singh, sensing that wrongdoing was afoot, wrote to Raja, objecting to the minister's policy and exhorting him to be transparent. Raja replied immediately, defending himself. On 3 January 2008, the prime minister acknowledged this letter—yes, 'acknowledged', as though he had acquiesced. This gave Raja the permission to go ahead and issue the controversial licences. In May 2010, the prime minister admitted that Raja had indeed written to him.

People wanted to know why their prime minister had fallen silent after having objected initially to the policy. In those dark months, people had desperately wanted to clutch on to an honest man. They thought they had found one in selfless, ethical Manmohan Singh. Everyone conceded that the prime minister was personally honest, but they insistently asked about the value of a leader who was himself upright but whose government was corrupt. It confirmed that the most important quality in a leader was determination—more important than even intelligence and personal integrity, both of which their prime minister possessed in abundance. They concluded sadly that Manmohan Singh the leader was a failure.

The prime minister's silence raised questions over his integrity in some people's minds, just as it had in the case of the venerable Bhishma, the respected and selfless grandfather in the *Mahabharata*. Bhishma too had remained silent when Draupadi was being disrobed by his grandchildren. When Draupadi had insistently looked at him in the assembly and questioned the 'dharma of the ruler', no one had replied. Everyone, including Bhishma, had remained silent. Then Vidura had scornfully spat out at the immorality of silence. Quoting Rishi Kashyapa, he had said that when a crime occurs, half the punishment goes to the guilty, a quarter to his ally and another quarter falls to those who remain silent.

Loyalists in the Congress party wondered why these corruption scandals had surfaced all together in 2010–11. A respected commentator suggested that it may have been 'cosmic punishment' for not pursuing the dharma of reform. The middle class had hoped in 2004, when the Congress-led coalition came to power and installed a 'dream team of reformers' at the helm, that the momentum of the reforms would continue. Not only had the reforms slowed down but they in fact stopped after 2009. None of the political leaders in the coalition government had tried to build public support for the basic principles of reform—competition and free enterprise. The Congress party was itself deeply divided. Manmohan Singh, the leader of the government, favoured reforms; Sonia Gandhi, the leader of the party, did not. She won—and so did corruption.

When corruption scandals broke, people blamed them on liberalization. In an opinion poll reported by *India Today*, 83.4 per cent of the people in eight major cities believed that corruption had gone up after liberalization.

People still did not understand that corruption persisted because the economic reforms were incomplete. Each time something went wrong people wanted the heads of those in power. No one thought of reducing their discretion. Because they had not understood the root cause of corruption, their instinctive reaction was to have more laws, give even more authority to officials, and reduce their own freedom.

PREMATURE WELFARISM WORSENS CORRUPTION

The day after the government announced its flagship National Rural Employment Guarantee scheme in 2005, I received an e-mail from a Chinese friend in Beijing. He said that the Chinese leadership would never contemplate such a 'make work' scheme. 'It would bankrupt us,' he said. The Indian government's new law *guaranteed* a hundred days of employment each year to the rural poor to be funded by the state.

My friend is a respected businessman and a senior official in the Communist Party. He is also a Buddhist and has watched India's rise over the years with a degree of sympathy. 'We create jobs in China by building roads,' he wrote. 'A road creates opportunities for productive, permanent jobs as villagers learn to travel and trade between their village and the town. We have learned bitterly from the days of Mao that job-creating schemes create bogus jobs because no one is accountable for the result. We built many roads in Mao's days under "make work" programmes, but all those roads got washed away after the first rainfall.' I wrote back saying that I endorsed the idea of an affordable safety net for the poorest but I opposed this NREGA scheme because there were too many moral hazards entailed in its execution, especially by the Indian state which had a poor record of implementing such programmes.

Prime Minister Manmohan Singh would have agreed with my Chinese friend that the road to prosperity lay in building infrastructure, giving people the opportunity to learn skills and encouraging investment. As a Cambridge-trained economist, Dr Singh knew that 1 per cent of GDP borrowed from the banks to finance this programme would crowd out private investment, push up interest rates, lower the economy's growth rate—and, saddest of all, eat into real jobs. Since this new law required paying minimum wage, 'make work jobs' would divert people from productive to unproductive jobs. But he was helpless because he owed his position to Congress president Sonia Gandhi, who knew there were votes behind welfare programmes.

The lower bureaucracy and local politicians, meanwhile, smelled an opportunity. For decades they had perfected the art of creating fake muster rolls and thus siphoned away funds from such programmes. No one spoke out in Parliament for fear of being called 'anti-poor'. MPs only proposed amendments that would make graft easier. Sonia Gandhi's husband, Rajiv Gandhi, had famously claimed that only 15 per cent of the funds reached the beneficiaries of such programmes. Over the years I had read studies in the *Economic and Political Weekly* that showed that the

poor never received more than 30 per cent. Even Jean
Dreze, the spirit behind NREGA, confessed that the muster
rolls were either absent or fudged in five out of six states
that he had studied. 'Loot for work' was his headline
above a thoughtful article in the *Times of India*. Manisha
Varma, Solapur's collector, had just uncovered a 'jobs
fraud' in her district worth Rs 9.1 crore. All this should
have placed a man of conscience like Manmohan Singh
in a dilemma. How could he personally steer a law
in Parliament when he knew that more than half of the
Rs 40,000 crore of the hard-earned savings of the Indian
people may not reach the beneficiaries? The states knew it
too and were unwilling to contribute even 10 per cent of
its cost.

As competitive markets began to replace the institutions
of the 'licence raj' after 1991, the reformers in succeeding
governments tried to also curb populist giveaways. But
they failed. Bad habits are hard to change, and two decades
later electricity was still being given virtually free to farmers
in many states and such 'agricultural connections' had
exploded to include non-farmers. The number of families
with cards that showed they were 'below the poverty line'
(BPL) and entitled to government-subsidized food and
other benefits had ballooned. In relatively prosperous
Karnataka, 83 per cent of all families had these cards
when data showed that the poor were less than 25 per
cent. According to official estimates, approximately half
the foodgrains from the government system 'leaked out'
through corruption. This meant that around Rs 20,000
crore was ripped off annually. The government's response

to this was to propose an even greater swindle called the 'food security programme'.

The same dismal story repeated itself in the subsidy on energy. Because diesel was artificially priced—around 40 per cent lower than petrol, depending on the city—car manufacturers in India did a thriving business in diesel cars, and the state subsidy ended in the pockets of the middle class. It had been intended for the poor on the assumption that the poor rode in diesel-powered buses and consumed food carried by diesel-powered trucks. The shift to diesel had been going on for years despite the environmentalists' lament about diesel being more polluting. Kerosene was priced even lower, almost a fourth of the cost of petrol, and it was freely used to adulterate both petrol and diesel. Estimates of adulteration varied from a third to a half and had led one nationalized oil company, Bharat Petroleum, to create an advertising campaign, claiming that its petrol was 'pure, for sure'. From time to time this scandal situation hit the headlines, confirming a nexus among truckers, oil company employees, policemen and local politicians. It was a similar tale in cooking gas (LPG), which was widely diverted to the non-poor because of a dual price.

Subsidies had climbed to around 15 per cent of a much larger GDP in 2011. Some called it 'premature welfarism' because a nation with a per capita income of $1500 per annum could not afford to protect its people from life's risks as a nation with a per capita income of $15,000 could. It came at the cost of investment in infrastructure, governance and longer-term prosperity. One observer worried that India might meet the same fate as Brazil in the late 1970s, where excessive government spending set off hyperinflation, crowded out private investment and kept the country in a 'middle-income trap' for decades.

As a result of the 'make work' programme, agricultural wages had gone up by more than 20 per cent annually in the past few years and farmers were being forced to look for labour-saving options—which paradoxically added to the unemployment problem. Pressure was building to employ government-funded labour on private farms and one could only imagine the moral hazard. The Reserve Bank warned that wages, which were indexed against inflation in the employment scheme, had already pushed rural wage inflation by 15 per cent in 2011. As a result, India might not gain manufacturing jobs when China moved up the income ladder. But neither the 'do-gooders' nor the Congress party was deterred by the massive corruption in the supply of diesel, kerosene, electricity and cooking gas, as well as in 'make work' schemes and food distribution. Politicians felt there were still plenty of votes there.

A PRIMER FOR THE CORRUPTION FIGHTER

Many liberal democracies have faced the problem of graft. None has eliminated it but the successful ones have brought it down to a manageable level. The lesson is to raise either the capacity of the state or to limit its ambition. Since capacity building in a poor, soft democracy will be slow, it is wiser to limit ambition at this stage and focus on the core functions of governance. Quick and strong punishment to the corrupt has been a proven deterrent in all societies and eliminating judicial delay will do more than any single step. So will administrative, police and electoral reforms identified by innumerable commissions. Economic reforms are important as they reduce bureaucratic discretion and crony capitalism. Cash transfers to the poor are a better way to deliver benefits as they do not distort market signals, nor put pressure on capacity. Smart cards reduce corruption, as we have seen in the government's health scheme (Rashtriya Swasthya Bima Yojna—RSBY), and their use for delivering other services such as food rations and NREGA payments will definitely reduce corruption. So will the use of the Internet in delivering birth certificates and passports and other services by reducing the interface between the citizen and the official. Many of these ideas have been mentioned before so I have only summarized them here.

Anna Hazare and Arvind Kejriwal's answer to corruption is the Lokpal—an anti-corruption agency to catch crooks in high places. It is a clear, specific objective, and this is its virtue. A strong Lokpal is needed and its success will bring huge credibility to Hazare's movement. To be effective, the Lokpal should be lean, and focus only on the big fish, leaving the smaller ones to other institutions like the Vigilance Commission. It ought to have the power to initiate a case without government permission, and its decisions ought to be binding. The chief vigilance commissioner has failed because his organization has lacked these empowerments. Much depends on who becomes the

Lokpal. The Election Commission was mediocre until the determined T.N. Seshan came along, and he was followed by the outstanding J.M. Lyngdoh. The Lokpal's selection must be insulated from the politics of democracy. More than probity, he needs to be tough, determined and courageous.

There are two types of corruption—harassment-induced and collusive. In collusive corruption the bribe-taker and bribe-giver conspire—as in the 2G spectrum scam. Both must be severely punished. In harassment-induced corruption, an official denies a citizen his rightful due—a licence, a ration card, a building certificate—unless the latter gives a bribe. It is the most common form of corruption and the bribe-giver is the victim. In this unequal relationship, the citizen is more vulnerable as the official can actually close down his enterprise. Hence, Kaushik Basu, the former chief economic adviser to the government, suggested giving immunity to the bribe-giver from prosecution in order to encourage him to complain.

The Lokpal has a greater chance of success if the delivery of justice is speeded up simultaneously. The rich and influential, as we have observed, are able to drag criminal and civil cases for decades. A much quoted study in the *Economic and Political Weekly* tracked almost 3000 cases against corrupt officials over sixteen years in Karnataka. It concluded that the real problem was not the neutrality of the investigation agency (as Anna Hazare's team believed) but judicial delay. The answers have been highlighted by numerous commissions, but this is not the place to get into details of judicial reform. Quick and honest enforcement of contracts will also make India a better place to do business in. It is sobering to remember that India ranked 132 out of 183 countries in the World Bank/IFC Annual Doing Business report of 2011.

Corruption will shrink, as the Santhanam Committee suggested, if decision-making in the bureaucracy is transparent, discretion is reduced, rent-seeking opportunities are cut, officers punished for deliberate delay and punishment guaranteed to the guilty. This could be achieved if incentives changed from a seniority system—where everyone is promoted based on years of service—to rewarding good performance and punishing poor outcomes. This in turn needs a better assessment system for officers. Eight out of ten officers cannot be rated 'very good' or 'outstanding' in any service.

Similarly, the police force needs to be reformed along the lines recommended by police commissions. Officers need to be insulated from political pressure and have to be stopped from doing the dirty work of their political masters. Too many die in police custody, and forensic skills need to be upgraded instead of relying on third-degree methods. Finally, electoral reform is critical. The previous chapter highlighted the importance of fast-tracking the trial of elected legislators who face criminal charges, as this would deter criminals from entering politics. A modest electoral funding law that reimburses candidates for each vote received will be an incentive for honest persons to enter politics while discomfiting the frivolous.

Land is the biggest source of collusive corruption and the answer is to implement the second generation of economic reforms. It is not necessary to reinvent the wheel—we merely need to follow the best practices in the world related to land use, building certificates, equalizing circle and market rates, etc. Similarly, when awarding contracts for natural monopolies—mining, oil and gas, telecom spectrum—the solution, as already noted, lies in transparent, electronic auctions. A similar approach could be taken with government procurement. The more things are out in the open, the less are the chances of bribery. The Right to Information Act, as we have seen, is making the system more transparent already.

A government that cannot identify the poor wastes a lot in terms of universal subsidies that end up in the wrong pockets. A poor person with a secure online identity does not have to wait in an endless line in the sun, nor does he have to bribe an official who has monopoly on the paperwork. The harassment especially of young widows who try to get their pensions is a daily feature of life that few women complain about. A pilot project in Jharkhand has shown good results by linking the secure identity of a poor person, thanks to the outstanding UID Aadhaar project, with a bank account through the mobile phone with funds payable at any registered village store. It is far better than the government hoarding millions of tons of grain, part of which is annually eaten by rats.

Finally, fighting corruption means continuously building incentives to depersonalize relationships inside the state and creating loyalty to the larger national community. Strict enforcement of the law—the old lesson of danda-niti—helps. But eventually, the rule of law needs a change in 'habits of the heart'. Kejriwal is right when he focuses on the gram sabha in the village and the mohalla sabha in the city. When people govern themselves they begin to internalize the virtues needed to become good citizens.

POSTSCRIPT: KILLING OF 24x7 WATER

My promised account of Delhi's water debacle begins with an odd statistic. Surprisingly, Delhi has more water available than many famous cities in the world. In 2007 it had 300 litres of treated water available per person per day, compared to Paris with 150 or London with 171. Then why, I asked myself, did the people of Paris and London get water twenty-four hours a day while Delhi's residents got it only for four on an average? Guwahati in Assam sits on the Brahmaputra river but its residents get water for only two hours a day. The poor in India's cities depend on tankers. When the tanker is late there is a scramble and even a riot. Recently, there was news about such a tardy tanker driver who, fearing for his life, took off at high speed, and a child died in the chaos.

Because water comes intermittently, Indians learn to store it. Storage tanks cost money and are not cleaned regularly. This brings disease. Since water pipes are not under continuous pressure, they get broken when pressure is released—it is called the 'hammer effect'. Vacuum also develops in the pipe, and ground and sewage water enters through the cracks, thereby contaminating drinking water. It takes ninety minutes to re-pressure and dump the contaminated water, and much clean water is thus wasted.

Everyone in Delhi had a diagnosis for its water problem. Delhi's Jal Board said that 40 per cent of its water was stolen. Its zonal engineers wanted more pipes and infrastructure—lucrative contracts brought prosperity to engineers. Economists contended that Paris charged properly for its water, and hence Parisians didn't waste it. Delhi's water charges were so low that there was little incentive to conserve it. Besides, low tariffs ended up benefiting the rich and the middle class because the poor did not have taps that were metered. All these facts were true but the main problem was with Delhi's Jal Board itself. It was a fiefdom of politicians and its 20,000 employees (where comparable cities had no more than 5000). It did not meter water properly, encouraged theft, and was not accountable to customers.

Delhi's government, to its credit, recognized the problem and decided to act. The chief minister, Sheila Dikshit, accepted a World Bank plan to insulate the Jal Board from politicians and try giving water twenty-four hours a day in two of the twenty-two zones. It offered management contracts to World Bank experts, who planned to motivate Jal Board employees to reduce theft, extend taps to poor areas and become more responsive to customers. Although no one would lose a job, employees feared that they would now have to work transparently and opportunities for graft would shrink. The government took a loan from the World Bank for this project and this is when its problems began. A well-organized NGO, Parivartan, with antipathy for the World Bank, claimed that the process of hiring high-paid consultants had been manipulated. It raised fears of privatization and successfully mobilized public opinion through a very effective media campaign. Meanwhile, Sheila Dikshit was beleaguered, fighting critics against the recent privatization of power, and she did not want to open up another flank of attack. Thus, an excellent reform died and with it the prospect of water twenty-four hours a day, seven days a week, in Delhi.

It is not easy to reform in a democracy, I realized. Sheila Dikshit rightly understood that the answer is 'not to fix the pipes, but to fix the institutions that fix the pipes'. But she failed to win over the people in trying to reform the Jal Board. Vested interests—local politicians, bureaucrats and Jal Board employees—struck back. They manipulated Parivartan which became their spokesperson and managed to scare away Delhi's citizens from an excellent reform. Parivartan claimed that it was a representative of 'civil society' and had the right to enforce the people's will. This was untrue. In a constitutional democracy only elected governments are responsible for 'enforcing' that will. The truth is that politicians were not enthusiastic about the water reform—they were beneficiaries of the current system. Recall, the ancient Greeks were suspicious of democracy because ordinary people could be manipulated by demagogues and vested interests.

9

WHAT IS TO BE DONE?

*A state without some means of change
is without the means of its conservation.*

—Edmund Burke,
Reflections on the Revolution in France, 1790

'What is to be done?' is the question that Vladimir Lenin famously posed in 1902. It was in a political pamphlet, *Burning Questions of Our Movement*, inspired by the novel of the same name by the nineteenth-century Russian revolutionary Nikolai Chernyshevsky. Lenin argued that the working class could not become political simply by fighting economic battles with employers over wages, working hours and the like. He wrote, 'Class political consciousness can be brought to the workers only from without,' that is, only from outside the economic struggle, from outside the sphere of relations between workers and employers. 'From without' meant from the middle class or the bourgeois intelligentsia. His fateful answer to the question 'What is to be done?' was to form a political party or 'vanguard' of dedicated revolutionaries to spread Marxist political ideas among workers. This led to a split in the ranks in the Russian social democratic movement between the more moderate Mensheviks and Lenin's revolutionary Bolsheviks. The latter finally triumphed and went on to capture power in the Russian Revolution in October 1917.

With more modest ambition but a similar bias for action, I have advocated in Chapter Seven the setting up of a secular, liberal political party in India. The spirit, ideology and the working of this modern-day Swatantra Party is, of course, the opposite of Lenin's. This classical liberal party is one of a number of ideas scattered through this book which can help transform India's tottering state. When I embarked on this project I was not seeking prescriptions. I was attempting only to understand why India seemed to be stuck after the two best decades of its economic history. As I near its end, I find that what was essentially a project of self-cultivation has thrown up a number of actionable ideas. Hence, as a follow-up to the action-oriented 'Primer for the Corruption Fighter' in the previous chapter, I discuss a few principal remedies here.

Aside from a cri de cœur for a liberal party, some of the main action points that have emerged are as follows: reform the key institutions of governance—the bureaucracy, judiciary, police and Parliament—along the well-known lines articulated by numerous committees; encourage the federal trend and continue to decentralize power away from the Centre to the states; incentivize the states in turn to push power and funds downwards for more vigorous local self-government in villages and municipalities; promote civic education in citizenship and 'public dharma' in order to embed the values of our liberal Constitution so that they become over time 'habits of the heart'; energetically push the agenda for the second generation of economic reforms not only for growth but to achieve better governance; tap the awakening middle class, nudging it in the direction of active engagement with citizenship, civic life and the political process (rather than illiberal Anna Hazare-type street protests); restore the primacy of danda-niti, 'punishment', in the mindset of our nation state and thus recover the first lesson of raj dharma: the monopoly of violence given to the state is meant to protect the weakest. To these should be added the action-oriented plot in the 'Primer for a Corruption Fighter'. In this chapter I discuss some of these with the objective of helping make India a strong, liberal state.

THE CONSTITUTION AS A MORAL MIRROR

Anna Hazare's movement has proven once again that crowds might awaken people but they do not achieve the goal. Instead of the chanting multitudes inspired by a mystical faith in the collective popular will, let us turn for inspiration to one of the greatest moments in India's history. Between 1947 and 1949 a diverse assembly of deeply principled, sometimes brilliant, sometimes risk-taking men and women worked selflessly to create an outstanding modern Constitution. As they sought to reinvent the state in democratic terms, these nation builders wrestled constantly between the rationality of the state and its rule of law, and the deep-rooted 'primordial' loyalties of the Indian society. One of the most illustrious among them, B.R. Ambedkar, was head of the drafting committee. He was sceptical of crowds and of mass democracy, and diligently steered the constituent assembly towards a representative democracy—a republic—based on the rule of law.

A sensible beginning point in the quest for a strong, liberal state is to try and imagine the passion with which the founding fathers debated the principal ideas that became the pillars of our Constitution. The next step is to translate that fervour into one's own life, thereby transforming that document into a living thing. This means to put in practice the duties of citizenship in one's day-to-day life. Voting at elections is a minimum. Engaging in one's neighbourhood in volunteer activities even for a few hours a week is what impressed Tocqueville as he thought about the magic of America's democracy. This engagement will lead to connections with others: one discusses the life of the community—the condition of the roads, schools, street lights, garbage collection and other concerns. It is thus that civic life is born in a republic. So is the concept of a citizen as envisioned in our Constitution. When public-spirited individuals think of the community rather than being exclusively preoccupied with personal well-being, individual self-worth is formed.

The next stop on this expedition is to take the heroic leap into politics. Only when individuals of talent and 'superior intellect', as Tocqueville put it, move from the dogged pursuit of material comfort to public life will there be some hope for our democracy. Although it has lately been devalued, in part by Anna Hazare's movement, politics is the noblest of endeavours. Aristotle believed that the public life was more virtuous than the private one. In the *Mahabharata* Bhishma returned from his deathbed precisely to give the same message to Yudhishthira, who wanted to renounce the throne after the bloody war at Kurukshetra. Gandhi, Nehru and Patel also believed in the power of politics. As a result, India was blessed with an amazing first generation of political leaders. Sixty years later the nobility of politics has been replaced by money and criminality. The best shun politics, leaving it to the worst. It is now of critical importance for decent men and women to take the plunge into politics before criminals take it over completely. The best place to dive in, as I advised Shashi Kumar in Chapter Six, is one's own neighbourhood. Cervantes reminds us in *Don Quixote* that the universal lies in one's backyard, and it is as good a place as any to begin the political life.

To make the Constitution a moral mirror requires one to transmit its ideas to our generation, especially to the young. This will need translating the moral basis of the Indian political community into actionable language that will resonate with the ordinary person. One of the possible ways is to follow the inspirational lead of Mohandas Gandhi. He employed the vocabulary of the general restraint of universal sadharana dharma in order to 'sell' his liberal ideas during the freedom struggle. Nehru also tried to 'sell' liberal, democratic values to the people in countless speeches, but his appeal was a rational one of a westernized intellectual, and it had limited success. Certainly, no politician has tried it subsequently. The goal is to disseminate the ideas at the core of our democracy and inspire schoolchildren and college-goers as part of a broad citizenship project. Social media and technology are powerful tools in the hands of the young to mobilize it in quest of this goal. One must not merely instruct but ensure that action follows in behaviour. It is practice that leads to dharmic habits of the heart. Gradually these habits become a part of the character of the person. Robert Bellah shows in his book *Habits of the Heart* how inner states of human beings make outer states a reality and provide a collective language to a group. When that person grows up into a young man or woman, and when they have to appear in court, they will not commit perjury, and will instinctively train their eyes to look at the epigraph engraved in Sanskrit above the honourable judge, Satyameva Jayate, 'where there is truth, there is victory'.

GOD OF A LOWER WORLD

Having made the heroic mental leap to engage in politics, one next asks, what kind of politics? It is important to bring to politics the right mindset or 'moral temper'. The liberal temperament assigns the same moral worth to all human beings and places an individual above collective, social goals. It is sceptical of solutions beyond the test of human reason. John Locke, the father of classical liberalism, believed in life, liberty and property as the supreme values and that the state existed to protect them. In addition to these, classical liberals generally believe in individual rights, constitutional government, pluralism, toleration, autonomy and consent. They have a healthy fear of state power and a belief in limited government, expressed famously by Thomas Paine: 'Government even at its best is a necessary evil.' This is why Montesquieu's ideal of the 'separation of powers' is natural to a liberal. So is secularism, which in Europe means the separation of the Church and the state, but in India it was best expressed by Emperor Ashoka as 'respect for all faiths'.

I am a classical liberal, not a 'social liberal'. The latter emerged in the late nineteenth century with T.H. Green's distinction between 'positive' and 'negative' liberty. A social liberal is prone too easily to advocate state intervention in providing social and economic services. In India and some other countries such a person is called a 'left liberal'. I fear social liberalism because it can quickly turn into socialism and undermine not only human liberty but also a predictable, rules-based order. However, being a 'social liberal' is different from taking a liberal and tolerant view on social and cultural issues. And this is what I do.

The modern liberal temper was born in an intellectual revolution in eighteenth-century Europe, but its roots are ancient. In the West, they can be found in Pericles' incomparable Funeral Oration in ancient Athens. In India, they lie in raj dharma's separation of powers between the king and the Brahmin, as well as in the notion of a universal sadharana dharma, which inevitably awakens the sentiment of empathy in the human heart and leads one to identify with fellow human beings.

Although Edmund Burke was a conservative (and critical of liberal French revolutionaries), he proposed what I regard as the appropriate liberal moral virtue for a young person entering politics today in India. He called it 'prudence'. It suggests to me a sensible realism—to pursue only what is attainable. Unnecessarily demanding ideals get easily discredited. Prudence seems to be now an eighteenth-century virtue and without any high moral purchase these days. To our minds, it suggests someone who is self-interested and expedient. But I believe one can be 'prudent' when one's own interest is not involved. A 'prudent' mother is concerned about her child's welfare. A 'prudent' person looks at the future consequences of his actions. It is also a central virtue of a ruler guided by raj dharma, whose first duty is to protect his people. In the language of evolutionary biology, it is the virtue of 'reciprocal altruism': present a friendly face to the world but do not allow yourself to be exploited. It shuns moral perfection, avoids ideological extremes and strikes a middle path between the egoistic, amoral realism of Hobbes and the super-morality of a Gandhi or a Jesus. Hence, Burke called this virtue a 'god of a lower world'.

CRI DE CŒUR FOR A LIBERAL PARTY

Once the decision is made to take the plunge, the next question is: which political party? It is always better to improve existing institutions than to create new ones. It would be preferable to nudge one of the two major national parties towards a secular, free-market agenda of good governance. But that seems almost a hopeless prospect. The DNA of the BJP is not secular; the DNA of the Congress is statist, populist and socialist. Neither of the two has shown the commitment for institutional reform that is needed for good governance, let alone the ability to deliver it. The regional parties lack a national vision, except perhaps the Lok Satta in Andhra Pradesh, which in any case has not proven its electoral capability. The left parties do not believe in market-based outcomes. So, although the last thing India needs is a new party, it is unfortunately the only alternative for a young, aspiring, secular Indian in the twenty-first century.

Hence, I have advocated in Chapter Seven that we either revive the old Swatantra Party or start a new secular, liberal party. It would have a single-minded focus on the reforms of institutions and on the second generation of economic reforms. It would trust markets rather than officials for economic outcomes, thereby drastically reducing the discretionary authority of politicians and bureaucrats in microeconomic decision-making. This in turn would decrease the interface of citizens with the state and shrink the chances of collusive corruption. Thus, the country would begin to move away from crony capitalism and towards rules-based capitalism. The timing for such a party of aspiration is far more propitious than the 1960s of the Swatantra Party. The mindset of the nation has shifted in the past two decades from a command economy run by the state to one based on a competitive market. Its primary constituency, the middle class, is almost a third of the population and will be half the country in a decade. As the Anna Hazare movement has shown, it is impatient for good governance.

Adam Smith's 'invisible hand' is difficult to sell at the polls, however, precisely because it is invisible. This presents a problem. Economic and institutional reforms and fiscal responsibility are not winnable platforms because their benefits are not immediate but come in the long term. Here, a free-market party is inherently at a disadvantage over a populist or a socialist one which promises tangible, immediate 'giveaways'. Hence, market liberals have been successful either when they had a social or cultural agenda or were in coalition with parties with such an agenda. This accounts for the success of the Republicans in America or of the Conservatives in Britain. In India, it is imperative to be secular at this fragile point in the nation's history. Social and cultural appeals can prove to be dangerous and divide the nation. Both the Congress and the BJP have been divisive.

A possible solution to this dilemma is to follow Mohandas Gandhi's inspiration. That is, to bring both the market-based economic appeal and a rules-based governance appeal under the umbrella of high moral sadharana dharma. A party committed to 'doing the right thing' will instinctively resonate with an electorate sick of corruption. Such an appeal is secular in the best sense. It respects tradition while not being sectarian (unlike the empty secularism of the Marxist, who has contempt for tradition). Such an appeal also raises the bar for those who want to join the party. They would have to be public-spirited individuals who would be driven to politics by public interest, a concern for the community, rather than personal interests which motivate most politicians today. All democracies face this challenge. Tocqueville had warned Americans almost two centuries ago about the potential gap between private success and public failure when he observed that Americans were also too occupied with private success.

As the citizen of a poor, democratic country one must be concerned about reducing hunger and poverty. It is also important not to cede the 'inclusion' or 'social justice' platform to the Congress and the parties of the left. The overwhelming task is to prove to voters that open markets and rules-based government are the only civilized ways to lift living standards. When open markets are combined with genuine equality of opportunity via good schools and primary health centres, the result is shared prosperity for everyone.

Conspicuously absent in India's politics are disciplined party organizations, which help leaders in other democracies to mobilize support for specific programmes. Hence, there is an excessive reliance on the personal appeal of individual leaders to win elections. The liberal party should avoid this pitfall. It must create a grass-roots organization right from the start and manage it transparently like a modern organization. It should be 'bottom up' and not 'top down', and employ the powerful instruments of social media and technology. If such a 'bottom-up' organization is created, the party will be rewarded when it comes to pushing through programmes or when opposition mounts.

A NEW SPIRIT OF FEDERALISM

The sight of a weak prime minister humiliated repeatedly by a coalition partner in 2011–12 was too much for most Indians. Time and again Mamata Banerjee, chief minister of West Bengal, undermined the actions of Manmohan Singh's government which were approved by the Cabinet and were patently in the nation's interest. They ranged from an agreement with Bangladesh over sharing the waters of the Teesta river and foreign investment in the retail sector to a reformist railway budget. Even the most avid supporter of states' rights did not want to see central authority paralysed in this manner. Regional parties pulled the national coalition in different directions. Parliament was gridlocked, unable to pass laws. Courts were dictating policy. Timid civil servants were too scared to put pen to paper. Seeing this, people wondered how their proud democracy could have come to this pass.

The founding fathers of the Constitution could not have imagined such a crisis of authority and paralysis in decision-making. They had set out to make the Indian federation 'top down' rather than 'bottom up'. They called the

Constitution 'a Union of states', not a federation, and deliberately created a strong Centre. Granville Austin, who wrote the best book on the making of the Indian Constitution, says that their centralizing impulses were influenced by the experience of Partition and a worry that the princely states wanted to be independent. Nehru's socialist belief in the intellectual capability of a strong Centre to guide the states also played a role. This gave birth to the Planning Commission, a 'superbody' in the fearful words of Sardar Patel, which is not accountable to the Parliament but has dictated directly to the states for six decades, and is a source of much resentment in the states. Its consultative meetings with the states via the National Development Council have been only ceremonial, top-down affairs.

Several other factors in the 1970s contributed to the decline in Indian federalism. The personal centralization of power by Indira Gandhi weakened the federal nature of the Congress party. After the 'Indira wave' in 1972, the state Congress units surrendered the right to appoint their own chief ministers. Since then the high command at the Centre has damagingly made this decision. At the same time, state governors began to act in a partisan fashion. Governors were meant to be eminent persons, 'above party politics', but increasingly they became party loyalists and abused their discretion in imposing President's rule under Article 356 of the Constitution. 'Instead of becoming guardians of the federal system, governors became agents of its decline,' as the Rudolphs put it in *The Pursuit of Lakshmi*. But in the past few decades, the Centre has weakened as a result of coalition politics and power has shifted to the states.

The reality is that the running of India now is actually in the hands of the states and the regional parties. With the gridlock at the Centre, state governments have become more powerful. Chief ministers want more power to be transferred to the states. Voices have begun to ask, has India become too big to be managed as one unit, especially by a fractious coalition? There is a prime ministerial system in Delhi, but a de facto presidential one in most states. While the prime minister must be consultative, imperious state chief ministers get away with arbitrariness. Voters look less and less to the central government. Increasingly, the momentum for economic reform comes from the states, which control more than half of government spending. The rise of the regions is spreading the economic boom to every corner of the land, as new consumer subcultures emerge. But alongside there is a serious and unchecked rise of cronyism.

Collective action is a problem in all democracies. Some have suggested moving away from the Westminster parliamentary system to the American or the French presidential one as a solution. I am not persuaded. Both systems have had strong and weak governments during their history. The gridlock in Washington during Obama's presidency is an example of how a powerful, hostile Congress was able to weaken the American president. India, on the other hand, has had strong, decisive leaders— Indira Gandhi, Sardar Patel, etc. But now Indians are resigned to weak coalition governments for the foreseeable future. One of the causes appears to be too many parties. France has partially solved this problem through a system of run-off elections to ensure the winner has a majority. Germany does not provide state funding to a party that wins less than 5 per cent of the vote. Both these measures have helped reduce the number of parties, and these are the sort of solutions that we ought to consider.

There is no need for a new constituent assembly to review the structure of the existing Constitution. It has stood the test of time remarkably, demonstrating flexibility, especially in dealing with Centre–state issues of federalism. Granville Austin called its approach 'cooperative federalism'; Justice A.M. Ahmadi referred to it as 'pragmatic federalism'. A strong state in the Indian context is perfectly compatible with a federal structure in which the component states have great authority. Indeed, India's democracy has not only survived but has grown vigorous because power has devolved down to the linguistic states and local groups. Meanwhile, strong central governments in other countries have been the source of tyranny.

With power shifting to the states, strong and decisive regional leaders have emerged in recent years. Many have been delivering good governance, and attracting investments and jobs. One does not approve of all their actions but they are partially making up for a feeble Centre. I believe India's democracy needs to decentralize even more, using the excellent principle of subsidiarity. This is a concept that originated in the Roman Catholic Church but is currently used to good purpose in the European Union (EU). The principle simply says that a higher-level public agency should not do what can be done at a lower level. The competent authority should be the smallest, lowest and least centralized. This should be the motto of the 'new federalism' in India.

To make that new federalism work will require formal, binding institutional mechanisms. All the three major constitutional commissions set up on Centre–state relations—the Sarkaria Commission (1988), the Venkatachaliah Commission (2002) and the Punchhi Commission (2010)—have unanimously recommended such mechanisms. Currently, the National Development Council, which reviews the five-year economic plans, is ceremonial and the Inter-State Council hardly ever meets. These need to become genuinely empowered bodies and their decisions need to be binding. A good start is the idea to have a dispute resolution council for the planned goods and services tax. While political power has been wrested by the states, this is not the case with economic power. The direction for the future was signalled by the Centre's decision to give freedom to the states regarding foreign direct investment in retail. Unfortunately, this sensible decision became victim to the tantrums of Mamata Banerjee in November 2011 and was aborted. But it is clearly the right direction for India's new federalism.

Having said that, it is sobering to remember that devolving power to the states is not a panacea. Pratap Bhanu Mehta has highlighted the failure of the states in tackling basic problems, such as electric power and education. As already pointed out, the power situation is in a mess in most states and the main reason is the terrible state of the finances of its power utilities. This in turn is due to the supply of free power to farmers or its theft by politically connected elements. Similarly, education is in the hands of the states, and they have driven the sector to the ground. Not a single state has been able to create a university of national standards. The same could be said of the management of public health, water and agriculture. This is not an argument against devolving more power to the states, but it is a cautionary warning that the types of reforms we have been discussing at the Centre are also needed in the states.

Why stop with the states? India's new federalism requires that we embrace the principle of subsidiarity and give momentum to local self-government. Effective village panchayats and nagarpalikas have shown over the past two decades great ability to take decisive, transparent action, while reflecting the people's wishes. Corrupt individuals at the local level have been easier to spot, to shame and to change when they behaved badly. Cities need even more autonomy and their leaders need to be held more accountable; this is dramatically obvious in the pernicious growth of urban slums. The energetic pursuit of gram sabhas and mohalla sabhas is the key to embedding moral habits in the hearts and minds of Indians, thus strengthening the rule of law and reducing corruption. The thirteenth Finance Commission has also recommended direct tax devolution to the local governments, bypassing state governments. I have made my impassioned plea for local democracy in Chapter Four. Suffice it to add here that only 2 per cent of government expenditure is made through local bodies compared to almost 20 per cent in China.

Historically, other democracies have gone through similar fluctuations in the power of the Centre and the states. For the past forty years the United States has been in the midst of its own 'new federalism'. The American Constitution initially gave limited powers to the president. Over the years this power grew very large as the federal government's role expanded, especially in administering the welfare state. But since the 1970s American presidents, especially Nixon and Reagan, have deliberately wanted to make the federal government smaller and hand over more responsibility to the states. In contrast, more centralization might be needed in Europe to keep the whole together. Better economic performance on the periphery is only possible with tough rules dictated from the Centre. Oddly enough, Europe today is being refashioned in the image of Germany when India and the United States are pushing for more federalism.

With increasing power in the linguistic states, the Indian state is returning to its historical norm of 'ordered heterogeneity' of regional kingdoms united by a loose subcontinental empire. Selig Harrison's 1960 book, *India: The Most Dangerous Decades*, feared this trend and predicted that India would soon disintegrate into linguistic nation states. But this did not happen. Instead, Europe began to aspire to an Indian type of democratic, multicultural federalism through the EU. Just as India has been rewarded by a peace dividend from its federalism, the EU cannot also conceive of the prospect of war between its member states. Indian states are as large as European countries—Uttar Pradesh has more people than Germany and France combined—but Indian federalism has ensured that a dispute between Tamil Nadu and Karnataka over the water rights to the Krishna river could not have led to war. Had the linguistic states been independent nations there may have been dozens of wars between them in the past sixty years.

BALANCE COMPETITION WITH COOPERATION

Finally, a few words on a subject that requires a much longer discussion. 'Parties are inevitable in a democracy,' wrote Lord Bryce, the distinguished British intellectual, jurist and Liberal politician. But they need not be dysfunctional. India's political parties suffer from a number of failings that have together weakened the state. They are nepotistic, lack inner-party democracy, have weak organizational structure and have not learned to collaborate on issues of national importance. The Congress party sometimes behaves as though the party is supreme and more important than the government. Parties require the right balance between competition and cooperation in a democracy.

More than two hundred years ago, at the birth of the world's first modern democracy, Americans were also warned of the danger of 'factions'. James Madison, one of the authors of the Federalist Papers, expressed concern that excessive partisanship would paralyse the government. He felt that a lack of cooperation between legislators came from an excessive concern with self-interest and not enough with the common interest. Hence, the Federalist Papers underlined the importance of a deep commitment on the part of legislators towards the common good. This is not unlike a commitment to public dharma to which our founding fathers were deeply committed and which we must recover in our public life.

Arun Shourie's rule that I stated in Chapter Seven bears repeating: never oppose anything that you would do in office. To be in the Opposition, and not oppose requires character. To build that character and teach parties to cooperate, the famous Prisoner's Dilemma from game theory may be a good place to start. Playing that game repeatedly, it has been found, inculcates the virtue of 'reciprocal altruism' that evolutionary biologists have written much about. It is one reason human beings have not only survived but flourished through the evolutionary 'ascent of man'. It makes one realize that it pays not to be selfish. The world generally smiles back at those who present a friendly face. To make the unselfish move, however, does not imply that one turns the other cheek when confronted with mean behaviour. One reciprocates with 'tit for tat' and sends the right signal to the other side that one's default position is to cooperate, but not be exploited.

*

These are then some of the levers of action that might help us climb out of our present malaise and steer our country in the right direction. This is not the appropriate place for a comprehensive discussion on the reform of the institutions of the state that I have alluded to throughout the book. Nor is it the right place to discuss the complete agenda of the second generation of economic reforms which will do so much for prosperity and for governance. Clearly, what I have gone into is also not an exhaustive list of the issues, and I certainly do not have all the answers. I have simply sought to engage the reader to seek along with me 'what is to be done' in order to create a strong, liberal state in India so that our children and grandchildren can be proud citizens of one of the world's foremost democracies.

CONCLUSION
A Quest for a Strong, Liberal State

Is it the Constitution that has failed us, or we who have failed the Constitution?

—President K.R. Narayanan, speech to mark the fiftieth anniversary of the Republic, 27 January 2000

This book had a remarkable birth in the Arab Spring where in a strange, unplanned way, I found myself standing bewildered on a podium in Tahrir Square. I was forced to improvise a three-minute lesson for Egypt from India's democracy. In the fog of the moment a less than obvious feature of democracy—something I had not thought much about—flashed through my mind. So, I went on to extemporize about the 'rule of law' as I have recounted in the Introduction. Before coming to Egypt I had been depressed by the persistent failures of governance in India and the unhappy contrast between private success and public failure. But I had not connected these till that instant in Tahrir Square to India's fraying rule of law. Nor had I thought of the rule of law as lying at the heart of a successful liberal state. With the benefit of hindsight, I might have also added the other two pillars of a successful modern democracy—a strong executive capable of decisive action and making sure that the action was accountable to the people.

The other thing weighing on my mind before I arrived in Tahrir Square was why India seemed to have got stuck after two decades of reforms. The early signs of an economic slowdown were apparent and it was not only due to the world's depressed environment. There were obvious structural weaknesses, not in the economy but within India's polity. As I wrestled with these problems while writing this book over the past year, I started seeing a subtle but significant shift in my own perspective. From a somewhat laissez-faire position, I have come to believe firmly in the need for a strong, liberal state, which is, in fact, true to the original conception of the liberal state.

The French phrase 'laissez-faire' implies 'let it be' or 'leave it alone' and was first used, according to legend, in a meeting in 1680 between the powerful statist French finance minister Jean-Baptiste Colbert and a group of French businessmen. When the eager minister asked how the French state could be of service to the merchants, one of them replied: *laissez-nous faire*, 'Leave us alone.' In holding this position, I felt that I was within the ideology of classical liberalism, which has always advocated limited government in addition to constitutionalism, rule of law, due process, individual liberties and free markets. I had also been influenced by my friend Robert Nozick, the political philosopher at Harvard, who had proposed a minimalist state in his book *Anarchy, State, and Utopia*. He had argued that a distribution of goods is fair and just if brought about by free exchange among consenting adults and if the starting position of the agents was just. It did not matter if large inequalities emerged afterwards from the process of exchange. Nozick had thus challenged my teacher John Rawls, who had persuasively argued that 'social and economic inequalities are fair only if they help the least-advantaged member of the society'.

Socialism is obsessed with equality and the market is indifferent to it. One has to find a via media. Nozick had persuaded me that one should work hard to ensure a fairer starting position in India. This, of course, is not easy, as democracies around the world have discovered. The answer lies in a relentless focus on giving everyone access to good schools and health centres (rather than worry about reservations in jobs and universities). India has failed to do this, and it is, perhaps, as great a failure as governance. The Indian government has focused on quantity, but, as I have mentioned, the quality of government-run primary schools and primary health centres is atrocious. Given the limitations in capacity of the Indian state, I have come to believe that schools and health centres do not have to be run by the state but merely to be provided for financially, and managed as a public–private model, such as a system of vouchers.

A laissez-faire state, like a completely free market, has

never existed and so the real issue is the extent and quality of government regulation. This realization was central to the change in my thinking during the course of writing this book. The merchants who asked Minister Colbert to 'leave them alone' were either optimistic or naive. The state, I have come to believe, is a 'first-order phenomenon' and is needed not only to protect human beings, as raj dharma requires, but is also a condition for realizing their potential. The state achieves this primarily by protecting human liberty, striving for an equality of opportunity, but most of all by guaranteeing a predictable rules-based order. Having said this, I must confess that I still do fear state power, and believe in limited government. Yes, human beings are subject to social luck, but one has to accept a certain amount of humility about the ability of a state to re-engineer society if one wants to preserve liberty.

As I look back on what I have written in this book I cannot escape a feeling of asymmetry. There is plenty of evidence for 'India grows at night' but not enough of 'a liberal case for a strong case'. There are many distressing stories about the failures of government and the political class, but not enough about how good regulators contribute to national success. This may be perhaps because my ideological position changed while I was working on the book, and the change came about gradually and subtly. Moreover, I had personally suffered during the 'licence raj' and the scars from those wounds have still not gone away. I also counted on the fact that succeeding governments would keep liberalizing the economy, and that somehow the country's governance problems would go away as a result. So, I remained in denial about the vital need for the reform of institutions of the state. One forgets that the promise of both the revolutions of the early 1990s remains incomplete. The second generation of economic reforms and the deepening of local self-government have not happened and they are crucial to creating a strong, liberal order.

THE RISE OF INDIA

The economic rise of India has been the defining event of my life. It is not only good news for its 1.2 billion people, but also an instrument for the good in the world. At a time when western economies and their way of doing business is under a cloud, a large nation is rising in the East based on political and economic liberty, proving once again that open societies, free trade and multiplying connections to the global economy are pathways to lasting prosperity and national success. India has finally joined up with that great human adventure that began two hundred years ago in north-west Europe, which has brought about an amazing rise in the standard of living of the human race. Till then, the vast majority of humanity—'bipedal, scantily haired, language-blessed apes'—lived lives that were mostly 'poor, nasty, brutish and short', for 70,000 years or 99 per cent of human history.

Twenty years of capitalist growth since 1991 has made India one of the world's fastest growing economies. Although this growth has recently slowed from a scorching 9 per cent rate prior to the global financial crisis, India is likely to continue to grow at between 7 and 8 per cent a year for the next couple of decades. This means that a large majority of Indians will soon emerge from a struggle against want into an age when they will be at ease. Like many parts of Asia, India, too, will turn into a middle-class nation. This will not happen uniformly—Gujarat will be ahead of Bihar, but even Bihar will catch up. Indians tend to be self-reliant, ambitious and thrifty—these attitudes are conducive to high growth. Poverty will not vanish, but the number of poor will come down to a manageable level and, importantly, the politics of the country will also change.

The stubborn persistence of democracy in India over the past sixty-five years is an even greater achievement. Time and again, it has shown itself to be resilient and enduring—giving a lie to the old prejudice that the poor are incapable of the kind of self-discipline and sobriety that make for self-government. Not least is the contribution of Indian federalism in helping Indians live peacefully. In a world where armed strife is mostly within sovereign states and not between them and takes the form of civil war and ethnic cleansing, India's federal system has helped to negotiate cultural and ethnic differences within relatively peaceful bounds. India's federalism is a work in progress. It is still trying to cope with the dichotomy expressed by a Tamil writer, 'Tamil is my mother, India is my father'. In this gendered metaphor, the writer conveys the warmth, care and affection that are born in one's home space, which becomes the 'rule of life' (that Justice Krishna Iyer spoke about in Chapter Three). But the mother's instinct for partiality must be disciplined by an equal loyalty to a rational, impartial rule of law represented by the impersonal central national government in Delhi.

The troubled history of third world countries after the Second World War shows that state formation must precede nation-building and economic development, and not the other way around. The Government of India Act, 1935 was the starting point in forming the contemporary Indian state. India's constitution makers were so impressed with its liberal nature that they took almost 250 articles verbatim from it and inserted them into their new Constitution. But the state that has emerged is not a European import. It has been built on the day-to-day practice under the bright Indian sun for over eight decades after 1860 of a liberal rule of law, and four decades of gradual parliamentary growth. Two, it contains the legacy of Mughal rule which influenced some British colonial institutions that continue till today. Three, it follows the classical conception of the Indian state whose main purpose is to protect the 'ordered heterogeneity' of Indian society. Despite the appearance of a centralized modern state, contemporary India is in fact loosely structured, segmentary, with considerable sharing of powers with the regional states. The regional kingdom was a central reality of Indian history and its contemporary expression is today's linguistic state. Not unlike other subcontinental empires— Mauryas, Guptas, Mughals and the British—the Centre continues today to negotiate the proper relationship with the states through a 'new federalism'. Four, it recognizes the pre-eminence of the primordial loyalties of a strong

Indian society, which has always limited the potential for tyranny by the state, but also undercuts the individualism inherent in our liberal Constitution. While pushing for some social engineering via affirmative actions on behalf of the historically disadvantaged, the contemporary state, like the ancient Hindu king, also protects the customs of the heterogeneous, self-regulating orders of the diverse groups of Indian society as another expression of the ancient principle of 'ordered heterogeneity'.

State formation is a continuing process. India's has also been influenced positively by seventeen years of Jawaharlal Nehru's rule and negatively by sixteen years of Indira Gandhi's. Early on, it was impacted by the death of Subhas Chandra Bose in August 1945, who might have taken the state in an authoritarian direction. But also the demise of the decisive Sardar Vallabhbhai Patel in December 1950, who if he had lived longer might have set the tone for a stronger liberal state. Despite its flaws, I believe India is more than Ramachandra Guha's 'phipty phipty' democracy. My Egyptian adventure made me realize that India does, indeed, offer lessons for aspiring democracies. It has kept generals out of politics, a thought uppermost in Egyptian minds but non-existent in Indian minds. Indians live together in peace with greater liberty than in almost any other developing nation. The nation is secular and plural and has given space to the minorities and the low castes, and they do not feel insecure. And over the last two decades it has also become a rapidly growing economy which is lifting millions out of poverty.

Some years ago, Fareed Zakaria, the Indian-American

political commentator, coined the term 'illiberal democracy'. The expression was designed to describe a class of states that did hold free and fair elections and saw an alternation of political parties but lacked many of the other attributes of liberalism—most important, they did not respect civil and political rights. There is no imminent danger of India joining the ranks of those states, and that too is an achievement. Democracy is now solidly anchored in India, and so a degree of accountability is assured. The trick is to make that accountability a daily, hourly reflex at all levels. Not easy!

INDIA'S CODE WORD

Some nations possess a code word which, like a key, unlocks their secrets. That word is 'liberty' in America's case; *égalité*, 'equality', in the case of France; for India it is 'dharma'. Some of the best and the worst deeds in these nations can only be understood when seen in the light of these words. Dharma can mean many things as we have seen—duty, law, justice, righteousness—but mostly it is about doing the right thing. The ideal that still exists in the Indian imagination is of a ruler guided by dharma. The outraged reaction of the people to the corruption scandals in 2011 was: 'Dharma has been wounded.' Just as America's founding fathers were obsessed with liberty, so were many of India's founders attached to dharma, so much so that they placed the dharma chakra, 'the wheel of dharma', at the centre of the nation's flag. They were clear that the nation-building project was a profoundly moral one.

Like P.V. Kane, I too regard the Constitution as a 'dharma text' and this is where I began my quest for a strong, liberal state. India's code word is important to my project. Fixing India's democracy entails not only the reform of institutions but also the moral core underlying our democracy. It requires a change in people's mindset, what we have been referring to as 'habits of the heart'. Early on in the freedom struggle, Mohandas Gandhi discovered that the liberal language of western constitutional morality did not resonate in a deeply traditional society. But the moral language of dharma did. So, like a consummate myth-maker, he resuscitated the universal ethic of sadharana dharma from the dharma texts. His project was not unlike that of the Buddhist emperor Ashoka in the third century BCE, who had also embarked on a programme to build 'habits of the heart' based on 'dhamma' (dharma in Pali), consisting of edicts which he had engraved on pillars throughout his empire. Both men understood that nation-building entails myth-making. Gandhi was surprised to find how quickly his 'dharma campaign' resonated with the masses. He may not have been able to end untouchability but he did breathe life into the movement for freedom, which had hitherto been a forum for westernized debating.

It may seem strange to want to invoke tradition, especially when that tradition has been responsible for so much unjust hierarchy and social injustice. But it is a question of how one reads the past. Nation builders and revolutionaries have always known that history is ever ready to be used in the service of the future. Gandhi was aware that dharma is a pliable concept. So, he deliberately side-stepped the hierarchical concept of svadharma and the social concept of duties specific to one's caste, and evoked instead the universal values of sadharana dharma. This sadharana dharma, as already discussed, is no 'respecter of persons', and is consistent with the ideal of 'blindfolded' justice conceived in our Constitution. Dharma, after all, has given coherence to people's lives for centuries, reduced uncertainty and provided the self-restraint needed for a successful polity. By appealing to tradition, I am deliberately trying to break the present divide in India between the vast majority of the Indian people who are religious and lead traditional lives and modern secularists, especially of the left, who tend to dub such religious people as superstitious, bigoted and communal.

THE RISE AND FALL OF GOVERNANCE

India's state evolved from a tribal society much like it did anywhere else. The passage from tribal society to the state brought prosperity and security but diminished human freedom. It unwittingly brought about a hierarchical society and greater stratification, and reduced the dignity of the individual. Everywhere a few became masters and the rest became slaves and serfs. A feudal society emerged in medieval Europe, but India's unique answer to hierarchy was an intricate caste system. The West eventually responded to hierarchy by giving birth to the modern constitutional state, a revolutionary moment in human history when for the first time human beings began to rule themselves on the basis of strong institutions with a rule of law that guaranteed equal rights and a degree of accountability. This state took time to mature as the new modern nations gradually built and enhanced the capacity of their modern institutions.

In India, the modern state surfaced in the 1860s after the British Crown took over direct rule. Robust institutions of a modern, centralized bureaucratic state evolved over almost a century during the British Raj. Democratic accountability was achieved with independence in 1947, when India acquired all three pillars of a strong liberal state—a strong central authority, the institutions of the rule of law and accountability to the people. State-building continued through the decade of the 1950s—a singular achievement of Jawaharlal Nehru. The full-bodied institutions helped the new nation establish universal franchise.

It is not surprising that India became an untidy democracy rather than a tidy autocratic state. It was being true to its plural character of diversity and its historical temper. Amartya Sen attributes India's democratic success to an old tradition of public reasoning. He explains in *The Argumentative Indian* that reasoning and public argumentation has shaped India's social world and the nature of its culture. 'It has helped to make heterodoxy the natural state of affairs in India,' he says. He believes there is an intimate connection between public reasoning and the development of democracy, and this seems reasonable.

Democracy is inherently a weak form of government. Pressure on institutions began soon after Independence. India embraced a socialist ideology and this added to the stress on governance. Politicians began to give away free electricity to farmers and cheap rice to the poor in exchange for votes, and the country quickly changed from a constitutional to a populist democracy. A regime of subsidies on fuel, food, energy and fertilizers added to fiscal anxiety. The ideology of socialism expanded the functions of the state far beyond its capacity. It conjured a vision of a limitless state. 'Licence raj' was one of its consequences and, when combined with Indira Gandhi's disrespect for constitutional norms, this resulted in grave damage to the institutions. The decline has continued till today when crony capitalism has become a reality. India has become a flailing state, which is both too weak and too intrusive. It is all gummed up and little gets done.

In the midst of a flourishing economy, Indians are held hostage to corruption, governance failure and shoddy public services. The new middle class has awakened, however, and it insistently asks uncomfortable questions: why does it take eight years to build a road in India and ten to get justice? Why are teachers absent in government schools and colleges? Why do so many legislators have criminal charges against them? Why are state employees not accountable? To many minds the sight of private success and public failure has left the impression that India might be able to manage despite a corrupt, bungling state.

This is a mistake, as I have pointed out. Even markets

need a strong rule of law and a network of regulations and regulators to enforce it. In the past two decades good regulators have contributed to India's economic success, just as bad regulators have impeded its growth. One must not succumb to the peculiar fantasy of the American right that a nation's success derives simply from keeping the government out of the way.

JEFFREY SKILLING AND JUDGE LAKE

It is in response to this crisis in governance that I have tried to make a liberal case for a strong state. When I try to imagine such a state, I am reminded of a courtroom scene in the United States, recounted a few years ago with some elegance by Malcolm Gladwell in a *New Yorker* essay. I have tried to recall that scene on the afternoon of 23 October 2006, and retold it briefly in my own words:

> Jeffrey Skilling sat before Judge Simeon Lake in a courtroom in Houston, Texas, waiting to be sentenced. Skilling was no ordinary criminal. He had been head of the giant energy company Enron, which the stock market had valued as the seventh-largest corporation in the United States and Fortune magazine had ranked among the 'most admired' in the world. It had collapsed five years ago, and Skilling had been convicted by a jury for fraud two months earlier. Everything he owned had already been given away to recompense shareholders.
>
> Impeccably dressed in an expensive blue suit, Skilling was surrounded by a battery of extremely high paid lawyers. Outside, the world awaited the judge's sentence,

which would be conveyed by a battalion of TV cameras scrambling around the courthouse. The judge asked the defendant to get up. He then sentenced him to 292 months in prison.

One of Skilling's lawyers rose at this point and requested the judge to lower the sentence by ten months. Judge Lake must have wondered if the lawyer had heard him properly. But the lawyer explained that by the rules of the Bureau of Prisons relating to good behaviour, Skilling would qualify to serve probably the rest of his life in a 'lower facility'. After all, the lawyer said, Skilling wasn't a murderer or a rapist.

'No,' said the judge.

This is an example of how a strong, liberal state behaves. In India, an investigation lasts for years, charges are then filed, a trial is finally held and guilt is established, but then years go by without anything happening, and people lose interest. Weak enforcement is the soft underbelly of the weak Indian state, whose chief victims are the poor and the vulnerable. This is ironical, for danda, 'punishment', is the reason for the state to exist, according to both raj dharma and the classical liberals. India must restore primacy to danda-niti in the paradigm of our nation state. It is in keeping with a sensible realism of the Burkein public virtue of 'prudence' that I proposed in the previous chapter as being central to the temper of the ruler and the ruled in a strong, liberal state. Enacting a strong Lokpal is consistent with this moral sentiment but if the existing laws are enforced the role of the Lokpal would rightly be a limited one.

HISTORY IS NOT DESTINY

Chapters Eight and Nine have defined an agenda to make India a strong, liberal state. Since it has historically had a weak state, it will be more difficult to make it strong. However, even though the past does matter, it does not mean that one is trapped in it. Time and again India has changed, often by successfully borrowing new ideas and making them its own. History is not destiny, as they say.

But the wholesale reform of state institutions is a daunting prospect in any nation. Fortunately, many have done it, and with great success. Lant Pritchett of Harvard's Kennedy School asks us to imagine what it would be like if we were plunked down in Chicago in the 1920s. He would have found a hundred reasons to be pessimistic:

> Social conflict was everywhere, racism embedded and institutionalized, the police was corrupt, organized crime was thriving, economic progress was bifurcated between fabulous wealth and abject poverty, there were threats to public health, immigrants who couldn't even speak the language had poured in, and politics were brutal and 'machine' dominated.

Almost a century years later that cynicism turned out to be misplaced. Chicago went on to reform, did so continuously and became a successful, modern, well-governed city. India or at least some of its states could do the same. Some of the societies we admire, such as the UK, also suffered from poor governance. Britain had a corrupt administration in the early nineteenth century, honeycombed with nepotism and patronage. But then, good leaders emerged—Gladstone and Disraeli in the nineteenth century and Margaret Thatcher in the twentieth. They had the courage to fight vested interests and implement governance reforms.

If India is lucky, it might also throw up a strong leader who is a reformer. But since there is no guarantee of this happening in a democracy, the next best hope is to create a demand for reform as well as a constituency for it. Since the demand for reform is unlikely to come from within the state, one must depend on society. After two decades of rapid economic growth, a sizeable middle class has emerged, as we know, and it has now attained dignity. The extraordinary support garnered by Anna Hazare's movement in 2011 showed that an imperceptible but profound change is under way in India's traditional society. A newly awakened middle class backed by an assertive media will no longer accept a civic life shaped only by those who are powerful or by calculations of who stands to lose or gain.

People in the end obey the law because they think it is fair and just, that it applies equally to all, and because they get morally habituated to it. It thus becomes a form of self-restraint. Eventually the habit becomes character. Hence, the demand for governance reform must emerge out of an Indian moral core. And so we return once again to the Indian code word: dharma. Dharma imposed this moderation of temper in pre-modern India as Common Law did in pre-modern England. It might help us to recover constitutional morality today.

'Constitutional morality,' warned B.R. Ambedkar in the constituent assembly, 'is not a natural sentiment. It has to be cultivated. We must realize that our people are yet to learn it. Democracy in India is only a top dressing on an Indian soul, which is essentially undemocratic.' Since the time Ambedkar spoke, India's democracy has turned from a 'constitutional' to a 'populist' one, and his warning is all the more significant. The only legitimate way to recover dharma, as we noted in the previous chapter, is through the hard work of day-to-day politics.

Reforming corrupt government institutions is never easy. But the task cannot be put off any longer. In Chapter Four, I compared the crisis-ridden Hastinapur in the *Mahabharata* with today's flailing Indian state. Just as we have a problem with our corrupt institutions of governance, the kingdom of the Bharatas had a problem with the self-destructive Kshatriya institutions of its time, and it had to wage a civil war at Kurukshetra to cleanse them. There are impatient voices in India today that are prepared to wage such a Kurukshetra-like war in order to bring accountability into public life. This was apparent in the clamour surrounding Anna Hazare's movement for a Lokpal in 2011. There is thus an urgency to the task, but it should not be addressed through mobs on the street but through institutional reform. However, Anna Hazare's cautionary message is that if the political class is not up to enacting those reforms then it better be prepared for a bloody civil war.

The sole life which a human being can lose, they say, is the one he is living. While winning or losing depends mostly on one's private life, the state can make a difference—it can make that life more predictable and secure through rules-based governance. Politicians make promises but there is no point in promising the future: it has to happen today. This means that good persons must enter politics and transform the institutions that are crying out for change. Until then, the best one can do is to keep dreaming of that great spectacle—greater than the sea and the sky—of a government run by men and women of restraint acting on the basis of the rule of law while remaining accountable to the people.

SELECT BIBLIOGRAPHY

Ambedkar, B.R. *The Essential Writings of B.R. Ambedkar*. Edited by Valerian Rodrigues. Delhi: Oxford University Press, 2002.

———. *Writings and Speeches*. 18 vols. Edited by Vasant Moon. Bombay: Government of Maharashtra, 1979–2007.

Anderson, Benedict. *Imagined Communities*. London: Verso, 1983.

Anderson, Perry. *Passages from Antiquity to Feudalism*. London: New Left Books, 1974.

———. *Lineages of the Absolutist State*. London: New Left Books, 1977.

Austin, Granville. *The Indian Constitution: Cornerstone of a Nation*. 1966. Reprint, Oxford: Oxford University Press, 1999.

Axelrod, Robert. *The Evolution of Cooperation*. New York: Basic Books, 1984.

Aziz, Abdul. *The Mansabdari System and the Mughal Army*. Delhi: Idarah-I-Adabiyut-I Delli, 1952.

Badaoni, as cited in *The Abul-Fazl-i-'Allami*, The A' in-I Akbari. Translated by H.F. Blochmann and H.S. Jarrett and further annotated by Jadunath Sarkar. 2nd ed. Calcutta: Asiatic Society of Bengal, II (1927): 256.

Baechler, J. *The Origins of Capitalism*. Oxford: Blackwell, 1975.

Basham, Arthur L. *The Wonder That Was India: A Survey of the Culture of the Indian Sub-Continent before the Coming of the Muslims*. London: Sidgwick and Jackson, 1954.

Bayly, C.A. *Rulers, Townsmen and Bazaars: Indian Society in the Age of British Expansion, 1780–1870*. Cambridge: Cambridge University Press, 1983.

——. *Indian Society and the Making of the British Empire*. Cambridge: Cambridge University Press, 1988.

——. *Recovering Liberties: Indian Thought in the Age of Liberalism and Empire*. Cambridge: Cambridge University Press, 2012.

Berman, Harold J. 'Religious Foundations of Law in the West: An Historical Perspective'. *Journal of Law and Religion* 1(1): 3–43.

Berman, Sheri. 'Civil Society and the Collapse of the Weimar Republic'. *World Politics* 49(3): 401–29.

Béteille, André. 'The Politics of "Non-Antagonistic" Strata'. *Contributions to Indian Sociology*, n.s., III, December 1969.

——. *The Idea of Natural Inequality and Other Essays*. Delhi: Oxford University Press, 1983.

Bhargava, Rajeev. *The Promise of India's Secular Democracy*. New Delhi: Oxford University Press, 2010.

Birla, R. *Stages of Capital: Law, Culture, and Market Governance in Late Colonial India*. Durham, NC: Duke University Press, 2009.

Bloch, Marc. *Feudal Society*. Chicago: University of Chicago Press, 1968.

Brass, Paul R. *The Politics of India since Independence*. Cambridge: Cambridge University Press, 1990.

Braudel, F. *The Wheels of Commerce*. Vol. 2 of *Civilization and Capitalism*. London: Book Club Associates, 1982.

Brecher, Michael. *Nehru: A Political Biography*. Oxford: Oxford University Press, 1959.

Buhler, Georg. *The Laws of Manu*. Reprint, Delhi: Motilal Banarsidass, 1975.

Burke, E. 'Speech to the Electors of Bristol'. 1774. In *Select Works of Edmund Burke*. Edited by J. Payne. Indianapolis: Liberty Fund, 1999.

Chandra, Bipan. *India's Struggle for Independence*. New Delhi: Penguin Books India, 1988.

Chao, Paul. *Chinese Kinship*. Boston: Routledge, 1983.

Chatterjee, Partha. *The Nation and Its Fragments*. Princeton: Princeton University Press, 1993.

Claessen, H.J.M., and P. Skalnik. *The Early State*. The Hague: Mouton & Co., 1978.

Collier, Paul. *The Bottom Line: Why the Poorest Countries Are Failing and What Can Be Done About It*. New York: Oxford University Press, 2007.

Constituent Assembly Debates 1946–1950. 12 vols. Delhi: Parliament of India, 1954.

Constituent Assembly Debates: Official Report. 12 vols. Delhi: Publications Division, 1946–50.

Dahl, Robert. *Democracy and Its Critics*. New Heaven and London: Yale University Press, 1989.

De Soto, Hernando. *The Other Path: The Invisible Revolution in the Third World*. New York: Harper, 1989.

Derrett, J. Duncan M. *Religion, Law, and the State in India*. London: Faber, 1968.

——. *History of Indian Law (Dharmasastra)*. Leiden: E.J. Brill, 1973.

Dirks, N. *Castes of Mind: Colonialism and the Making of Modern India*. Princeton, NJ: Princeton University Press, 2001.

Doornbos, Martin, and Sudipta Kaviraj. *Dynamics of State Formation: India and Europe Compared*. Thousand Oaks, CA: Sage Publications, 1997.

Dumont, Louis. 'The Conception of Kingship in Ancient India'. *Contributions to Indian Sociology* 56 (1961).

——. *Homo Hierarchicus: The Caste System and Its Implications*. Chicago: University of Chicago Press, 1980.

Engels, Friedrich. *The Origin of the Family, Private Property, and the State, in Light of the Researches of Lewis H. Morgan*. New York: International Publishers, 1942.

Etienne, Balazs. *Chinese Civilization and Bureaucracy*. Edited by Arthur Wright. New Haven: Yale University Press, 1964.

Fukuyama, Francis. *Trust: The Social Virtues and the Creation of Prosperity*. New York: Free Press, 1995.

——. *State-Building: Governance and World Order in the 21st Century*. Ithaca: Cornell University Press, 2004.

——. *The Origins of Political Order: From Prehuman Times to the French Revolution*. New York: Farrar, Straus and Giroux, 2011.

Fustel de Coulanges, Numa Denis. *The Ancient City*. Garden City, NY: Doubleday, 1965.

Gandhi, M.K. *Hind Swaraj and Other Writings*. Edited by A.J. Parel. Cambridge: Cambridge University Press, 1997.

Gellner, Ernest. *Culture, Identity, and Politics*. New York: Cambridge University Press, 1987.

Ghoshal, U.N. *A History of Indian Political Ideas*. New York: Oxford University Press, 1959.

Gladwell, Malcolm. *What the Dog Saw and Other Adventures*. New York: Allen Lane, 2009.

Gokhale, G.K. *Speeches of Gopal Krishna Gokhale*. 4th ed. Madras: G.A. Natesan and Co., 1920.

Gonda, J. *Ancient Indian Kingship from the Religious Point of View*. Leiden: E.J. Brill, 1969.

Goody, J. *The Oriental, the Ancient and the Primitive*. Cambridge: Cambridge University Press, 1990.

Government of India, Ministry of Home Affairs. *Seventh Report of the National Police Commission*. Delhi, 1982.

Goyal, S.R. *History of the Imperial Guptas*. Allahabad: Central Book Depot, 1967.

Guha, Ramachandra. *Indian after Gandhi: A History of the World's Largest Democracy*. London: Macmillan, 2007.

Guha, Ranajit, and Gayatri Chakravorty Spivak. *Selected Subaltern Studies*. New York: Oxford University Press, 1988.

Habib, Irfan. *The Agrarian System of Mughal India, 1556–1707*. Delhi: Oxford University Press, 2000.

Haggard, Stephan, Andrew MacIntyre, and Lydia Tiede. 'The Rule of Law and Economic Development', *Annual Review of Political Science* 11 (2008): 205–34.

Hamilton, Alexander, James Madison, and John Jay. *The Federalist Papers*. Edited by Clinton Rossitor. New York: Penguin, 1961.

Harrison, John A. *The Chinese Empire*. New York: Harcourt, 1972.

Harrison, Selig. *India: The Most Dangerous Decades*. Princeton, NJ: Princeton University Press, 1960.

Hart, H.L.A. 'Are There Any Natural Rights'. *Philosophical Review* 64 (1955).

Hayek, Friedrich. *Law, Legislation and Liberty*. Chicago: University of Chicago Press, 1976.

Heesterman, J.C. *The Ancient Indian Royal Consecration*. The Hague: Mouton & Co., 1957.

Hegel, G.W.F. *The Philosophy of History*. 1956. Translated by J. Sibree. Mineola, NY: Dover, 2004.

Hobbes, T. *Leviathan*. Cambridge: Cambridge University Press, 1996.

Huntington, Samuel P. *Political Order in Changing Societies*. 1968. With a New Forward by Francis Fukuyama. New Heaven: Yale University Press, 2006.

Jenkins, R. *Democratic Politics and Economic Reform in India*. Cambridge: Cambridge University Press, 1999.

Jennings, Ivor. *Some Characteristics of the Indian Constitution*. Oxford: Oxford University Press, 1953.

Kane, P.V. *History of Dharmasastra*. Vols. 1–5. Poona: Bhandarkar Oriental Research Institute, 1962.

Kangle, R.P. *The Kautiliya Arthasastra*. 3 vols. Bombay: T.V. Chidambaram for the University of Bombay Studies, 1960–65.

Kaviraj, Sudipta. 'On the Enchantment of the State: Indian Thought on the Role of the State in the Narrative of Modernization'. *European Journal of Sociology* 46(2): 263–96.

Khan, Rashiduddin. *Federal India: A Design for Change*. New Delhi: Vikas Publishing House, 1992.

Khilnani, Sunil. *The Idea of India*. New York: Farrar, Straus and Giroux, 1998.

Koestler, Arthur. *The Lotus and the Robot*. New York: Macmillan, 1962.

Kohli, Atul. *Democracy and Discontent: India's Growing Crisis of Governability*. Cambridge: Cambridge University Press, 1990.

Kosambi, D.D. *The Culture and Civilisation of Ancient India in Historical Outline*. London: Routledge, 1966.

Kothari, Rajni. *Politics in India*. New Delhi: Orient Longman, 1970.

Kremer, Michael, Karthik Muralidharan, Nazmul Choudhary, and Jeffrey Hammer. 'School Absences in India: A Snapshot'. *Journal of European Economic Association* III (2–3): 658–67.

Kulke, Hermann. *The State in India 1000–1700*. Delhi: Oxford University Press, 1995.

Lal, Deepak. *The Hindu Equilibrium: India c. 1500 B.C.–2000 A.D.* New York: Oxford University Press, 2005.

——. *The Hindu Equilibrium*. Vol. 1. Oxford: Clarendon Press, 1988.

Lariviere, Richard W. 'Justices and Panditas: Some Ironies in Contemporary Reading of the Hindu Legal Past'. *Journal of Asian Studies* 48(4): 757–69.

Lingat, R. *The Classical Law of India*. Berkeley: University of California Press, 1973.

Lipset, S.M. *Political Man*. London: Heinemann, 1959.

———. 'Some Social Requisites of Democracy: Economic Development and Political Legitimacy'. *American Political Science Review* 53 (1959): 69–105.

Locke, John. *The Second Treatise of Government*. Indianpolis: Bobbs-Merrill, 1952.

Mahabharata. Book 12. Translated by James Fitzgerald. Chicago: Chicago University Press, 2004.

Maine, Henry. *Ancient Law: Its Connection with the Early History of Society and Its Relation to Modern Ideas*. Boston: Beacon Press, 1963.

Maitland, Frederic W. *The Constitutional History of England*. Cambridge: Cambridge University Press, 1961.

Malhotra, Inder. *Dynasties of India and Beyond*. New Delhi: HarperCollins, 2003.

Mayne, Sumner Henry. *Village Communities in the East and West*. London: John Murray, 1895.

McCloskey, Deirdre N. *Bourgeois Dignity: Why Economics Can't Explain the Modern World*. Chicago: Chicago University Press, 2010.

McCrindle, J.W. *Ancient India as Described by Ptolemy*. Calcutta: Chuckervertty, Chatterjee and Co., 1927.

Mehta, Bhanu Pratap. *The Burden of Democracy*. New Delhi: Penguin, 2003.

Mehta, U.S. *Liberalism and Empire: A Study in Nineteenth-Century British Liberal Thought*. Chicago: University of Chicago Press, 1999.

Melvin, Richter. *The Political Theory of Montesquieu*. New York: Cambridge University Press, 1977.

Menon, V.P. *The Story of the Integration of the Indian States*. New York: Macmillan, 1956.

Migdal, Joel. *Strong Societies and Weak States: State–Society*

Relations and State Capabilities in the Third World. Princeton: Princeton University Press, 1988.

Mill, J.S. *Utilitarianism: On Liberty, Representative Government.* Letchworth: The Aldine Press, 1957.

——. *On Liberty and Other Writings.* Edited by S. Collini. Cambridge: Cambridge University Press, 2005.

Mishra, B.B. *The Indian Middle Classes.* London: Oxford University Press, 1961.

Mookerji, R. *Local Government in Ancient India.* Oxford: Kessinger Publishing, 1919.

Moore, Barrington Jr. *Social Origins of Dictatorship and Democracy: Lord and Peasant in the Making of the Modern World.* Boston: Beacon Press, 1967.

Morris-Jones, W.H. *The Government and Politics of India.* 3rd rev. ed. London: Hutchinson, 1971.

Mukerjee, Radhakamal. *Democracies of the East: A Study in Comparative Politics.* New Delhi: Radha Publications, 1923.

Myrdal, Gunnar. *Asian Drama: An Inquiry into the Poverty of Nations.* 3 vols. New York: Pantheon, 1968.

Naipaul, V.S. *India: A Million Mutinies Now.* London: Vintage, 1998.

Nandy, Ashish. *Traditions, Tyranny, and Utopias: Essays in the Politics of Awareness.* Delhi: Oxford University Press, 1987.

Nehru, Jawaharlal. *The Discovery of India.* Delhi: Oxford University Press, 1989.

North, Douglass C. 'Institutions and Economic Growth: An Historical Introduction'. *World Development* 17(9): 1319–32.

Nozick, R. *Anarchy, State, and Utopia.* Oxford: Basil Blackwell, 1974.

Oakeshott, M. *Rationalism in Politics and Other Essays.* New and expanded ed. Indianapolis: Liberty Fund, 1990.

Olivelle, P. *The Dharmasutras*. New York: Oxford University Press, 1999.

Olson, Mancur. *The Logic of Collective Action: Public Goods and the Theory of Groups*. Cambridge, MA: Harvard University Press, 1965.

——. *The Rise and Decline of Nations*. New Heaven: Yale University Press, 1982.

Paine, Tom. *Common Sense, Rights of Man, and Other Essential Writings*. New York: Signet Classics, 2003.

Pannikar, K.M. *In Defence of Liberalism*. Bombay: Asia Publishing House, 1962.

Plamenatz, J. *On Alien Rule and Self-Government*. London: Longmans, 1960.

Polanyi, Karl. *The Great Transformation: The Political and Economic Origins of Our Time*. Boston: Beacon Press, 1957.

Pollock, Frederick, and Frederic W. Maitland. *The History of English Law before the Time of Edward I*. Cambridge: Cambridge University Press, 1923.

Pritchett, Lant, and Michhael Woolcock. 'Solutions When the Solution Is the Problem: Arraying the Disarray in Development'. Washington, DC: Center for Global Development Working Paper 10, 2002.

Przeworski, Adam. *Democracy and Development: Political Institutions and Material Well-Being in the World, 1950–1990*. Cambridge: Cambridge University Press, 2000.

Putnam, R.D. *Making Democracy Work*. Princeton, NJ: Princeton University Press, 1993.

Rawls, John. *A Theory of Justice*. Cambridge, MA: Harvard University Press, 1971.

Raychaudhuri, Hemchandra. *The Political History of Ancient India: From the Accession of Parikshit to the Extinction of the Gupta Dynasty*. New Delhi: Oxford University Press, 1996.

Robert, Bellah. *Habits of the Heart: Individualism and Commitment in American Life.* Berkeley and Los Angeles: University of California Press, 1985.

Rodrik, Dani, and Arvind Subramanian. 'The Primacy of Institutions (and What It Does and Does Not Mean)'. *Finance and Development* 40(2): 31–34.

Rousseau, Jean-Jacques. *Discourse on the Origin and the Foundation of Inequality among Mankind.* New York: St. Martin's Press, 2010.

Rudolph, I. Lloyd, and Susanne Hoeber Rudolph. *In Pursuit of Lakshmi: The Political Economy of the Indian State.* Chicago: University of Chicago Press, 1987.

———. *The Realm of Institutions: State Formation and Institutional Change.* New Delhi: Oxford University Press, 2008.

———. 'The Subcontinental Empire and the Regional Kingdom in Indian State Formation'. In *Region and Nation in India.* Edited by Paul Wallace. pp. 40–59. New Delhi: Oxford University Press, 1985.

Sachau, E.C. *Alberuni's India.* Vols 1 and 2. Reprint. Delhi: S. Chand & Co., 1964.

Sastri, K.A. Nilakanta. *The Colas.* Rev. ed. Madras: University of Madras, 1955.

Sax, William S. 'Conquering Quarters: Religion and Politics in Hinduism'. *International Journal of Hindu Studies* 4(1): 39–60.

Schram, Stuart R. *The Scope of State Power in China.* New York: St. Martin's Press, 1985.

Schumpeter, J.A. *Capitalism, Socialism and Democracy.* New York: Harper & Row, 1950.

Scott, James C. *Seeing Like a State: How Certain Schemes to Improve the Human Conditions Have Failed.* New Haven: Yale University Press, 1998.

Secondat, Charles de, Baron de Montesquieu. *The Persian Letters.*

Translated by John Davidson. London: Routledge and Sons, 1923.

Sen, Amartya. *Development and Freedom*. Oxford: Oxford University Press, 1999.

——. *The Argumentative Indian: Writings on Indian History, Culture and Identity*. London: Allen Lane, 2005.

——. 'Democracy as a Universal Value'. *Journal of Democracy* 10 (1999): 3–17.

Shah, Parth J., and Naveen Mandava. *Law, Liberty and Livelihood: Making a Living on the Street*. New Delhi: Academic Foundation in association with the Centre for Civil Society, 2005.

Sharma, R.S. *Aspects of Political Ideas and Institutions in Ancient India*. Delhi: Motilal Banarsi Dass, 1968.

——. *Social Changes in Early Medieval India, c. AD 500–1200*. Delhi: Motilal Banarsi Dass, 1969.

Shiva Rao, B. *The Framing of the Constitution: Select Documents*. Vol. 1. 1967. Reprint, Delhi: Universal Law Publishing Co., 2004.

Shourie, Arun. *Governance and the Sclerosis That Has Set In*. New Delhi: Rupa & Co., 2004.

Sivananda, Swami (Tr.). *The Brihadaranyaka Upanishad*. Rishikesh: Divine Life Society, 1985.

Smiles, Samuel. *Self-Help*. New York: Oxford University Press, 2008.

Smith, Adam. *The Theory of Moral Sentiments*. 1759. Reprint, Indianapolis: Liberty Fund, 1982.

——. *An Inquiry into the Nature and Causes of the Wealth of Nations*. 1776. Reprint, Indianapolis: Liberty Classics, 1981.

Srinivas, M.N. *Social Change in Modern India*. Bombay: Allied Publishers, 1966.

Stein, Burton. 'The State and the Agrarian Order in Medieval South India: A Historiographic Critique'. In *Essays on*

South Asia. Edited by Burton Stein. Honolulu: University of Hawaii Press, 1975.

———. 'All the King's Mana: Perspectives on Kingship in Medieval South India'. In *Kingship and Authority in South Asia*. Edited by John F. Richards. pp. 115–67. Madison: University of Wisconsin Press, 1978.

———. 'State Formation and Economy Reconsidered'. *Modern Asian Studies* 19(3): 387–413.

Steinbeck, John. *Cannery Row*. New York: Penguin, 2002.

Stokes, E.M.C. *The English Utilitarians in India*. Oxford: Clarendon, 1959.

Strayer, R. Joseph. *On the Medieval Origins of the Modern State*. Princeton: Princeton University Press, 1970.

Thapar, Romila. *From Lineage to State: Social Formations in the Mid-First Millennium B.C. in the Ganga Valley*. Bombay: Oxford University Press, 1984.

———. *Cultural Pasts*. Delhi: Oxford University Press, 2000.

———. *Early India: From the Origins to AD 1300*. London: Allen Lane, 2002.

The Law Code of Manu (Manava Dharmasastra). Translated by Patrick Olivelle. New York: Oxford University Press, 2004.

The Mahabharata of Krishna-Dwaipayana Vyasa. 2nd ed. 13 vols. 1884–96. Reprint, Delhi: Munshiram Manoharlal, 1970.

Tilly, Charles. *The Formation of National States in Western Europe*. Princeton: Princeton University Press, 1975.

Tocqueville, Alexis De. *Democracy in America*. 1835. Reprint, London: Collins, 1968.

Tyler, Tom R. *Why People Obey the Law*. New Haven: Yale University Press, 1990.

Weber, Max. *The Protestant Ethic and the Spirit of Capitalism*. New York: Scribner, 1930.

———. *The Religion of India: The Sociology of Hinduism and Buddhism*. Glencoe, IL: Free Press, 1958.

Weiner, Myron. 'India's New Political Institutions'. *Asian Survey* 16 (1796).

Wink, A. *Al-Hind: The Making of the Indo-Islamic World*. Vol. 1. Delhi: Oxford University Press, 1999.

Wittfogel, Karl A. *Oriental Despotism: A Comparative Study of Total Power*. New Haven: Yale University Press, 1957.

Woodruff, Philip. *The Men Who Ruled India*. 2 vols. New York: Schocken, 1967.

Zakaria, Fareed. *The Future of Freedom: Illiberal Democracy at Home and Abroad*. New York: Norton, 2003.

ACKNOWLEDGEMENTS

My happiest task is to thank those who have made this book possible. I owe a great debt of gratitude to many thinkers who have helped shape my thinking over the years. But as this is not an academic work, I have not bothered to clutter the text with footnotes. I also want to thank practitioners and friends, who have helped shape my thinking, either through conversations, writings or their comments to a draft of this book. In alphabetical order they are: Rajeev Bhargava, André Béteille, Shivashish Chatterjee, Paul Courtright, Ashok Desai, Francis Fukuyama, Charles Harper, David Housego, Janaki Kathpalia, Tejinder Khanna, Madhav Khosla, Daniel Kurtz-Phelan, Pratap Bhanu Mehta, Prakash Menon, Joydeep Mukherji, Ralph Nicholas, Philip Oldenburg, Anup Pahari, Tom Palmer, Anthony Parel, Lant Pritchett, Mahesh Rangarajan, Tirthankar Roy, Lloyd and Susanne Rudolph, Sanjeev Sabhlok, Razeen Sally, Vijendra Sawhney, Hardayal Singh, Jay Sokhi, Frank Trentmann, J.S. Verma and Rob Young.

I especially want to thank my assistant, Shiju Chacko, for his patient help with research and readying the book for the press; my editor at Penguin, Udayan Mitra, who lent wonderful support throughout in countless ways; and finally, my wife, Bunu, who is always there and makes it all possible.

INDEX